THE SORCERER OF BAYREUTH

RICHARD WAGNER, HIS WORK AND HIS WORLD

BARRY MILLINGTON

The Sorcerer of Bayreuth

Richard Wagner, His Work and His World

285 ILLUSTRATIONS, 165 IN COLOR

OXFORD

UNIVERSITY PRESS

VISTA GRANDE
PUBLIC LIBRARY

Oxford University Press is a department of the University of Oxford.
It furthers the University's objective of excellence in research, scholarship,
and education by publishing worldwide. Oxford is a registered trade mark
of Oxford University Press in the UK and in certain other countries

Published in the United States of America by
Oxford University Press
198 Madison Avenue, New York, NY 10016, United States of America

First published in the United Kingdom in 2012 as *Richard Wagner:
The Sorcerer of Bayreuth* by Thames & Hudson Ltd, 181A High Holborn,
London WC1V 7QX

Library of Congress Cataloging-in-Publication Data
Millington, Barry.
 The sorcerer of Bayreuth : Richard Wagner, his work and his world /
Barry Millington.
   p. cm.
 Includes bibliographical references and index.
 ISBN 978-0-19-993376-1
1. Wagner, Richard, 1813–1883. 2. Composers—Germany—Biography.
3. Wagner, Richard, 1813–1883—Criticism and interpretation.
4. Opera—19th century. I. Title.
 ML410.W1M57 2012
 782.1092—dc23[B] 2012017940

Text pages designed and typeset by Fred Birdsall with
assistance from Bob Birdsall, Fred Birdsall studio

9 8 7 6 5 4 3 2 1

Printed and bound in China by C & C Offset Printing Co. Ltd.

Contents

Preface

A sorcerer is one who weaves enchanting spells, and the time-honoured perception that Wagner's music has the capacity to cast a spell on the listener, to transport him or her to realms of unimaginable ecstasy, long ago earned him the sobriquet that forms the title of this book. Already in Wagner's own time there were fellow artists such as Charles Baudelaire who described the experience of listening to Wagner's music as one of being engulfed, of being intoxicated: he even compared it to the effect of a stimulant. And since then, devotees without number have succumbed to the hedonistic delights of music that is in every way incomparable.

The designation 'sorcerer' also has a pejorative connotation, however, as Nietzsche, who was the first to use it with regard to Wagner, was well aware. Those spells can be woven round the listener without their consent; and might there actually be something dangerous in the brew? There is certainly a very potent element in his works, to judge by the passions they arouse when their content is under discussion.

The perplexing ideology of their creator similarly causes endless dissension, yet so rich are the works, and so problematic their composer, that the exegetical challenges seem to be endlessly renewable. The present book attempts to grapple with these issues and to present them in a new light, drawing on scholarship of recent years that has yielded some fascinating results and in some cases positively demanded a radical reappraisal of the subject. Examples are recent studies of Cosima Wagner, of Otto and Mathilde Wesendonck, of Wagner's fetishistic tendencies, his compositional process and his own self-promotion as a 'brand', and of the subsequent members of the Wagner clan (notably Winifred, Wieland and Wolfgang). There has also been some sterling musicological work done on the thirteen operas that form the core of Wagner's oeuvre, while the discipline of film studies has thrown up some intriguing insights into their proto-cinematic nature. Hovering like a dark cloud, never quite banished, is the baleful legacy of Wagner – specifically the question of his anti-Semitism and the extent to which it is integral to the works themselves. Here, too, there has been some valuable scholarship of late.

All these issues are tackled here in an original format that (it is hoped) will illuminate the subjects under discussion. The material is presented as a series of chapters, each exploring a theme through text, illustrations and documents, and thus departs from the conventional formats of illustrated biography and documentary study. At times, the results of this reappraisal may seem surprising, even sensationally so. It is a mark of how comprehensively Wagner has entered the popular imagination, for better or for worse, that there are so many misconceptions about him. For far too long the same tired clichés, based on received opinion, have been recycled. There could be no better opportunity than the bicentenary of Wagner's birth to demolish some of these stereotypes once and for all. They serve only to impede understanding of Wagner as a historical figure and of his inexhaustible works.

Postcard with a portrait of Wagner by Dietze.

1 Father of the Man: Paternity and Childhood

Do you think he perhaps has musical talent?
Ludwig Geyer, the day before he died

The days immediately preceding Wagner's birth were eventful ones in war-torn Saxony. Napoleon was advancing, but as the weeks and months passed the allied nations of Austria, Prussia and Russia were putting up stout resistance.

Thus stood affairs at sunrise on the 22nd of May, when the youngest son of Police-actuary Wagner greeted the light of this turbulent world with his earliest cry, in the house of the White and Red Lion [*sic*] on the Brühl at Leipzig. The cannon thunder of the two preceding days had scarcely rolled away from the field of Bautzen [90 miles east of Leipzig]: Napoleon had been left with a barren victory, a loss of 25,000 in killed and wounded, and neither prisoners nor field-guns taken.[1]

The Battle of Nations at Leipzig, 18 October 1813, showing the Monarch Hill (centre) and Leipzig itself (background).

So reported Carl Friedrich Glasenapp, one of Wagner's earliest biographers; and while his account is a graphic reminder that the sound of

The Brühl in the Jewish quarter of Leipzig, where Wagner was born.

gunfire provided a terrifying backdrop to daily existence for Saxons in those days, it leaves much unsaid. The Brühl, for example, was the name of a wide street in Leipzig, but also of a district, part of the city's Jewish quarter. So the 19th century's most prominent scourge of Jewry drew his first breath in a tenement that rubbed shoulders with the lodgings, shops and synagogues of the very people he was so catastrophically to anathematize.

But was this child really the 'son of Police-actuary Wagner', i.e. Carl Friedrich Wagner, the municipal official who died in a war-related outbreak of typhus that swept Leipzig that November? Or was his father actually Friedrich's close friend, the actor and painter Ludwig Geyer, who supported the family in its hour of need and brought up Richard as his own? (The boy was even called Geyer until the age of fourteen, reverting to Wagner some years after Geyer's death.) Friedrich's widow, Johanna Rosine, already pregnant with Wagner's younger sister, Cäcilie, married Geyer quite soon after Friedrich's death, on 28 August 1814, and moved with him to Dresden. But, although Richard bore an undeniable resemblance to Cäcilie, that cannot be taken as evidence of Geyer's paternity, because he also shared physiognomical characteristics with his elder brother Albert, whose birth long preceded Geyer's arrival on the scene.

Postcard showing the Red and White Lion, in which Wagner was born on 22 May 1813.

The truth of Wagner's paternity remains tantalizingly unknown and unknowable. Perhaps more important is the fact that Wagner thought Geyer might well have been his father. But notwithstanding insinuations by Nietzsche and other contemporaries, there was no truth to the suggestion that Geyer might have been Jewish, and his Protestant lineage has been established definitively.

The mystery was not all on Wagner's paternal side, however. His mother, too, was an enigma to him. Until a few decades ago it was thought that Johanna Rosine was probably the illegitimate daughter of Prince Constantin of Saxe-Weimar-Eisenach. The story may have been fabricated by Johanna herself, and Wagner, too, liked to think he may have had royal blood in his veins. But in 1985 Martin Gregor-Dellin published an article demonstrating that Johanna was in fact a mistress of the prince.[2] A humble baker's daughter in Weissenfels, she had caught the roving eye of Prince Constantin who, in the time-honoured fashion of his sex and class, seduced and abandoned her. More precisely, he died suddenly on a campaign in 1793, and Johanna, then aged nineteen, was granted 50 thalers[3] by the ducal council appointed to deal with such matters, with the ruling that she be 'left to her fate'. Johanna, who was nothing if not resourceful, set about reinventing herself. The modest house in the Brühl where the prince had lodged (and no doubt seduced her) became a 'select seminary', while the aristocratic connection was remembered as a 'high-born fatherly friend' or even 'a Weimar prince'. She adjusted her maiden name from Pätz to Perthes, lowered her age by four years, and within five had married the respectable, middle-class police registrar to whom she was to present ten children (Richard was the ninth; one died in infancy and another at the age of four). Not even her first husband, Friedrich, appears to have been told the truth about her past – a fact not lost on Wagner, who was to write an opera about a woman forbidden to enquire about the name or origins of her bridegroom.

For Wagner the enigma surrounding his mother symbolized her unknowability and remoteness:

Her chief character trait appeared to be a wry sense of humour and a good temper … . The anxieties and pressures of bringing up a large family (of which I was the seventh surviving member), the difficulties in obtaining all we needed, and at the same time satisfying, despite her very limited means, a certain inclination for ostentation were not conducive to a warm tone of motherly tenderness for her family. I can hardly ever remember being cuddled by her; in fact there were never any displays of tenderness in our family, whereas a certain restless, almost wild, boisterousness appeared very natural.[4]

Wagner retained a deep affection for his mother, however, and was much moved by her death in 1848.

His stepfather, on the other hand, was a warm and outgoing man by all accounts:

Cameos of (from left to right) Wagner's stepfather, Ludwig Geyer; sister Cäcilie; brother Albert; and the composer himself, as drawn by his friend Ernst Benedikt Kietz in 1840–42.

He took his art seriously, but enjoyed life so long as fresh vitality and vigorous energy flowed in his veins. He was the heart and soul of a lively circle of friends of both sexes, whom the hospitable man liked most of all to entertain in his own home and who were kept in constant good humour by his merry, sparkling wit. Little family parties turned into imaginative puppet shows, and later even dramatic performances, all of which he organized himself, making the costumes and writing the texts.[5]

Dresden as it looked in Wagner's childhood. Carl Gregor Täubert's etching shows the Altstadt and the bridge over the Elbe.

Geyer died when Wagner was only eight, and that fact, combined with the somewhat peripatetic lifestyle dictated by the thespian ambitions of his sisters, meant that he was continually being shunted around. Evidently his parents found him a recalcitrant child. Geyer exerted the firm hand of discipline – using a whip on one occasion – and terrified him even more by the personas he adopted in his melodramatic presentations. At the age of seven Wagner was packed off to stay for a year with Pastor Christian Wetzel at Possendorf, near Dresden, at which time he had a few piano lessons. Homesick and unloved, he could not wait to make the journey back to Dresden – three hours as it was on foot. But after a brief return to Possendorf, following Geyer's death, he was taken to stay with his uncle Karl at Eisleben, where he was obliged to live with the bachelor gold-smith and his elderly grandmother. When Karl, some ten months later, decided to get married, Wagner was taken in briefly by another uncle, Adolf, before entering the Dresden Kreuzschule on 2 December 1822. Here, the exploits of mythological Greek heroes made a greater impact on him than the irksome rules of grammar and the principles of mathemat-ics. Though hardly a model pupil, he worked industriously at the subjects that interested him. For a few years his home life was relatively stable, and the physical proximity of his sisters and the trappings of their theatrical activities stimulated him in more than one way:

Everything that went to produce theatrical performances remained for me full of mystery, an attraction amounting to intoxication, and while I sought with my playmates to imitate performances of *Der Freischütz*, and applied myself with great enthusiasm to the production of costumes and masks through grotesque painting, it was the more delicate costumes of my sisters, on which I often saw my family working, that exerted a more stirring effect on my imagination: just touching these objects could cause my heart to beat wildly. Despite the fact that, as I have mentioned, there was little tenderness in our family, particularly as expressed in loving hugs, the predominantly feminine environment must have strongly influenced my emotional development.[6]

Wagner's mother, Johanna Rosine (painted here by Ludwig Geyer). Wagner complained that she rarely expressed her love physically, though he felt her death keenly.

Rosalie, Wagner's beloved eldest sister. She was a gifted actress whose thespian activities did much to inspire in him a love of the theatre.

In 1826, by which time Wagner was a tender thirteen years old, the family moved to Prague, where his eldest sister Rosalie, the chief breadwinner, had secured a good post at the theatre. The boy was once again farmed out to the family of some schoolfriends. Little wonder that *Heimat*, physically expressed love, and substitute mother and father figures were to loom so large in his operas.

2 Learning the Craft: Youthful Apprenticeship

Probably you will never write fugues or canons.
What you have achieved, however, is self-sufficiency.
  Wagner's teacher Weinlig summarizes his pupil's progress

Having spent most of his fourteenth year apart from his family, Wagner moved back to his native city of Leipzig in December 1827, where several members of his family had by now also returned. In the first month of the new year he entered the Nicolaischule; his enrolment there was an emotional milestone, in that he now abandoned the name Geyer and called himself Richard Wagner. Displaying from this early age a penchant for ambitiously conceived tragic drama, he worked on a five-act play called *Leubald* (1826–28), effectively his first opus. As Wagner himself later acknowledged, the somewhat macabre plot, involving murder on an industrial scale, rolled *Hamlet*, *Macbeth* and *King Lear* – not to mention Goethe's *Götz von Berlichingen* – into one. 'The plan was quite stupendous,' he recalled: 'forty-two people died in the course of the play and I found myself obliged to bring most of them back as ghosts, since otherwise I should have run out of characters in the later acts.'[1] His intention had been to write incidental music for this hair-raising blockbuster in the style of Beethoven's *Egmont*, but if any was written it has not survived.

A lively scene in the marketplace of Leipzig, *c.* 1800.

On entering the Nicolaischule Wagner was obliged to swallow his disgust at having to lay aside Homer – of whom he already translated twelve books, he tells us in *Mein Leben*, his autobiography – in order to take up 'the easier Greek prose writers' once more. But it was also during this period that he deepened his acquaintance with his uncle Adolf. The latter was a liberal-minded, erudite man, well versed in both the Classics and German literature. He had met Schiller, Fichte and Tieck, and been commended also by Goethe. The day Adolf handed over to Wagner the modest library that had belonged to his brother Friedrich (Wagner's father) was a memorable one for him. It was Uncle Adolf who introduced him to, and fired him with enthusiasm for, the Greeks, Shakespeare, Dante and much more besides.

With a view to writing music for *Leubald*, Wagner borrowed from the library a treatise on composition by Johann Bernhard Logier, and in the autumn of 1828 began also to take harmony lessons (initially in secret) from a local musician, Christian Gottlieb Müller. When he came to write an account of his early years for a periodical in 1843, Wagner played down the seriousness of this initial tuition, but to judge from a letter of that period it was anything but a breeze:

I had the good fortune of being taught by the most sincere & strict of teachers; my lessons with Herr Müller proved to be a series of almost oppressive demonstrations of an almost pedantically strict sincerity; he inured me to the most injurious and discouraging attacks on my youthful endeavours, teaching me to see in such criticism only instructive demonstrations of sincerity, even when these latter did not always spring from the purest of sources.[2]

During this time he completed his first compositions, two piano sonatas and a string quartet, none of which has survived. An event also took place that proved to be a formative experience for the young Wagner. One of

The Nicolaischule in Leipzig, which Wagner attended from 1828 to 1830. Now abandoning his stepfather's name of Geyer, he launched his career as Richard Wagner with the bloodcurdling drama *Leubald*.

Adolf Wagner, the composer's uncle – a well-read man who inculcated a love of both classical and German literature in his nephew.

Christian Gottlieb Müller, the 'sincere & strict' composition teacher with whom Wagner studied from 1828 to 1831.

the leading singers of the day, Wilhelmine Schröder-Devrient, was in Leipzig making a series of guest appearances. She was then, Wagner tells us in *Mein Leben*,

at the very peak of her artistic career – youthful, with a warmth and beauty such as I have never seen in any woman on the stage since. She appeared in *Fidelio*.

When I look back on my whole life I can think of hardly any event which I could set beside this as being comparable in its effect on me. Any man who can remember this wonderful woman from that period of her life must somehow be able to bear witness to the almost primeval warmth which such a humanly ecstatic performance as that of this incomparable artiste must certainly have radiated over him. After the performance I raced round to one of my acquaintances to write a short letter in which I declared irrevocably to the great artiste that from that day my life had acquired its true meaning, and if one day in the world of art she should hear my name mentioned with praise, she should remember that on this evening she made me what I hereby swore I intended to become.[3]

The declaration is an eloquent one, and only marginally diminished by the fact that it was not as Leonore in *Fidelio* that Wagner saw Schröder-Devrient on this occasion, but (in all probability) as Romeo in Bellini's *I Capuleti e i Montecchi*. Whether it was simply a case of two separate but

MADAME SCHRÖDER-DEVRIENT als ROMEO.

Ach, eitles Hoffen! verschlossen für meinen Jammer   Ahi vana speme! è sorda
Ist das Ohr der Geliebten.   La fredda salma di mia voce al suono......

Wilhelmine Schröder-Devrient as Romeo in Bellini's *I Capuleti e i Montecchi*. It was this appearance that endowed the young Wagner's life with 'its true meaning', according to a note he dashed off to the singer.

The celebrated Thomasschule in Leipzig. Wagner enrolled there in 1830 but devoted more time to dissipated student escapades than to scholarly pursuits.

memorable experiences converging in Wagner's memory, or whether the name of the composer was consciously adjusted, the better to blaze a trail of destiny that linked his own name with that of his hero Beethoven, can no longer be ascertained.

In 1830 Wagner left the Nicolaischule and enrolled at the Thomasschule, also in Leipzig. Over the summer he underwent a short period of violin tuition, but, according to the teacher, a violinist in the Gewandhaus orchestra by the name of Robert Sipp: 'He caught on quickly, but was lazy and unwilling to practise. He was my very worst pupil.'[4] In the second half of that year, Wagner produced four more compositions, all overtures, all (again) now lost. Beethoven was a major inspiration at this time, and Wagner undertook a piano transcription of the Ninth Symphony, which he offered to Schott for publication (the offer was courteously declined). On Christmas Day 1830 an overture of his in B flat was actually performed in Leipzig – an occasion that failed to yield the expected satisfaction. The work acquired the nickname 'Drum-beat Overture' on account of a highly innovative feature: after each four-bar melodic phrase, a fifth bar was inserted consisting simply of a loud stroke of the timpani on the second beat. The longer the piece lasted, the more amusement it caused the audience, and when it came to an unusually abrupt conclusion the general merriment was unconfined. Wagner fled the theatre humiliated.

He was not to be deterred, however, and more works flowed from his pen the following year, 1831: a set of seven pieces for Goethe's *Faust* for voice and piano, including Wagner's only example of a melodrama (resurrected in recent years), and a piano sonata in B flat for four hands. In February that year he matriculated at Leipzig University but continued with his private musical studies, transferring to another teacher, Christian Theodor Weinlig, in the autumn. These lessons too were downplayed in later years, but the fact is that under Weinlig's tutelage Wagner acquired a soundly based technique of harmony and counterpoint. Master and pupil evidently hit it off personally too. As Wagner related in a letter to his sister Ottilie the following spring:

Christian Theodor Weinlig, the local cantor whose lessons in harmony and counterpoint set the young composer on his path.

I should have explained that for more than six months I have been a pupil of the local cantor Theodor *Weinlig*, who, with some justification, may be regarded as the *greatest living contrapuntalist* and who, at the same time, is so excellent a fellow that I am as fond of him as if he were my own father … . The extent to which he cares for me is proved by the fact that when, at the end of half-a-year's lessons, our mother asked him what his fee was, he replied that it would be unreasonable of him to accept any payment, such was the pleasure it had given him to teach me: my hard work and his high hopes for my future were sufficient of a reward for him.[5]

This new course of study bore fruit with two compositions for piano: an inventive Sonata in B flat, this time for two hands, published as op. 1, and a Fantasia – a more individual, if somewhat wayward, piece. A more ambitious, indeed Beethovenian, work was the so-called Grosse Sonate in

A major, followed later the same year (1832) by a Symphony in C major. Weinlig was far more open to the idea of Wagner having his pieces performed than Müller had been, and, indeed, the symphony was given in Prague that November. Beethoven was once again the model, and the ten orchestral hammerblows that open the work may be seen as at once a recollection of the 'Eroica' and an attempt to outdo it. The slow movement recalls the Andante of Beethoven's Fifth and the Allegretto of the Seventh, while the finale owes something to the finale of Mozart's 'Jupiter' Symphony. It is a fine student work, occasionally played today, and Wagner retained a lifelong affection for it, conducting it in a private performance at La Fenice, Venice, to celebrate his wife Cosima's birthday in 1882. An amusing, if more jaundiced, view of the work was provided by Friedrich Wieck, the father of Clara Schumann. As Clara reported to her future husband, Robert:

On Saturday father went to the 'Euterpe' [a music society run by Wagner's first composition teacher, Christian Müller]. I say, Herr Wagner has outstripped you; they played a symphony by him which is supposed to have resembled the A major symphony of Beethoven to a tee. Father said: the symphony by F. Schneider [a highly regarded composer of the time], which was done in the Gewandhaus, could be compared to a horse and cart which took *two days* to get to Wurzen, kept straight on the road and a dozy old driver with a big peaked cap kept muttering to the horses, 'Come on, gee up, giddyup, giddyup'. But Wagner drove his gig up hill and down dale and was in the ditch every minute. But he got to Wurzen in *one day*, even though he was black and blue all over.[6]

In September and October of 1832 Wagner stayed with Count Pachta on his estate at Pravonin, near Prague. He had already encountered Pachta's

A page from the last movement of Wagner's piano transcription of Beethoven's Ninth Symphony, offered to Schott for publication but politely rejected.

attractive illegitimate daughters a few years previously. Now nineteen and sporting a beard, Wagner catapulted into an infatuation with the elder, dark-haired sister, Jenny. To his chagrin she failed to reciprocate, and even made him aware of her indifference in some painful way on which he did not elaborate. This romantic interlude did not entirely distract him from work, however: while at Pravonin he conceived an opera, to be called *Die Hochzeit* (The Wedding), and like *Leubald* a somewhat grisly story of murder and revenge. The original idea for the story came from a study of medieval chivalry by Johann Gustav Büsching called *Ritterzeit und Ritterwesen*. The scenario was outlined by Wagner as follows:

A frenzied lover climbs to the bedroom window of his friend's bride, where she is waiting for her bridegroom; the bride struggles with the madman and finally hurls him into the courtyard below, where he breaks his neck and dies. At his funeral the bride with a cry sinks lifeless upon his corpse.[7]

Wagner began to sketch a novella on the subject, adding a mysterious old organist to the cast of characters. A mystical relationship was developed between the said organist, the frenzied young man and the tragic bride. The organist was, in Wagner's words, 'to be found dead on his bench at the organ, after playing an impressive requiem and expiring during an endlessly prolonged triad at its close'. The novella was not completed, but Wagner pursued the story and fashioned an opera libretto from it, pointing up the theme of feuding families and incorporating close-to-the-knuckle autobiographical references in the process. Only an introduction, chorus and septet were written; of particular note is the septet, which is in seven real, skilfully interlocking parts, unfolding wonderfully lyrical lines that coalesce in imaginative, poignantly expressive harmonies. The poem is lost, though several of the characters' names (Ada, Arindal, Lora and Harald) were taken over into Wagner's next operatic project, *Die Feen*.

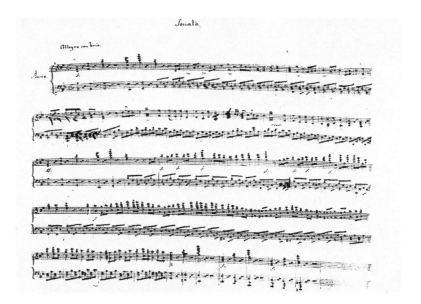

Opening of the Piano Sonata in B flat, op. 1, Wagner's earliest surviving work for the instrument and his first published piece.

3 Earning his Keep: First Professional Appointments

I am resolved to become a perfect epicure in respect of my art, nothing for posterity, but everything for our contemporaries & for the present moment.
Wagner to Theodor Apel

Albert Wagner was a singer, actor and stage manager. A man of some influence at the provincial theatre in Würzburg, he was able to pull a few strings on behalf of his brother.

It was thanks to his brother Albert, a tenor at the theatre in Würzburg, that Wagner was able to secure a post there as chorus master. Having arrived, frozen, in an open-top farmer's cart in the January of 1833, he soon came to grips with the demands of a small provincial theatre. Because he was still legally under age, three family members (mother, sister Rosalie and brother Albert) were required to act as guarantors for the purposes of his contract, which stipulated the following:

Richard Wagner's chief duties will be as chorus master, but if necessary he will also be expected to make himself useful as required in walk-on and spoken parts in plays, tragedies and ballets, and for this both he and the guarantors of his diligence have given their permission and consent.[1]

In fact, just preparing the chorus kept him sufficiently occupied. Two new grand operas, Marschner's *Der Vampyr* and Meyerbeer's *Robert le Diable*, were on the schedule, and both left their mark in different ways on his own future work. Marschner's *Hans Heiling*, for all that Wagner was dismissive of its weaknesses, was another novelty – it had received its world

The Marienberg fortress and Old Main Bridge of Würzburg, the city where Wagner held his first professional appointment as chorus master.

premiere in Berlin just a few months before its Würzburg performance – and was echoed in later Wagner works. He also had the opportunity to get to know operas by Beethoven, Paer, Cherubini, Rossini and Auber during this period.

Somehow Wagner found the time to write the music for his first complete opera, *Die Feen*, as well. There was hard drinking to be done too, with results that would today have him in trouble for neglect:

My brother and his wife left Würzburg after Easter in order to give guest performances elsewhere. I remained behind with their children – three young girls of the tenderest age – which put me in the extraordinary position of a responsible guardian, a role in which I did not exactly distinguish myself at this time … . I often took myself off into the surrounding countryside, making merry with Bavarian beer and Franconian wine. A beer garden called *The Final Blow*, situated on a pleasant hill, bore witness almost nightly to my wild, enthusiastic carousing and exuberance. On those warm summer nights I never got back to my three fosterchildren without having put the world and art to rights in appropriately ecstatic fashion.[2]

Costume design for the Fairy King, produced by Joseph Flüggen for the first performance of *Die Feen*. In fact the opera was not premiered until 29 June 1888, under the musical direction of Hermann Levi in Munich.

Portrait of Heinrich Laube – author, critic, theatre director and representative in the Frankfurt National Assembly.

The job in Würzburg came to an end in January 1834, at which point Wagner returned to Leipzig where he came again within the orbit of the firebrand writer Heinrich Laube, whom he had already met through his sister Rosalie. Laube was a leading figure in the Young German movement, which also embraced such figures as Heinrich Heine, Karl Gutzkow, Ludolf Wienbarg and Ludwig Börne. Taking their inspiration from the French Utopian Socialists, especially the Saint-Simonians, and from the July Revolution of 1830, which spread from Paris to various German cities including Leipzig, the Young Germans called for the unification of Germany, abolition of censorship, constitutional rule and the emancipation of women. Radical notions such as these put them at odds with both church and state, and it was the hedonistic, sensual enjoyment of life they advocated that found expression in Wagner's second opera, *Das Liebesverbot* (The Ban on Love). A summer holiday in Bohemia, during which Wagner and his friend Theodor Apel indulged themselves to excess with food, drink, creature comforts and uninhibited intellectual debate, resulted in a prose sketch for *Das Liebesverbot*, based loosely on Shakespeare's *Measure for Measure* but relocated to the sunny Mediterranean.

No sooner had Wagner returned from his Bohemian jaunt than he was offered the job of musical director of a theatre company run by a dissipated impresario by the name of Heinrich Bethmann. The company, which mounted opera as well as drama, was based in Magdeburg, but was playing that summer in Bad Lauchstädt, an attractive spa town not far from Leipzig. Wagner took himself off there to reconnoitre. His confidence was not inspired by the sight of the decrepit Bethmann, walking the streets in dressing gown and nightcap, nor by the toothless skeleton of the theatre attendant. But what decided him to decline the post there and then was the demand that he put on a *Don Giovanni* the following Sunday, without the benefit of a prior rehearsal, since the visiting orchestra (municipal bandsmen from Merseburg) were not willing to rehearse on the Saturday.

The Schlackenburg near Teplitz, where Wagner sketched his second opera, *Das Liebesverbot*, while on holiday with his friend Theodor Apel.

Requiring overnight accommodation in the town before returning to Leipzig, however, Wagner was directed to the same lodgings as one of the company's leading actresses, Christine Wilhelmine Planer, known as 'Minna'. Meeting her by chance at the door, he was smitten by her blue eyes and dark wavy hair, her charm and composure. He took the room and announced that he would conduct *Don Giovanni* after all. The performance – his début as an opera conductor – went well, but it was the discovery of Minna that persuaded him to stay with the company. That there was a sexual frisson between them is clear, and a comment in a letter to one of Wagner's friends – 'she has given me a couple of moments of sensual transfiguration, – it was marvellous'[3] – suggests that they lost little time in consummating the relationship. Three-and-a-half years older than he was, Minna had suffered a bitter experience as a fifteen-year-old, when she had been seduced and abandoned by a guards captain, Ernst Rudolph von Einsiedel. Her pregnancy was concealed and her daughter, Natalie, brought up as her sister. Perhaps as a result, she was not anxious to commit herself to Wagner, or to anyone else. Admirers flitted in and out of her dressing room, offering her marriage, and in one case (Alexander von Otterstedt) painting her portrait. But she was sweet on Wagner too, as an anecdote retailed in *Mein Leben* illustrates:

As I returned to my groundfloor room late one night via the window, having failed to take the house key with me, the noise of my entry drew Minna to the window above mine. Still standing on the windowsill, I begged her to allow me to say good night to her. She hadn't the least objection to that but it had to be done via the window as her room had already been locked by the servants and no one could get in that way. She facilitated my handshake in friendly fashion by leaning out with the upper part of her body so that I could grasp her hand while standing at my window.[4]

On another occasion, when Wagner was hiding in his room suffering from the disfiguring complaint of erysipelas, Minna was happy to visit and nurse him. Left, finally, with a rash round his mouth, he lamented that she was unlikely to favour him with a kiss, whereupon she surprised and delighted him with just that.

The two of them moved with the Bethmann company when it visited Rudolstadt in Thuringia. Here Wagner set to work on another symphony, this time in E major – only to abandon it in the middle of the second movement – and the libretto of *Das Liebesverbot*. Moving back with the company to its home base in Magdeburg, he secured a performance of his friend Apel's play about Christopher Columbus, celebrating the great navigator's heroic voyage of discovery and the opening up of a new continent. Wagner's own incidental music featured some interesting pictorialism in the swirling waves and the vision of the promised land, the latter atmospheric effect achieved by three pairs of trumpets playing what he described as a Fata Morgana theme. The six trumpets eventually combined in a triumphant climax to the work.

The actress Minna Planer, Wagner's first wife. Alexander von Otterstedt's portrait captures something of her wide-eyed, vivacious charm.

But the highlight of the season occurred towards its end, when in April 1835 the distinguished actress Wilhelmine Schröder-Devrient, by whose stage presence Wagner had first been struck several years back, arrived for a series of performances under him. So successful was their artistic collaboration that the soprano generously offered to give an extra benefit concert in his aid. He assembled a large orchestra, including doubled and trebled brass, and a mighty array of percussion and cannon effects, for Beethoven's 'Battle Symphony'. But the locals, perhaps not believing that Schröder-Devrient would really turn up, and probably deterred also by the high prices charged to recoup the costs, stayed away, leaving the great soprano to sing Beethoven's *Adelaide* to a half-empty hall. Worse was to follow. The audience's eardrums had only just recovered from the massive brass forces of the *Columbus* Overture, combined with the excessive reverberation of the hall, when they were assailed again by the cannons and muskets of the 'Battle Symphony'. Schröder-Devrient, who had graciously occupied a front-row seat to hear the remainder of the concert, fled from the hall in distress, followed by the rest of the audience, leaving Wellington's victory to be celebrated, as Wagner wryly noted, 'in an intimate exchange between the orchestra and myself alone'.[5]

Touring Bohemia and south Germany that summer in search of local talent, Wagner had two experiences that were to bear fruit several decades later. The first was the discovery of the small Bavarian town of Bayreuth, attractively illuminated in the evening sun. The second was a nocturnal street brawl in Nuremberg, into which Wagner found himself swept up. One of the things he found most memorable about it was that it came to an end 'as if by magic', on the sound of a punch received by one of the participants, straight between the eyes. Three decades later it was to

A concert in Magdeburg of the kind satirically described by Wagner as an hors d'oeuvre to the main event.

The Green Hill of
Bayreuth, much as it
might have looked to
Wagner on his first
glimpse, in 1835.

be the sound of the Nightwatchman's horn that would dispel a similarly frenzied fracas in *Die Meistersinger*.

The frustrations of being a musician in Magdeburg in the 1830s were revealed by Wagner in an anonymous report submitted to a journal edited by Robert Schumann. Laying on the irony like a patissier icing a cake, he pretends that concerts are merely a front for subversive political activity:

I go into a well-lit hall, everything is laid on as you would expect, they play symphonies, concertos, overtures, they sing arias and duets and spare no effort to make you think it is a genuine concert. But a politically trained eye soon notices something wrong: the indifference, the boredom, the restlessness in the auditorium; you realise that the whole thing is a blind, set up to deceive the spies and informers; the nearer the concert gets to the end the more eagerly the eyes of the conspirators are turned to a great closed door. What is behind it? During the adagio of the symphony you can hear plates being rattled in the next room … . The concert is over, everyone gets ready to go, respectable people like myself take their hats, and then the suspicious door is opened and tell-tale smells float into the hall, the conspirators throng through the door together – I am politely turned away.[6]

Anonymous silhouette
of Wagner, 1835.

Performing to an audience whose expectations were gastronomic rather than aesthetic was hardly a new experience for musicians, of course, but such blatant philistinism was bound to rile the idealist in Wagner.

Meanwhile he and Minna were settling into the pattern of mutual torment and tolerance that was to mark their thirty-year marriage. Minna was playing hard to get at this stage, and when she left to take up an engagement at the Königstadt Theatre in Berlin he indulged in a positively operatic outpouring of self-pity:

Minna, I cannot begin to describe the state I'm reduced to, you have left me, and my heart is broken; I am sitting here, scarcely in possession of my senses, weeping & sobbing like a child. Dear God, what am I to do; how & where shall I ever find consolation & peace of mind! ... Minna, Minna, what have you done to me! – I am at present sitting in my room, with my thoughts buzzing round in my head; – an emptiness which is hideous, – nothing but tears, grief & misery. – How are you feeling yourself? – A large beautiful city, ––––oh – I can't go on! –[7]

Similar letters were torn off every day from 4 to 12 November (1835), promising Minna marriage, financial assurance, the world. She finally capitulated and returned to Magdeburg within a fortnight of leaving. It was another year before they eventually tied the knot. Despite their tender feelings for each other, they were hardly suited by temperament or education to be partners. Wagner required a muse-cum-sounding board who could understand and support his visionary conception of art. Minna was content to give up her acting career in exchange for material security, and the biggest disappointment in her life was that Wagner would not settle for the stable existence of a Kapellmeister. Such incompatibilities were presaged when, the day before their wedding, they visited the officiating priest, who opened the door to find them squabbling and on the point of separating. The comical aspect of the situation was appreciated by all, however, and the ceremony went ahead on 24 November 1836.

The following spring Wagner was appointed music director at the Königsberg Theatre, but his new role certainly did not bring financial security, since the theatre was on the verge of bankruptcy. And in fact Minna left him, briefly, for a merchant called Dietrich. Wagner tracked her down at her parents' house in Dresden; although she was not prepared

The apartment in a suburb of Riga where Wagner composed the first two acts of *Rienzi*. The writing desk is placed between the two windows; on the right is a hired grand piano, and on the left a divan.

to return immediately, she did agree to stay with him for a time in lodgings outside the city, at Blasewitz. There he read Edward Bulwer-Lytton's novel about the Roman demagogue and last tribune Rienzi, which provided him with both the subject and the inspiration for a five-act grand opera in the French style.

A more satisfactory post then came his way in the form of the musical directorship of the theatre in Riga, the Livonian capital colonized by Germans. In the hope that this would provide both the artistic satisfaction he craved and the financial security he acknowledged was essential for his marriage, Wagner made the Baltic crossing alone in August 1837, to be joined by Minna and her sister Amalie, who had accepted a singing engagement at the theatre. The cosiness of this little ménage was enhanced further, for a brief period, by the adoption of a baby wolf.

In Riga Wagner began to set to music a text he had been working on, probably in Königsberg, with the curious title *Männerlist größer als Frauenlist oder Die glückliche Bärenfamilie* (Man's Cunning Greater than Woman's Cunning, or The Happy Bear Family). Sitting with pipe in mouth, clad in dressing gown and Turkish fez, he started to write a Singspiel based on the text, inspired by the *Arabian Nights*. Although he completed only two numbers, the style, reminiscent of French *opéra comique* and Italian *opera buffa* as well as German Singspiel, had an attractive light quality that Wagner was never again to essay in his operas.[8]

Riga turned out to be a cultural backwater – though Wagner was able to rehearse and/or conduct there operas by Auber, Beethoven, Bellini, Boieldieu, Cherubini, Meyerbeer, Mozart, Rossini, Spohr and Weber, among others – and after a contractual wrangle with the authorities he decided to try his luck in the very home of grand opera: Paris.

View of the market of Les Halles, Paris, *c.* 1828, by Giuseppe Canella I. The insalubrious Rue de la Tonnellerie, in which Wagner lived when he first came to Paris in 1839, was close by.

Wagner was heavily in debt and his passport had been impounded; the departure from Riga therefore had to be clandestine. Accompanied by their Newfoundland dog, Robber, he and Minna made their exit one night via a ditch marking the border, under the noses of armed Cossack guards; they reached the Prussian port of Pillau (now Baltiysk), where they were smuggled on board a small merchant vessel, the *Thetis*, bound for London. The stormy sea crossing may well have inspired or coloured the composition of *Der fliegende Holländer* (see Chapter 5: The Eternal Wanderer), which Wagner worked on once he had reached the French capital. He and Minna would remain there for a dismal, penurious two and a half years, undertaking hack work arranging operatic potpourris, severely undernourished and only narrowly avoiding a spell in the debtors' jail. Despite Wagner's later protestations to the contrary, it seems that Meyerbeer, the reigning monarch in the world of grand opera, did try to help the struggling younger composer. It was partly through Meyerbeer's influence that *Rienzi* was accepted not in Paris but by the Dresden Hoftheater, where it was performed to immense success in October 1842. By this time, however, Wagner had had to concede defeat in the heartland of grand opera: by the spring of that year he and his wife had already packed their bags and begun to prepare their return to the fatherland.

Postcard of Rienzi, showing the sword-wielding people's tribune astride a charger with patricians in the foreground.

4 Under the Yoke: Kapellmeister in Dresden

I have placed myself in harness.
Wagner to Samuel Lehrs

Der fliegende Holländer, staged at the Dresden Court Opera in January 1843, was not quite the resounding success that *Rienzi* had been the previous autumn. But it was enough to ensure that its composer was a strong candidate for a musical directorship at the king of Saxony's court, two such posts having fortuitously become vacant not long after Wagner and his wife had arrived back in Germany after their miserable sojourn in Paris. In fact, Wagner was by no means sure he wanted to submit to the yoke of court service and become a liveried retainer at the mercy of royal officialdom. However, the prospect of a decently paid job, with security for life (or so he thought), appealed greatly to the couple after their privations abroad.

Having turned down the subordinate post of Musikdirektor, or assistant conductor, Wagner accepted the job of Kapellmeister, which entailed responsibility for all the court's musical activities, including opera and orchestral concerts. The task was to be shared with another Kapellmeister, Karl Gottlieb Reissiger, with whom Wagner was technically on equal terms, as demonstrated by their respective contracts.

Two months into his royal service, Wagner was reporting back buoyantly to his Parisian friend Samuel Lehrs:

I shall be able to make only the odd journey out there [to the spa at Teplitz, modern Teplice] this summer now that I have placed myself in harness. But I cannot complain, it is an easy yoke to bear – and where it chafes, it will also yield. I am treated here with some distinction, of a kind that has almost certainly never been accorded anyone else in similar circumstances. Only six months ago I was still a vagabond who would not even have known where to get hold of a passport – whereas I now have tenure for life with a handsome salary and the prospect that it will continue to increase, and I control a sphere of influence such as has been granted to few men. No secret is being made of the fact that I am expected to undertake a thorough artistic reorganisation of the musical life here, as a result of which all the proposals I care to make are accepted unconditionally.[1]

Wagner's enthusiasm turned out to be misplaced in certain key respects, however. Reissiger, having won for Dresden the reputation of the finest opera house in Germany, had become indolent and attempted to palm off his more tedious duties onto his younger colleague. Nor was Wagner

Playbill for the premiere of *Der fliegende Holländer* at the Dresden Court Opera, which starred Wilhelmine Schröder-Devrient as Senta.

1ste Vorstellung im vierten Abonnement.

Königlich Sächsisches Hoftheater.

Montag, den 2. Januar 1843.

Zum ersten Male:

Der fliegende Holländer.

Romantische Oper in drei Akten, von Richard Wagner.

Personen:

Daland, norwegischer Seefahrer.	—	—	Herr Risse.
Senta, seine Tochter.	—	—	Mad. Schröder-Devrient.
Erik, ein Jäger. —		—	Herr Reinhold
Mary, Haushälterin Dalands.	—	—	Mad. Wächter.
Der Steuermann Dalands.	—	—	Herr Bielezizky.
Der Holländer. —		—	Herr Wächter.

Matrosen des Norwegers. Die Mannschaft des fliegenden Holländers. Mädchen.

Scene: Die norwegische Küste.

Textbücher sind an der Casse das Exemplar für 2½ Neugroschen zu haben.

Krank: Herr Dettmer.

Einlaß-Preise:

Ein Billet in die Logen des ersten Ranges und das Amphitheater . . 1 Thlr. — Ngr.

[price list]

Die Billets sind nur am Tage der Vorstellung gültig, und zurückgebrachte Billets werden nur bis Mittag 12 Uhr an demselben Tage angenommen.

Der Verkauf der Billets gegen sofortige baare Bezahlung findet in der, in dem untern Theile des Rundbaues befindlichen Expedition, auf der rechten Seite, nach der Elbe zu, früh von 9 Uhr bis Mittags 12 Uhr, und Nachmittags von 3 bis 4 Uhr statt.

Alle zur heutigen Vorstellung bestellte und zugesagte Billets sind Vormittags von 9 Uhr bis längstens 11 Uhr abzuholen, außerdem darüber anders verfügel wird.

Der freie Einlaß beschränkt sich bei der heutigen Vorstellung blos auf die zum Hofstaate gehörigen Personen und die Mitglieder des Königl. Hoftheaters.

Einlaß um 5 Uhr.   Anfang um 6 Uhr.
Ende gegen 9 Uhr.

Gottfried Semper's imposing Court Theatre at Dresden, where *Rienzi, Der fliegende Holländer* and *Tannhäuser* were all given their first performances.

correct in his impression that radical proposals to reorganize the musical life at court would be welcome – a fact that would lead to an irreconcilable rift between him and the management.

Initially, though, things went well, even if Wagner's health was not of the best. As he graphically reported to his sister Cäcilie in October 1843:

I'm at present suffering a particularly bad attack of piles; my bowels are in ruins, & the result is a permanent feeling of nausea & a rush of blood to my head. I intend undergoing a thorough course of treatment next spring & hope then to be rid once & for all of this tiresome affliction.[2]

One of Wagner's responsibilities was to provide music for ceremonial occasions, as he did with the chorus *Der Tag erscheint* (The Day Appears) on the unveiling of a memorial to King Friedrich August I in June 1843. That the composition of such occasional music was not necessarily galling to Wagner at this stage is demonstrated by an event the following year. When the popular monarch Friedrich August II returned to Saxony from England, Wagner risked breaching protocol by organizing a spontaneous tribute. Neither Wagner's superior, the Intendant, Baron von Lüttichau, nor Reissiger was amused, but the latter was mollified by an invitation to conduct, while Wagner took his place among the tenors. In fact, Wagner seems to have derived as much pleasure from the whole incident as the king, especially when he was able to organize a dramatically effective recessional (the king had actually asked for a repeat performance, but then, on account of a severe toothache, asked for it to be shortened).

Friedrich August II of Saxony, the popular monarch whose Kapellmeister Wagner became in 1843.

An early success of Wagner's was his conducting of Gluck's *Armide*. Shortly afterwards (on 6 July 1843) there followed a performance of a so-called 'biblical scene' of his own composition. Under the title *Das Liebesmahl der Apostel* (The Love-Feast of the Apostles), it formed part of a gala concert given by the male choral societies of Saxony. A vast chorus of 1,200 amateur singers and an orchestra of 100 gathered in Dresden's Frauenkirche and, although Wagner gave an upbeat account of it to his sister Cäcilie at the time ('The singers ... greeted me afterwards with shouts of vivat! & hurrah whenever they caught sight of me; there was no end to the general rejoicing'), his recollection many years later in *Mein Leben* was rather less enthusiastic, referring to the 'comparatively feeble effect' produced by the work.

A formative influence in Wagner's youth had been the music of Carl Maria von Weber, and he vigorously supported a campaign to have the composer's remains transferred from London, where he had died, to his home town of Dresden. After much bureaucratic obstruction, the ceremony finally took place on a December night in 1844, accompanied by a torchlit procession and funeral music written by Wagner. The following morning he delivered a stirring oration and conducted an ensemble of male voices in a setting of a poem written by himself.

Wagner made good use of the galleries in the Dresden Frauenkirche for the massed choirs of his biblical oratorio *Das Liebesmahl der Apostel*. Destroyed by fire bombing in World War II, the Frauenkirche has since been restored to its full glory.

The disembarking of Weber's remains at Hamburg en route for Dresden.

Mention should be made of the library that Wagner built up while living in Dresden. The catalogue, published in 1966, attests to the catholicity of his literary interests, both ancient and modern. Among the authors to be found there, mostly in German translation, were Aristophanes, Byron, Calderón, Chaucer, Dante, Gibbon, Goethe, Hegel, Homer, Horace, Lessing, Molière, Ossian, Plato, Schiller, Shakespeare, Sophocles, Tacitus, Thucydides, Virgil and Xenophon.

Wagner's library also included volumes he carried with him on a fruitful excursion to take the waters at Marienbad (now Marianske Lanske) in the summer of 1845. Editions of Gottfried von Strassburg's *Tristan*, the Parzivâl and Lohengrin epics, and a number of volumes on the life and times of the medieval cobbler-poet Hans Sachs were among them. Thus it can be seen that the subjects of *Lohengrin* and all the great music dramas to follow the *Ring* – *Tristan und Isolde, Die Meisteringer von Nürnberg* and *Parsifal* – were already germinating in his mind during this period.

In the meantime Wagner's latest opera, *Tannhäuser*, was staged successfully under his own direction in October 1845, after which he set himself the task of itemizing the reforms he deemed necessary in the musical establishment at the Dresden court. His recommendations included changes in the policy of hiring orchestral players, a rationalization of their workload, an increase in their salaries, and improvements in the layout of the orchestra so that players could hear each other and see the conductor clearly. He also suggested a series of winter orchestral concerts and the establishment of two concert halls, adaptable for other purposes. All very reasonable and, indeed, practicable, one might think. But Wagner scarcely endeared himself to his superiors by describing them as 'philistines' (Lüttichau's expertise was in fact not in the arts but in forestry), and after waiting a year for a response he was finally told that his proposals had been rejected.

It was a bitter blow. The realization that his ideas for reform of the institution were not welcomed after all was inescapable. Wagner's acute disappointment is evident in a letter to his friend and colleague Ferdinand Heine:

I am so full of utter contempt for everything connected with the theatre as it stands at present that – being unable to do anything about it – I have no more ardent desire than to sever all links with it, and I regard it as a veritable curse that my entire creative urge is directed towards the field of drama, since all I find in the miserable conditions which characterize our theatres today is the most abject scorn for all that I do.[3]

One of the officials with whom Wagner did not see eye to eye was Karl Gutzkow, appointed Intendant of the Court Theatre in 1846. Gutzkow was a writer (he had belonged to the literary Young Germany group banned in 1835), but was now in charge of the opera and theatre at court. Wagner perceived his administration as interference and complained that this 'journalist' was bringing the opera into disrepute through his incompetence and intriguing. Gutzkow, for his part, had little sympathy

Sepia drawing by F. Tischbein made after the premiere of *Tannhäuser*. It shows Wilhelmine Schröder-Devrient as Venus and Joseph Tichatschek as Tannhäuser.

The interior of the Dresden Court Theatre. Note the audience socializing in their boxes – an ostentation Wagner was to prohibit at Bayreuth – and the conductor with his back to some members of the orchestra.

with Wagner's drift towards a hybrid form of music drama: for him, 'opera must stay opera and drama drama'. He went on, in his reminiscence of later years, to register his disapproval of Wagner's aesthetic in extraordinary terms:

At every performance of a Wagner opera that I heard (I was present later at the first performance of *Lohengrin* in Weimar) I heard the most exaggeratedly demonstrative applause, the beginning of this claque which has been organized throughout Germany and which Wagner, Liszt and others will one day have to answer for in the history of art. Behind me in the audience there was a German–Russian family, literally going crazy with wild fanaticism and making an unbelievable contribution to the Wagner cult. In Dresden they set the tone for this adulation. Women in high society, licentious natures, and men of effeminate character then made the propagation of Wagnerian music in other places and in the same manner their particular concern.[4]

There was certainly a hugely enthusiastic audience – whether consisting predominantly of licentious women and effeminate men is not known – for a special event masterminded by Wagner in 1846. The occasion was the annual Palm Sunday benefit concert held in aid of the royal orchestra's widows' and orphans' fund. To the horror of the trustees, Wagner proposed to mount a performance of Beethoven's Ninth Symphony, still regarded at that time as the work of a madman. So successful was he in whetting the appetite of the public with tantalizing press announcements that the receipts actually exceeded those of all previous years. Thanks to Wagner's meticulous rehearsal schedule (the cellos and basses had twelve special sessions to perfect the difficult recitative-like passage at the start of the finale) and bold reorganization of the performing space, the concert was also an unqualified artistic success.

The following year Wagner mounted a production of Gluck's *Iphigénie en Aulide* in an edition he prepared himself. Favourably impressed by

Philipp Stölzl's 2010 production of *Rienzi* for the Deutsche Oper, Berlin, emphasized the totalitarian aspects of the story through iconographical references to Nazi propaganda.

Gluck's progressive tendencies – especially his abandonment of regular melodic periods – Wagner endeavoured to 'improve' the dramatic flow of the work still further by means of preludes, postludes and transitions. At this time also he studied Aeschylus (in particular the *Oresteia* trilogy), Aristophanes, and many other Greek authors in German translation.

A plan to put on *Rienzi* in Berlin met with mixed success. The opera did indeed reach the stage of the court theatre, but it was not received well by the Berlin press; to add insult to injury, Wagner was not paid for the two months of rehearsals, nor did the production achieve the desired effect of securing a commission for *Lohengrin* from the king of Prussia.

Early the next year, on 9 January 1848, Wagner's mother died in Leipzig. Though Wagner was not close to her, her death came as a blow. His sense of loneliness now that the last link with his family had been broken (his siblings were all now occupied elsewhere) was mitigated to some extent by work on *Lohengrin* and preparations for a series of three orchestral and choral concerts in Dresden. Artistic conditions at the court were becoming increasingly irksome, however. The constant thwarting of Wagner's radical schemes, combined with ongoing financial problems (his Kapellmeister's salary was less than generous) and the cutting of his last remaining family ties, conspired to foster a general sense of dissatisfaction. Wagner was ripe for the surge of revolutionary activity that was about to break in Germany.

5   The Eternal Wanderer: *Der fliegende Holländer*

The longing for peace amid the storms of life
         Wagner

On the face of it, the eponymous Flying Dutchman is the figure around whom Wagner's opera revolves. It is *his* torment, *his* redemption, that form the backbone of the story. In recent years, however, scholarship has made us aware of just how crucial a figure Senta is, and on closer examination it appears that, both musically and conceptually, a Senta-centred reading pays rich dividends.

Certainly Senta's Ballad, the song in Act II in which the heroine mesmerizes her audience of fellow spinning-girls with her song about the pale sea captain who plies the world's oceans for eternity in his ship with blood-red sails and a black mast – punishment for a blasphemous, hubristic oath – was one of the work's earliest numbers to be written. It was on board the vessel *Thetis*, during his flight from creditors in Riga, that Wagner had the initial inspiration for the work. Or so he tells us in his slightly fanciful autobiographical account. Having braved a violent storm in the Skagerrak, he reports, they had taken shelter in a Norwegian fjord:

Senta with factory seamstresses in a post-war Soviet bloc setting: Tim Albery's 2009 production for Covent Garden.

A feeling of indescribable well-being came over me as the sailors' calls echoed round the massive granite walls while they cast anchor and furled the sails. The sharp rhythm of these calls clung to me like a consoling augury and soon shaped itself into the theme of the [Norwegian] sailors' song in my *Fliegender Holländer*. Already at that time I was carrying around with me the idea of this opera and now, under the impressions I had just experienced, it acquired a distinct poetic and musical colour.[1]

In actual fact Wagner's story was originally set not in Norway at all, but in Scotland, though that does not necessarily undermine the validity of his claim that the stormy voyage and its aftermath were inspirational influences. What we do know for sure is that, even before setting down his

In Hugo L. Braune's illustration, the gruesome Dutch sea captain and the blood-red sails of his vessel evoke the demonic aura of Wagner's maritime opera.

poem for the opera in Meudon, just outside Paris, in May 1841, Wagner had begun to compose some music for it. The first numbers to be written included, as one would expect, the chorus of the Norwegian sailors, but also the chorus of the Dutchman's crew and, crucially, Senta's Ballad. This would probably have been between May and July 1840, a year after the *Thetis* voyage. Perhaps Wagner had jotted down musical ideas in the meantime, but there is no evidence of that. The rest of the score was drafted fairly rapidly after the poem, by 22 August 1841, and the full score was completed by 19 November.

The centrality to the drama of Senta's Ballad has long been debated. On the one hand we have Wagner's testimony, as set down a decade later in his 'Communication to my Friends':

I remember that before I proceeded to write *Der fliegende Holländer* at all, I first sketched Senta's second-act Ballad, composing both the text and the melody; in this piece I unwittingly planted the thematic seed of all the music in the opera: it was the poetically condensed image of the whole drama, as it was in my mind's eye; and when I had to find a title for the finished work I was strongly tempted to call it a 'dramatic ballad'. When I came eventually to the composition, the thematic image I had already conceived quite involuntarily spread out over the whole drama in a complete, unbroken web; all that was left for me to do was to allow the various thematic germs contained in the Ballad to develop to the full, each in its own direction, and all the principal features of the text were arrayed before me in specific thematic shapes of their own making.[2]

This is an account that needs to be treated with some caution, since by the time he wrote the 'Communication', in 1851, Wagner was well on the way to creating his 'artwork of the future': the through-composed music drama as opposed to opera with separate numbers. On the other hand, it is also the case that elements of Senta's Ballad appear elsewhere in the work, often in important numbers, for example the Dutchman's Monologue, Erik's Dream, the Act II duet for Senta and the Dutchman, and the finale. In a recent study of Wagner's female characters, from Senta to Kundry, Nila Parly points out that, although Senta's Ballad tells of the Dutchman's destiny, 'it is primarily an expression of *her* psyche, *her* longing'. Moreover, the Ballad 'reverberates throughout the entire opera, having influence that can be felt in even the tiniest detail', with the result that Senta effectively 'takes the lead role in the opera' in purely musical terms.[3] The Dutchman, of course, dominates in terms of the text and the drama as a whole, but his big Act I monologue, for all its expressive force, is self-contained and has no musical ramifications beyond the monologue itself. Significantly, the Dutchman's Monologue makes no appearance in the overture, which is based almost entirely on ideas to be found in Senta's Ballad.

Nevertheless, it is the elemental world of the storm-tossed mariner that is conjured up in the overture: its glassy open 5ths (surely a reminiscence of the opening of Beethoven's Ninth Symphony) on wind and strings provide a bracing aural backdrop for the striding theme of the Dutchman (also based on 5ths, and their inversion, 4ths). The rolling waves and the

sound of wind whistling through the rigging are also graphically depicted
– indeed, this is Wagner's most vivid piece of tone painting to date. It is
after the curtain rises that we hear most clearly the sailors' calls echoing
round the massive granite walls of the Norwegian fjord, just as Wagner
described it. A pair of horns – the first *forte*, the second *piano* – reiterate a
series of such calls to suggest the receding effect of an echo. Eventually a
steersman is left on watch, battling with sleep. He launches into a folklike
mariner's song, but his increasingly fragmented line and the orchestral
interspersions tell us that he has lost the battle. The blood-red sails of the
Dutchman's ship appear in the distance, heralded by open 5ths, tremolos
and his striding theme. The Dutchman's Monologue ('Die Frist ist um'
– The term is up) begins in recitative-like mode before a powerful arioso

Wagner and his
steersman aboard the
Thetis, weathering a
storm in the Skagerrak,
as imagined by an
illustrator for *National
Geographic* magazine
(1944).

The blood-red sails of
the Flying Dutchman's
ship in the early
modernist, geometric
setting of the historic
Kroll Opera production
(1929).

is initiated over a rolling-wave accompaniment. The expressive force of this latter section ('Wie oft in Meeres tiefsten Schlund' – How often into the ocean's deepest maw) is enhanced in two ways: by irregular phrase patterns (the first eight-bar period consists of a five-bar and a three-bar phrase instead of the usual four plus four), and by the way the shape of the phrases suggests the Dutchman's alternating rising hopes and consequent dejection. The central section of the monologue ('Dich frage ich' – I beseech you) uses tremolo to rather different effect, to convey more generalized mental agitation. It was surely this passage Berlioz had in mind when he noted in his *Memoirs*:

> The score of the *Dutchman* I thought remarkable for its dark coloration and certain storm-effects perfectly motivated by the story; but I could not help noticing as well an excessive use of the *tremolo*, which is the more disturbing in that it had already struck me in *Rienzi* and that it implies a certain intellectual laziness on the part of the composer, against which he is not sufficiently on his guard. Of all orchestral effects, sustained *tremolo* is the one you get tired of most quickly; what is more, it requires no imagination at all on the part of the composer when there is no striking idea above or below it.[4]

A fair comment, one might think, though Wagner redeems himself in the monologue's final section ('Nur eine Hoffnung soll mir bleiben' – One hope alone remains to me), with its sweeping vocal phrases (marked in places to be intensified with portamento) and hammerblow orchestral accompaniment.

Daland welcomes the Dutchman against a quasi-19th century backdrop recalling Arnold Böcklin. Peter Konwitschny's 2006 production of *Der fliegende Holländer* ironically references German Romanticism, but the Dutchman himself might have stepped out of a painting by Frans Hals.

When the Dutchman encounters the Norwegian skipper, Daland, shortly after, and offers his treasure for a night under Daland's roof with daughter thrown in, we are not surprised to have some music in lighter mode. Daland's 'Wie? Hör' ich recht?' (What? Did I hear right?) introduces a number of toe-curling banality, with a harmonic scheme and regularity of phrase worthy of the most superficial models from which Wagner was busily distancing himself. All very well, perhaps, as an ironic comment on the one-dimensional, money-grubbing sea captain, until the Dutchman enters in the same mode – indeed, with the main tune in all its glorious vulgarity.

A more traditional representation, by Michael Echter (1872), of the encounter between the desperate Flying Dutchman and the grasping merchant Daland.

Passages such as this remind us that in *Der fliegende Holländer* Wagner was still very much in thrall to traditional genres while struggling to find his own identity. Senta's Ballad in Act II is a perfect illustration of the dichotomy. On the one hand, such a ballad is a traditional topos in 19th-century opera: Jenny's in Boieldieu's *La dame blanche* and Emmy's in Marschner's *Der Vampyr* (both well known to Wagner) are just two examples. On the other hand, Wagner elevates it – not least in his post-hoc rationalization quoted above – to a position of crucial importance in the opera. Coming, too, as it does immediately after the metrical chattering of the Spinning Chorus (another generic number, for which Wagner seems to have lifted an exact phrase from a spinning song in *La dame blanche*[5]), Senta's Ballad lifts us out of the mundane, bourgeois, domestic sphere of the spinning maidens and into another world altogether: a world where one might dare everything, risk not just one's life but one's immortal soul, in search of an experience not granted to ordinary mortals.

Generally speaking, there is a striking contrast between the characterization of the 'exterior', public world of Daland, Erik, the Norwegian sailors and the maidens on the one hand, and the 'interior' world of the imagination inhabited by Senta and the Dutchman on the other. The 'exterior' world is depicted by traditional forms and harmonies, of which Daland's music represents an extreme example. Erik's two set pieces are another: 'Mein Herz voll Treue bis zum Sterben' (My heart faithful to death) in Act II and the cavatina 'Willst jenes Tags du nicht dich mehr entsinnen?' (Do you no longer remember that day?) in Act III both fall into regular, tuneful phrases, adorned with turns, cadenzas and other conventional features. Little wonder Senta gives him such short shrift.

Senta holds her audience of fellow spinners enthralled with her story of the cursed Dutch sea captain. Gouache by Ferdinand Leeke, 1894.

Paradoxically, however, it is with Erik, the boring huntsman, that one of the opera's most progressive passages is associated. It occurs in the second act, in what the score refers to as a 'duet' for Erik and Senta. Erik is recounting to Senta a dream he has had, in which her father brings home a stranger resembling the seafarer in the picture hanging on the wall: 'Auf hohem Felsen' (On a high cliff). Against an evocative background of horns and tremolo strings, Erik begins his narrative 'in a stifled voice', on repeated notes – in other words, he is reliving his dream. As the narrative progresses and he describes the foreign ship he saw ('seltsam, wunderbar' – strange, wondrous) his vocal line becomes fragmented, dictated solely by the experience he is recounting rather than by the demands of conventional phrase structure. Senta, who has sunk 'into a kind of magnetic slumber', empathizes with the vision so strongly that she appropriates it as her own. Her vocal line and his become indistinguishable, the one growing out of the other.

This is the most advanced word-setting anywhere in *Der fliegende Holländer* and as far from a conventional duet as it would be possible to imagine. Even the duet at the end of Act II for Senta and the Dutchman, for all its splendid music, is relatively traditional in form. Choral ensembles – which Wagner was (theoretically, at least) to banish from the 'artwork of the future' – are still present, as witness the Sailors' Chorus

The Dutchman's crew take on a ghoulish aura in Tim Albery's 2009 production for Covent Garden.

Preis' deinen Engel und sein Gebot!
Hier steh ich, treu dir bis zum Tod!

Senta, faithful to death, leaps from a cliff in a bid to release the Flying Dutchman from his curse. Illustration by Hugo Braune.

ending Act I and the Spinning Chorus in Act II. The extended chorus work in Act III, however, is far more progressive, breaking out of formal constraints to convey the struggle between the rival crews. The act begins with the conventional world of the Norwegian sailors, carousing on board their ship, and gradually emboldened to taunt the invisible Dutch crew. The latter finally strike up in ghostly chorus, setting the scene for an electrifying confrontation between increasingly apprehensive Norwegians and the original sailors from hell – a battle won inevitably by the latter, with cackles of diabolical laughter.

6 Desperately Seeking Venus: *Tannhäuser*

The opera with a lot of girls at the beginning
Neville Chamberlain

Tannhäuser (Johan
Botha) is tempted
by fleshly delights
in Tim Albery's
2010 production for
Covent Garden. Note
the incorporation
of proscenium and
theatrical décor to
suggest the merging
of art and life.

Saint and sinner, Madonna and whore, flesh and spirit: these are the traditional binaries around which Wagner's *Tannhäuser* is constructed. Oscillating between sacred and profane love, represented by Elisabeth and Venus respectively, *Tannhäuser* negotiates this dialectical opposition, finally breaking out of the straitjacket of stereotypes. Venus and her realm may be banished at the work's conclusion, but the libidinal life force she embodies has by then made a transformative impact on the ossified attitude to sexuality exemplified by the knights and minstrels of Wartburg society. Even so, it is one of the more curious paradoxes of Wagnerian opera that the composer, regarded as the quintessential purveyor of excessive sensuality in art, appears to repudiate the unbridled eroticism with which he is irredeemably associated. That paradox lies at the heart of the conception of *Tannhäuser*.

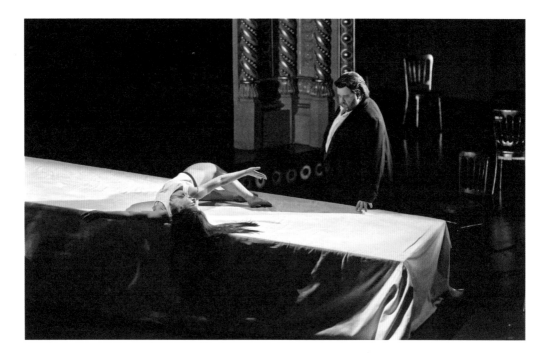

A Romantic view of
Venus's seduction
of Tannhäuser, with
classical references.
Painting by Otto
Knille, 1873.

Two of the chief sources for the medieval stories of Tannhäuser and
the song contest at the Wartburg were Ludwig Tieck's *Der getreue Eckart
und der Tannenhäuser* (The Faithful Eckart and Tannenhäuser, 1799) and
E. T. A. Hoffmann's tale *Der Kampf der Sänger* (The Singers' Contest),
from his *Serapions-Brüder* cycle (1819–21). Tieck's Tannenhäuser, like
Wagner's, dallied in the Venusberg, but found its pleasures stifling.
Hoffmann's story, by contrast, deals with a song competition at the
Wartburg in which the participants include Wolfframb von Eschinbach
and Heinrich von Ofterdingen. In his autobiography, Wagner tells how a
chance encounter suggested to him the possibility of a drama that fused
the separate stories of Tannhäuser and his cupidinous dalliance in the
Venusberg with the song contest at the Wartburg:

I was suddenly gripped by a quite different subject. This came to me quite by
chance through a folk book about the Venusberg. All I regarded as inherently
German had attracted me with ever-increasing force and impelled me to look
for its deepest meaning with enthusiastic longing, and here I suddenly found
it in the simple retelling of the legend, based on the ancient, well-known ballad
of Tannhäuser. Of course I already knew the basic outlines of the story from
Tieck's version in his *Phantasus*; yet his conception of the subject had led me
back in the direction of fantasy, as evoked for me by Hoffmann, and I had in no
way felt myself tempted to attempt an adaptation of the material for dramatic
purposes. The element in the folk book which made such an impact on me was
the connection, if only fleetingly set forth, of Tannhäuser with the contest of
song at the Wartburg. I was also familiar with this through Hoffmann's story in
his *Serapions-Brüder*; but I felt that the writer had a distorted view of this old
material and I now wanted to form a more authentic picture of this attractive
legend for myself.[1]

Landgrave Hermann I of Thuringia and his wife, Sophia, preside over a singing contest in an illustration from the 14th-century Manesse Codex.

Sebastian Baumgarten's controversial production of *Tannhäuser* for Bayreuth (2011) debates modern obsessions with science and technology. Designer Joep van Lieshout's vision of the Wartburg features an eco-recycling complex complete with alcohol processor.

The folk book in question was almost certainly Ludwig Bechstein's collection of Thuringian legends, *Der Sagenschatz und die Sagenkreise des Thüringerlandes* (1835–38), which erroneously and anachronistically associated the two stories. At about the same time, as Wagner goes on to describe, his friend Samuel Lehrs drew to his attention a scholarly paper by C. T. L. Lucas arguing (the theory has not subsequently been accepted) that one of the competitors at the Wartburg, Heinrich von Ofterdingen, was to be identified with Tannhäuser the minnesinger.

A third source is also worth mentioning: Heinrich Heine's essay *Elementargeister* (Elemental Spirits), which appeared in 1837 in the third volume of *Der Salon* and contained a characteristically ironic poem about Tannhäuser. Wagner was less than impressed by the irony – that was not his style – but he very probably gleaned a good deal of incidental detail on the Tannhäuser legend from Heine.

Retiring to Aussig (now Ustí nad Labem) in the Bohemian mountains, Wagner developed a prose draft of his text in the summer of 1842. The finished libretto followed in spring 1843 and then, after having sketched a number of individual sections of the work, Wagner elaborated two complete drafts, apparently worked on in tandem (summer/autumn 1843 to January 1845). The overture was written last, and the full score completed on 13 April 1845.

In 1842 Wagner took himself off on a ramble in the Bohemian mountains that lasted several days, making a prose draft of *Tannhäuser* while on the Schreckenstein. Ludwig Richter's 1835 depiction of the mountain dates from just a few years earlier.

For all that Wagner claims to have found Tieck's version of the legend unsuitable, its impact on his conception can clearly be seen. Tieck's Tannenhäuser is seduced so ungovernably by the scent of roses that he stoops to embrace the bushes – apparently heedless of their thorns – kissing the flowers 'on their red mouths'. Rosy mists and scents also loom large in Wagner's Venusberg (as shown by the detailed stage directions for the opera's first scene). But Tieck's eroticism is even more explicit:

A bevy of naked girls surrounded me invitingly, perfumes swirled magically around my head, as out of the most intimate heart of nature there resounded a music which cooled with its fresh waves the yearning of wild carnal desire. A terror, which crept so stealthily across the fields of flowers, heightened the ravishing music.[2]

Tieck's description thus evokes music that both ravishes the senses and cools carnal desires. And that is precisely what we have in Wagner's Bacchanale. As the sexual frenzy finally dies down, we hear the 'fresh waves' of that cooling music in the C major woodwind chords that accompany the calls of the distant sirens; the harmonies given to the latter are

A postcard showing Tannhäuser's face composed of the minstrel himself, Venus and her roseate attendants.

calm yet seductive. As usual, Wagner wants it both ways: even as unbridled sensuality is condemned in his text, the music celebrates it in no uncertain terms. And this is only the first of many contradictions in Wagner's *Tannhäuser*. In the Bacchanale composed for the Paris production of 1861, youths, nymphs, bacchantes, fauns and satyrs disport themselves to the accompaniment of voluptuous harmonies. Nothing in any of Wagner's earlier works approaches this licentious orgy for its shameless stimulation of the senses – visual and olfactory as well as aural.[3] These revellers, by the way, represent the lower orders banished to the Venusberg along with the classical gods at the arrival of Christianity, according to legend.

Nonetheless, there was a curiously puritanical streak in Wagner, which caused him to react against unfettered eroticism. In his 'Communication to my Friends' he tells us that he was longing

to find satisfaction in some more elevated and noble element which, unlike the immediately recognizable sensuality in life and art which was all around me in the present, I conceived as being something pure, chaste, virginal and inaccessibly and unfathomably loving. And what else could this loving desire be, this noblest of sentiments which it was in my nature to feel, but the longing to vanish from the present, to perish in that element of infinite love which was unknown on earth, in a way that only death seemed able to achieve?[4]

This is no pious or Christian sentiment, he hastens to add. Rather it was an aspiration for a higher form of love, something more spiritual – a love that perhaps could not be realized in this world. It is this form of idealized love that Elisabeth, in Wagner's opera, might have offered, had she lived. For Elisabeth is not the plaster saint she was for too long made out to be in traditional stage productions. On the contrary, she is subject to genuine stirrings of passion. These are alluded to first in her duet with Tannhäuser in Act II. 'Where have you been all this time?', she asks him, now he has returned to the bosom of his fellow minstrels. 'Far from here in distant, distant lands,' he replies, but tactful amnesia has set in about the Venusberg: 'all recollection has suddenly vanished,' he says. Elisabeth goes on:

But what a strange new world of feeling
awoke in me when I heard you!
At times it seemed I'd die of sorrow,
and then my heart would burst with joy,
with feelings I had not experienced,
and longings I had never known![5]

– as authentic an evocation of first love as any in Wagner's operas.

When, later in the act, Tannhäuser shocks the assembled company with his stated intention to slake his lusts, a stage direction coyly notes that Elisabeth should exhibit 'a conflict of feelings of rapture and anxious surprise'.[6] By the third act, it is true, Elisabeth has been drained of any sexual longing she might have had: now her life is given over to prayer and expiation. Or, as another stage direction has it, 'her way leads to heaven, where she has a high purpose to fulfil'.[7] For all her sensual potential, then, Elisabeth's primary role is as one pole in a binary pairing with Venus.

What is predicated here, however, is not a choice between eros and renunciation, as often used to be assumed. Rather it is an elevation – an *Aufhebung*, to use the Hegelian term for what results from the clash of thesis and antithesis – into something nobler. Carnality is not so much vanquished as embraced and ennobled, a point that emerges clearly from Wagner's own programme note for the overture (the original version, ending with the Pilgrims' Hymn):

It is the shout of jubilation of the Venusberg itself, redeemed from the curse of unholy desire, which we hear amidst the hymn to God. Thus all of life's pulsating forces seethe and leap to the song of redemption; and both disseevered elements, spirit and senses, God and Nature, embrace in the hallowed unity of love's redeeming kiss.[8]

It was surely by reason of this transcendence of Venusberg that Wagner was originally minded to entitle his work *Der Venusberg* (The Mount of Venus) – until he was persuaded of the likelihood of ribald jokes by the less pure-minded.

What recent studies have suggested is that it is not so much carnality that is overcome in *Tannhäuser* as patriarchal oppression. This is seen most clearly in the gathering of Wartburg society in Act II. The march that announces the arrival of the knights, nobles and their ladies is introduced by military-style fanfares, and the chorus that unfolds is as grandiose and self-satisfied as these representatives of high society themselves.

Wolfram holds Tannhäuser back from the welcoming arms of Venus and her attendants, as Elisabeth prays for his soul. Undated gouache by Franz Stassen.

A medieval setting for the Hall of Song, sketched by Philippe Chaperon for the Paris production of 1861.

The song contest provides an opportunity for the minstrels Wolfram von Eschinbach, Walther von der Vogelweide and Biterolf to pontificate on the form of chivalric love that defined and regulated sexual relations in the medieval era and, *mutatis mutandis*, in Wagner's time too: men determined the ordering of society with their laws regarding property and marriage, while women, decoratively ensconced on their pedestals, were freed from the obligation of having sexual feelings of their own.

But Tannhäuser's celebration of 'true love' is not exactly a radical feminist vision either: rather it is a yearning for the indulgence of bodily desire. Patriarchy subsists in the Venusberg as well as in the Wartburg. Tannhäuser's real sin, as Nila Parly perceptively suggests, may be that he loves only himself. His self-indulgence has a strongly narcissistic flavour, and indeed it was for the 'sin of pride', he tells Wolfram on his return from Rome, that he sought forgiveness. Evidently, having left the Venusberg of his own volition, but finding himself oppressed by the reactionary mores of the Wartburg, he began to turn his lustful, selfish gaze on Elisabeth. Understanding the needs of others is a vital part of the process of self-enlightenment, and the redemption effected by Elisabeth is in essence,

Parly notes, a turning away from this self-absorption towards a selfless, empathetic love.[9]

The formal numbers – aria, duet, chorus – that characterized conventional opera are still in evidence in *Tannhäuser*, but their integrity is eroded even further than was the case in *Der fliegende Holländer*. Declamatory recitative is more prevalent and reaches its apogee in the extended solo for Tannhäuser in Act III, known as the 'Rome Narration'. As Tannhäuser relates the circumstances of his journey – his fervent state of mind in setting out, his memory of Elisabeth, the pilgrims' heavy burdens, his encounter with the pope – music and text are meshed more scrupulously than anywhere else in the work. Awkward accentuations are avoided, and the ever increasing intensity of the dramatic situation is mirrored in the pitch and inflections of the vocal line.

At the opposite end of the spectrum is Wolfram's celebrated aria 'O du mein holder Abendstern' (O Star of Eve), also in Act III, with its regular four-bar phrases, while the Act II love duet for Tannhäuser and Elisabeth, for all its sectional character, sets the traditional demands of melodic interest and metrical regularity above dramatic projection. However, whereas the natural accentuation of words is blatantly disregarded in the duet, in Wolfram's aria it is treated with all due respect. It is here, then, and even more so in the Rome Narration, that we can sense Wagner edging his way towards the kind of musico-poetic synthesis that was one of the distinguishing features of his mature music dramas (see Chapter 10: The Rise and Fall of Valhalla).

Theatrical conventions are undermined in Stefan Herheim's production of *Tannhäuser* (Oslo, 2010): references to *Carmen*, *Aida*, *Magic Flute* and other operas abound in the Bacchanal.

Tannhäuser confessing his sins to Pope Urban IV, as depicted by Ferdinand Piloty the Younger on the walls of Neuschwanstein Castle.

Elsewhere, though, the vestiges of conventional opera make their presence felt. Indeed, one could regard the whole of the final section of Act II, from the assembly of the guests to the end of the act, as an exemplar of the typical pattern of a mid-19th century Italianate finale. At the climax of the latter occurs the classic interruption to a choral ensemble – in this case the intervention of Elisabeth, pleading for Tannhäuser's life – followed by a more reflective passage for her (in B minor) and an adagio prayer (in B major). Elisabeth's simple eloquence moves everybody. Tannhäuser, 'crushed with remorse', sinks to the ground with a heartfelt cry of grief. Then, in a double chorus, the minstrels and knights take up the theme of Elisabeth's prayer, hailing this intervention by an 'angel'. Tannhäuser's interjections of 'Erbarm' dich mein!' (Have mercy!) were originally intended to carry over the flood of the entire ensemble; later Wagner allowed the other voices to be omitted if necessary. The Landgrave, introduced with due solemnity, steps into the centre and announces that a band of pilgrims, their sins far more trivial than Tannhäuser's, is about to leave for Rome. The chorus takes up a melodic fragment of the Landgrave's and, urging Tannhäuser himself to depart for the papal city, brings the act to an appropriately Italianate conclusion.

7 Swansong to Traditional Opera: *Lohengrin*

Lohengrin is the favourite opera of all sensitive ladies.
Eduard Hanslick

With the final panel of his triptych of Romantic operas – *Der fliegende Holländer, Tannhäuser, Lohengrin* – Wagner reaches a crucial juncture in his career. For *Lohengrin*, while rooted in the genres of French and Italian grand opera that still dominated the continent, already bears the seeds of the radically ambitious new genre, the music drama, with which Wagner was about to change the course of operatic history.

Thus, on the one hand, there are in *Lohengrin* vestiges of recitative, aria, duet and chorus, not to mention the processions, calls-to-arms and spectacular tableaux in which grand opera excelled. On the other hand, we also find that Wagner is beginning to abandon the old number form and regular phrase structure of opera as it was then known in favour of through-composed paragraphs that fuse verse and music in an entirely new way.

As often with stylistic hybrids, there is a particular fascination with regard to *Lohengrin* in the tension between regressive and progressive elements. Much as we admire the passages of forward-looking writing (such as that for Ortrud and Telramund in Act II Scene 1), we also thrill to the noble sweep of the procession to the minster (also Act II) – straight out of the grand opera textbook, even down to the two melodramatic interruptions. Poised on the brink of the stylistic revolution about to be unleashed with the *Ring, Lohengrin* wraps the medieval legend of the Swan Knight in a cloak of rapturous, ethereal Romantic harmony.

It was in the fertile summer of 1845, while taking the waters at Marienbad, that Wagner familiarized himself with the Lohengrin legend. He had with him editions by Simrock and San-Marte of *Parzivâl* and *Titurel* by the poet Wolfram von Eschenbach (1170–shortly after 1220), and an edition of the anonymous epic *Lohengrin*.[1] In no time at all, he tells us in his none-too-reliable autobiography, the figure of Lohengrin 'stood suddenly revealed before me in full armour', the story 'complete in every detail of its dramatic shaping'.[2]

Supposedly undergoing a water cure in Marienbad, Wagner had been attempting to follow his doctor's instructions by freeing his mind of the *Lohengrin* material (by setting down an idea that was to form a scene in *Die Meistersinger von Nürnberg*, as it happens). It was in vain, however:

The traditional 19th-century representation of the Grail Knight and his supernatural mode of transport (see following page) are ironically referenced in Stefan Herheim's 2009 *Lohengrin* for the Staatsoper, Berlin. Klaus Florian Vogt is the flying Lohengrin.

Ludwig Schnorr von Carolsfeld, the first Lohengrin, painted himself as the Grail Knight. His avian vehicle is seen in the background, as is a Romantically medieval castle worthy of Ludwig II.

The hydropathic establishment at Marienbad where, according to Wagner's own account, he had the inspiration for *Lohengrin* while in the bath.

No sooner had I stepped into my midday bath than I was seized with such a desire to write down *Lohengrin* that, incapable of remaining in the bath for the prescribed hour, I sprang out impatiently after just a few minutes, scarcely allowing myself the time to get dressed again properly, and ran like a madman to my lodging in order to set down on paper what was obsessing me.[3]

It is an appealing account: a Eureka moment in the bath of a hydropathic establishment, with Wagner running down the corridor, half naked, dripping wet, desperate to get the *Lohengrin* scenario down on paper. In similar cases, musicologists have felt obliged to contradict Wagner's account in the interests of historical exactitude. In this case, there is no evidence to contradict Wagner's story; and, as it happens, the prose scenario he set down on 3 August while at Marienbad is remarkably close to the final version of the poem he subsequently worked out when he got back to Dresden.

The scenario produced by Wagner was strongly coloured by prevalent ideas to which he was exposed at the time – notably those associated with Young Germany, a radical literary and political movement that promoted republican and democratic ideals, and those of the philosopher Ludwig Feuerbach. The Lohengrin story revolves around a trope familiar from fairy tales, known as the 'Forbidden Question'. Elsa is told that her rescue by a knight is conditional on her refraining from asking her saviour's name or origins. She fails to keep the bargain, and Lohengrin is finally forced to reveal his identity as the Grail Knight and to leave Elsa and her compatriots behind. On the face of it, the story has a misogynistic streak: idle female curiosity has got the better of Elsa, and she is duly punished. But this is not how Wagner saw the situation. For him, the forbidden question is the *necessary* question, the one that any faithful lover should ask of his or her partner.

It was through Elsa, Wagner claimed in his essay 'A Communication to my Friends', that he first 'learned to understand the purely human

Ludwig Feuerbach's groundbreaking critique of religion was to have a profound impact on Wagner's works, beginning with *Lohengrin*.

In diesem Hause komponierte Richard Wagner im Sommer 1846 die Oper „Lohengrin"

Lohengrin-Haus Graupa bei Dresden

The so-called 'Lohengrin House' at Graupa, near Dresden, where much of the opera was composed.

element of love'. Lohengrin may have been answering the call of a damsel in distress, but he had his own needs. This is how Wagner put it:

Lohengrin sought the woman who would *trust* in him; who would not ask who he was or whence he came, but love him as he was, and because he was as he seemed to her. He sought the woman to whom he would not have to explain himself, or to justify himself, but who would *love* him unconditionally. He therefore has to conceal his higher nature, for it is precisely in the non-revelation of this higher – or more correctly heightened – essence that the true security subsisted that he was not admired and marvelled at for it alone, nor humbly worshipped as one beyond all understanding. On the contrary, he longed not for admiration and worship, but for the one thing that could redeem him from his loneliness and quench his yearning: he longed for *love, to be loved, to be understood through love*.[4]

Longing for the love of such a woman (Wagner goes on), Lohengrin descended from his 'blissful, empty solitude' on hearing Elsa's cry for help. But 'there clings to him the telltale halo of his heightened nature'. Recognized as something suprahuman, he is now plagued by the thought that he is being worshipped rather than understood. Compelled to admit his special nature, he returns to the lonely sphere from which he came.

Elsa, for her part, is driven by her unalloyed, unconditional love to ask the question that cannot be avoided. She 'awakes from the thrill of worship into the full reality of love,' says Wagner, and loves Lohengrin with the unquestioning commitment that he believed was as necessary from men as from women. As a result, Wagner tells us, Elsa 'made a complete revolutionary of me'.[5]

What, then, does the Forbidden Question represent in *Lohengrin?* The fact that Elsa is proscribed from enquiring after Lohengrin's name or origins suggests at best insecurity, at worst that he has something to hide – which of course is precisely the tack taken by the villainess Ortrud, who persuades Elsa that her saviour's powers are malevolent. But just how trusting should a bride be? In these days of prenuptial agreements, with all possible areas of conflict staked out, it seems naïve to us to expect anyone to sign up to a contract in which the spaces for 'name' and 'place of birth' have to be left blank.

The idea that one partner should suppress all rational categories when confronted with the individuality of the other only really begins to make sense in the context of how Wagner himself saw these characters. The essay 'A Communication to my Friends', quoted from above, has to be treated with a degree of caution here, given that it was written in 1851, a good three years after *Lohengrin* was completed. By this time Wagner had indeed not just become 'a complete revolutionary', but had had to flee into exile. It could be argued, therefore, that he was inclined to read his revolutionary fervour into such works as *Lohengrin* completed before the barricades went up.

This seems to me a wilfully distorted way of understanding the creative imagination. Utopian revolutionism did not arrive in Dresden one

day in 1848 or 1849: radical ideas had long been circulating. More importantly, it is perfectly possible for visionary conceptions to take shape in a work of art before they are articulated in the political arena. This would explain Wagner's designation of Elsa as 'the Unconscious, the involuntary, in which Lohengrin's conscious, voluntary being yearns to be redeemed'.[6] What distinguishes Elsa, for Wagner, is the fact that she is in communion with nature, untainted by the world of industry and 'civilization' all around.

The influence of the humanist philosophy of Ludwig Feuerbach is also crucial here, for the figure of Lohengrin evidently appealed to Wagner not primarily as some kind of divine protector or saviour, but as a 'metaphysical phenomenon' whose contact with human nature could end only in tragedy; the Christian trappings of the legend were of essentially symbolic value to him.

Lohengrin, Wagner tells us, is 'the embodied wish of the yearner who dreams of happiness in that land far across the sea he cannot sense'.[7] His desire to relinquish divinity in favour of humanity seems, at first, a curious one. But the explanation is to be found in the humanism of the Young Hegelians, and in particular Feuerbach's *Essence of Christianity*. For Feuerbach, 'Man' – or, as we would now say, 'men and women' – represent the crowning achievement of God's creation. No longer was humanity to bend to the submissive yoke of religion and the established Church. So Lohengrin's desire to be human can be seen as a bid for the free, emancipated humanity aspired to later in the *Ring*.

Wagner makes clear, moreover, that the Lohengrin myth inspired him not because of its 'leanings towards Christian supernaturalism', but because it penetrated to the core of human longings. 'Anyone to whom *Lohengrin* is intelligible as nothing more than the category "Christian Romantic",' he said, 'understands only an incidental, superficial characteristic, not the essence of the phenomenon.'[8]

From the opening bars of the work it is clear that this is to be no conventional opera. Where *Der fliegende Holländer* and *Tannhäuser* were prefaced with more or less traditional overtures juxtaposing salient themes from the forthcoming opera in contrasted sections, that for *Lohengrin* is conceived rather like a single exhalation. The mystical sphere of the Grail is exquisitely conjured in the opening bars in an appropriately unorthodox way: a body of divided strings high up in their compass, alternating with four solo violins playing harmonics, and a chorus of flutes and oboes – a striking aural image for the shimmering of the Holy Grail. According to Wagner, the Prelude represented the descent from heaven of a host of angels bearing the Grail, and their return to heaven.

Ensconced in Zurich, where he had taken refuge from the authorities following his part in the insurrection in Dresden (see the next chapter), Wagner was powerless to get his new work onto the stage in his home city. Fortunately his new-found friend Franz Liszt could be prevailed upon to mount the premiere of the opera at the Hoftheater in Weimar, where he was Kapellmeister, on 28 August 1850. Liszt also mounted an effective PR

An ailing king presides over a wasteland in the dark, tragic conclusion of Keith Warner's production of *Lohengrin* (Bayreuth, 1999). Ortrud gloats in triumph as Lohengrin disappears from view.

Extract from the first act of *Lohengrin* in the second complete draft, dated 12 May 1847. Wagner here elaborated his initial draft, but it is still in piano score, with occasional *aides-mémoire* about instrumentation.

operation on behalf of his friend. Having ensured that the first review in the local paper was favourable by writing it himself – though in fairness his article, for the *Weimarische Zeitung*, was primarily about the work rather than the performance itself – he went on to pen a detailed appreciation of the opera in what would prove to be a landmark essay.[9]

One of the most important aspects of the score to which Liszt drew attention was its division into three groups – strings, wind and brass – according to the imperatives of character or plot. Within that division, Wagner deployed further ternary groupings, namely three flutes (one doubling piccolo), three oboes (two oboes and a cor anglais), three clarinets (one of them a bass clarinet), three bassoons, three trumpets, three trombones. (By comparison, *Der fliegende Holländer* and *Tannhäuser* both employed essentially double wind.) The result, in Liszt's purple prose, was as follows:

Among other advantages this ternary system admits of complete chords being attacked and sustained by instruments of the same *timbre*. It is this that gives light and shade to his orchestration in a new way, which he uses with the most exquisite art, harmoniously blending it, in a manner as new as it is impressive, with the declamation, upon which it is made to serve as a sort of comment. Wagner also makes great use of the violins in sub-divisions. In a word, instead of employing the orchestra as an almost homogeneous mass he separates it into different channels and rivulets, and sometimes, if we may venture to say so, into bobbins of different colours, as numerous as those of the lace-makers; as these do, mingling them, rolling them together, and like them producing from this surprising tangle a manufacture, an embroidery of marvellous and inestimable value, in which the broidery of a solid texture spreads itself out over the most diaphanous transparencies.[10]

Liszt goes on to discuss the ways in which Wagner's originality manifests itself:

In *Lohengrin* he has reserved quite a different palette for his principal characters. The more attentively one examines the score of this opera, the more clearly one perceives what an intimate relation he has established between his orchestra and his *libretto*. Not only has he, as we have said, personified in his melodies the sentiments and passions which he has brought into play, but it has also been his aim to invest their outline with a colouring appropriate to their character, and simultaneously with the rhythms and melodies which he employs, he has adopted a *timbre* peculiar to the personages which he has created. Thus the motive which first appears in the introduction, and recurs each time that allusion is made to the St. Graal [Holy Grail], or is developed as in Lohengrin's recital [Narration] towards the close when he declares his sublime mystery, is invariably confided to the violins. Elsa is almost always accompanied by wind instruments, which give rise to the happiest contrasts when they succeed to the brass. One is especially moved when, in the first scene, a pause follows the long speech of the King (whose role is throughout supported by trumpets and trombones, which then predominate in the orchestra), and when one hears this soft and airy murmur arising like the perfumed undulations of a celestial breeze to assure us, even before Elsa has appeared, of her spotless purity. The same instrumentation comes like a refreshing dew to extinguish the sombre flames of the duet of Friedrich and Ortrud, when Elsa appears in her balcony.[11]

It remains to say a few words about the contrasting styles of writing in *Lohengrin* with respect to the work's hybrid status mentioned at the beginning of this chapter. Both Elsa's Dream in Act I and Lohengrin's Narration in Act III start with the conventional phrase structure familiar from French–Italian grand opera: that is to say, regular four-bar phrases. But in each case, the narrator (Elsa or Lohengrin) has a literally marvellous tale to tell, a fact reflected in the spontaneous emancipation of their music: foursquare phrases morph into breathless narrative as the unfolding of the tale seizes the imagination of both teller and listener.

It is perhaps no coincidence that the baleful theme heard as Lohengrin abjures Elsa from asking about his origins, 'Nie sollst du mich befragen' (Never shall you ask me) – the Forbidden Question motif – is a striking anticipation of the leitmotif principle to be developed in the *Ring*. Just as the notion of a fateful question is central to the dramaturgy, so the

The wedding guests – and attendants – are colourfully attired in Hans Neugarten's 2010 production for Bayreuth. Lohengrin (Klaus Florian Vogt) holds aloft a wooden cross representing the minster.

motif recurs ubiquitously in the opera. The most 'advanced' writing in the work, however, occurs in the first scene of Act II, in which Telramund and Ortrud plot the downfall of Lohengrin. Here more than ever foursquare phrase structure gives way to expressively heightened arioso (somewhere between recitative and aria) inflected by motifs identified with a particular character or idea.

The prelude to Act III, with its excited triplets on strings (and, later, wind) and striding melody thundered out on brass, is a popular concert item. Following it is the even better-known Bridal March, a piece that has accompanied countless inamoratas up the aisle over the decades. One wonders how many of those blissful brides are aware of the tragedy shortly to follow in the opera. The irony that the Bridal March, inscribed indelibly in our culture with notions of conjugal contentment, actually heralds, in the work from which it is taken, a catastrophic breakdown in marital relations is only one of the piquant paradoxes in which Wagner's music abounds.

8   Revolutionary Road: Uprising in Dresden

*The sublime Goddess of Revolution comes thundering in on the
wings of the storm.*

Anonymous newspaper article attributed to Wagner, 1849

By the beginning of 1848 Europe was ripe for revolution. The first palpable manifestations of that revolt against the established order were seen in January in Sicily and southern Italy. From there it spread to Paris in February and Vienna in March. Then the people of Dresden, among them Kapellmeister Wagner, took to the streets demanding electoral reform and social justice.

The thirty-nine states of the German Confederation, set up in 1815 at the Congress of Vienna, were ruled by princes whose autocratic, often feudal, behaviour was increasingly resented by the populace. Constitutional reform had been on the agenda for many years, and the momentum created by these outbreaks of protest, inspired by the 'glorious revolution weather', as Theodor Fontane described it, led rapidly to the election of a German National Assembly in Frankfurt. The Assembly survived only thirteen months, but decades later participants and observers recalled the exhilarating atmosphere of 'that marvellous day, when the bells rang throughout the city of Frankfurt, and the black, red and gold flags of liberal Germany bedecked all public buildings'.[1]

The historian Golo Mann describes the scene a touch more dispassionately:

There has never been a more highly educated parliament: more than a hundred professors, more than 200 learned jurists, writers, clergymen, doctors, burgomasters, civil servants, manufacturers, bankers, landowners, even a few master craftsmen and small tenant farmers – but not a single worker … . The world was good, the German people was great and good; and their old rulers were not so bad that it was not somehow possible to come to terms with them. The exponents of these noble ideas also had a high regard for themselves and the Assembly to which they belonged. The Hessian Heinrich von Gagern, a handsome, impressive man and a great orator who favoured the middle road, was elected president. He was chosen because the Assembly wanted to follow that road, the centre being by far the most powerful group.[2]

The delegate for Saxony was one Professor Wigard, for whose benefit Wagner set out in a letter of 19 May 1848 the measures he considered imperative if disaster were not to ensue. But just how radical was Wagner

in his outlook? Did he in fact wish for an overthrow of existing society, or did his revolutionary ideas merely amount to a self-interested programme of artistic reform? The truth is that for Wagner the two things were inseparable. In the same month that he proffered Wigard advice on social and constitutional reform, he also submitted to the relevant cabinet minister a 'Plan for the Organization of a German National Theatre for the Kingdom of Saxony'. The director of this proposed institution should, according to Wagner's plan, be elected by its staff, and by an association of dramatists and composers that was also to be inaugurated. A drama school was to be set up, chorus singers properly trained, the existing court orchestra expanded, salaries increased and its administration put under self-management. Inexplicably these proposals failed to find favour with either his superiors or his colleagues – though the suggestion that his co-Kapellmeister, Reissiger, should be 'promoted' to the innocuous sphere of church music, while the Intendant, Lüttichau, would be removed and all affairs placed under Wagner's own jurisdiction may have had something to do with it.

The wider perspective of social disaffection that Wagner shared with so many of his compatriots is evident from an even bolder statement he issued the following month. 'How do Republican Aspirations Stand in Relation to the Monarchy?' was the title of an article that appeared in the *Dresden Anzeiger* on 15 June. No author was credited, but he hardly needed to be, since Wagner himself had delivered a speech of that title only the day before, to huge enthusiasm at a public meeting organized by the revolutionary republican grouping known as the Vaterlandsverein.

The idealistic nature of this address is seen from Wagner's vision of a single, free *Volk*: a classless society rooted in the German soil. Such an emancipation of the human race would bring about a liberation from what Wagner regarded as the cause of all its misery:

We shall recognize that human society is maintained by *the activity of its members*, not through any supposed activity of *money*. We shall with clear conviction assert the principle, and God will enlighten us, enabling us to find the right *law* through which this principle can be put into practice. Then like a hideous nightmare this diabolical idea of money will vanish from us, along with all its loathsome concomitants of open and secret usury, paper swindles, percentages and bankers' speculations.[3]

Communism per se Wagner repudiates, on the grounds that a 'mathematically equal division of property and earnings' is both impractical and misconceived. Even so, his tirade was inflammatory enough to attract attention from the authorities. What perturbed them in particular was his conviction that the aristocracy was on its last legs, that the privileges of the court were coming to an end and that what the country needed was a people's militia dispensing with class distinctions. The emergent republic should, however, in his view, be presided over by the king of Saxony himself, as 'the first and truest republican of all'. If the latter suggestion has on the face of it as much merit as a proposal to abolish Catholicism but install the pope as archbishop of Canterbury, it is not quite as idiosyncratic as it seems. Bourgeois liberals of the type that convened at the National Assembly in Frankfurt sought constitutional and representative government, not revolutionary social change. Monarchs were often regarded as charismatic figureheads: it was the petty princes for whom they were gunning.

Wagner, like his meliorist brothers-in-arms, yearned for a new golden age, an idyllic world modelled on and illuminated by traditional German values:

Now we shall sail ships across the sea and found a young Germany here and there, fructify it with the outcome of our toils and struggles, and conceive and bring up the noblest, most godlike children. We will do it better than the *Spaniards*, for whom the new world became a priest-ridden slaughterhouse; otherwise than the *English*, for whom it became a grocery store. We will do it in the German manner and splendidly. From its rising to its setting, the sun will look down upon a beautiful, free Germany, and on the borders of the daughter-lands, as on those of the motherland, no downtrodden, unfree people shall dwell. The rays of *German freedom* and *German gentleness* shall warm and transfigure the Cossack and the Frenchman, the Bushman and the Chinaman.[4]

Hand in hand with this beatific, peaceable vision went a desire for extremist means bordering on terrorism to achieve it. One of Wagner's acquaintances in Dresden at this time was the actor and writer Eduard Devrient. Diary entries of his throw revealing light on the subversive tendencies of the composer:

[1 June 1848] After supper a visit from Kapellmeister Wagner; we again argued barbarously over politics. He wants to destroy in order to build anew; I want to transform the existing world into a new one.
[31 March 1849] Met Kapellmeister Wagner on the [Brühl] Terrace – another debate on his ideas for improving the world. He's still of the opinion that the destruction of property is the only way to achieve real civilization … . In the end he had to agree with me that only a moral improvement could remedy our misery and that this would yield the right form of government, according to the law of love.[5]

Another acquaintance of this period was August Röckel, who was both assistant conductor to Wagner at the Dresden court (until he was dismissed for subversive activities) and the founder editor of the republican journal *Volksblätter*. When the uprising came to an end in 1849 and Wagner made his escape into Swiss exile, Röckel was less lucky: he was arrested (along with another rebel, Otto Heubner, and others) and only narrowly escaped a death sentence, serving instead a thirteen-year term of imprisonment. Through Röckel Wagner also encountered the Russian anarchist Mikhail Bakunin at this time. There is no direct evidence that Wagner read the writings of Marx and Engels, but if he did – and it seems likely – it would probably have been on the recommendation of Bakunin, who knew them both.

The Brühl Terrace
in Dresden, where
Wagner and Eduard
Devrient 'argued
barbarously over
politics'.

The fact that Wagner was 'intimately acquainted with the leaders of the rising, Bakunin, Heubner and Röckel', was the first of seven charges held against Wagner in an official file compiled in 1856 and brought in evidence against him when he petitioned for an amnesty that year. The second charge is that Wagner was present at 'secret meetings ... believed to have been connected with the rebellion'. The next two accusations are as follows:

3. Wagner is further charged with having lent his garden for the purpose of a conference on the question of arming the populace, in which Röckel, Lieutenants Schreiber and Müller, Professor Semper, and others took part.

4. The notorious brassfounder Oehme, one of those mostly deeply implicated in the rebellion, and known more particularly for his attempts to burn down the Royal Palace, asserts that just before Easter 1849 Wagner and Röckel gave him an order for a considerable number of hand-grenades; these were said to be wanted for Prague, and were sent to the office of the *Dresdner Zeitung*. It seems, however, that they were never dispatched to Prague, as Oehme declares that on May 4, 1849, Wagner commissioned him to fill the grenades, which were still at the office of the *Dresdner Zeitung*.[6]

Charges 5 to 7 make further allegations about Wagner's movements around the time of the uprising. The evidence is clearly based on hearsay, government spies and informers, but in broad outline corresponds to what we know from other sources. Ascertaining the truth is difficult for a number of reasons: evidence given by apprehended fellow insurgents

such as Bakunin may have played down Wagner's role so as not to incriminate him, while Wagner's own later autobiographical account was written for the delectation of a king (Ludwig II), whose sensitivities had to be taken into account. Furthermore, posthumous hagiographers of Wagner (notably Houston Stewart Chamberlain) had their own reason to airbrush such subversive conduct from the official history books.

August Röckel was Wagner's assistant conductor in Dresden, but also a political firebrand. He was imprisoned for thirteen years for his part in the revolution, a fact to which we owe an important series of letters from Wagner.

Mikhail Bakunin, a Russian anarchist who played a major role in the revolution. He and Wagner enjoyed extended conversations on politics and art (Bakunin himself had compositional ambitions).

The warrant for Wagner's arrest. The description in the final paragraph (thirty-seven to thirty-eight years old, medium height, brown hair and spectacles) is incorrect in virtually every detail.

Politisch gefährliche Individuen.

Richard Wagner
ehemal. Kapellmeister und politischer Flüchtling aus Dresden.

Steckbrief.

Der unten etwas näher bezeichnete Königl. Capellmeister

Richard Wagner von hier ist wegen wesentlicher Theilnahme an der in hiesiger Stadt stattgefundenen aufrührerischen Bewegung zur Untersuchung zu ziehen, zur Zeit aber nicht zu erlangen gewesen. Es werden daher alle Polizeibehörden auf denselben aufmerksam gemacht und ersucht, Wagnern im Betretungsfalle zu verhaften und davon uns schleunigst Nachricht zu ertheilen.

Dresden, den 16. Mai 1849.

Die Stadt-Polizei-Deputation.

von Oppell.

Wagner ist 37—38 Jahre alt, mittler Statur, hat braunes Haar und trägt eine Brille.

Wagner's own idiosyncratic approach to revolutionism also muddies the waters. On 5 May 1849, for example, at the height of the insurrection, he climbed the tower of the Kreuzkirche to report on the movements of the troops for those attempting to coordinate the strategy from the city hall. His autobiographical account reports entertainingly how he spent the night up in the tower engaged in philosophical debate with a schoolmaster. No doubt he did, but that in no way diminishes his contribution to the struggle.

The danger to which insurgents were exposed is attested by eyewitness accounts such as that of Clara Schumann:

On *Thursday the 10th* [of May] we heard of the awful atrocities committed by the troops; they shot down every insurgent they could find, and our landlady told us later that her brother, who owns the *Goldner Hirsch* in the Scheffelgasse, was made to stand and watch while the soldiers shot one after another twenty-six students found in a room there. Then it is said they hurled men into the street by the dozen from the third and fourth floors. It is horrible to have to go through these things! This is how men have to fight for their little bit of freedom! When will the time come when all men have equal rights? How can it be that the nobility's belief that these men are different from us middle-class people can have become so ineradicably established over so many centuries![7]

The Kreuzkirche, Dresden, from the tower of which Wagner observed troop movements one night in May 1849, though his mind may have been more on Hegelian dialectics.

All that remained of the old opera house in Dresden, built by Gottfried Semper, after the insurrection of 1848–49.

Narrowly avoiding arrest, by missing the coach that carried Röckel, Bakunin and others into a trap at Chemnitz, Wagner scarcely realized at first what danger he was in, even contemplating a possible return to Dresden. A few days after the failure of the uprising he wrote to both Devrient and his wife, Minna, asseverating that the likes of them could never be true revolutionaries, for they lacked the necessary reckless determination:

It is not people like us who are destined to carry out this fearful task: we are revolutionaries in order to be able to *build* on new ground; what attracts us is not to *destroy* things but to *refashion* them, & that is why we are not the people that fate needs – these people will arise from within the lowest ranks of society; – we and others like us can have nothing in common with them. Look! *I herewith sever my links with the Revolution.*[8]

That mood of pessimism, tinged with characteristic idealism, was to hover over Wagner as he went into exile and would remain with him for most of the following decade.

9   The Zurich Years: Wagner's Exile in Switzerland

Do you know – Zurich?? – I have to go mad here!
    Wagner to Franz Liszt

For a composer as rooted in the culture and mythology of his native Germany as Wagner, the prospect of exile must have been bleak indeed. A warrant was out for his arrest, however, on account of his participation in the revolutionary uprising, and there was no choice but to leave Dresden as quickly as possible. He first made his way via Switzerland to Paris, but soon realized that the French capital was unlikely to be more receptive to him now than it had been a decade earlier. He settled instead in Zurich, where he was to remain for a good deal of his dozen or so years in exile.

There he established himself in a cultured community, supported by a circle of friends and admirers. Even in Dresden he had not enjoyed such popularity. Part of the attraction of Zurich was that the city had a tradition of welcoming radical intellectuals: the dramatist Georg Büchner, the poet Georg Herwegh, the architect Gottfried Semper and the historian Theodor Mommsen are just a few of the prominent people associated with the city in the first part of the 19th century.[1] Until at least the end of 1851 Wagner was still confidently expecting an uprising of some sort. His revolutionary activity, however, was now confined to the cerebral sphere, but what he began to formulate was a radical new aesthetics, involving a fundamental reappraisal of the role of art in society.

A major series of essays was begun in July 1849 with 'Art and Revolution', in which Wagner advocated an 'artwork of the future', one divorced from the realm of capitalist profit-making, the better for emancipated humanity to express itself. That concept of an 'artwork of the future' was then developed later that year in 'The Artwork of the Future', in which he proposed the reunification of the separate arts – music, dance and poetry (along with architecture, sculpture and painting) into a grand *Gesamtkunstwerk* or 'total work of art'.

By far the largest of this group of essays was 'Opera and Drama' (1850–51), a major theoretical work by any standards, setting out in detail how the text and the music of the new 'music drama', as it was to be called, were to be fused inextricably. Whereas conventional opera was characterized, to a greater or lesser degree, by a hierarchy of melody and accompaniment, the music drama would develop a new kind of melodic verse in which the vocal line would actually grow out of the poetic text.

Couched in theoretical and philosophical abstractions, these essays are dauntingly prolix, and their sense often difficult to follow – not least in the all-too-faithful standard English translations of William Ashton Ellis. Yet they are worth the effort for a true understanding of how Wagner wished to bring poetic ideas to vibrant dramatic life in the theatre.

Meanwhile, in the hope of alleviating two persistent bodily complaints, erysipelas (a painful skin condition) and constipation, he checked in at a hydropathic establishment at Albisbrunn, just outside Zurich. The somewhat drastic regimen was described by Wagner thus:

My daily routine is now as follows: 1st, half-past five in the morning wet pack until 7 o'clock; then a cold bath and a walk. 8 o'clock breakfast: dry bread and milk or water. 2nd, immediately afterwards a first and then a second clyster; another short walk; then a cold compress on my abdomen. 3rd, around 12 o'clock: wet rub-down; short walk; fresh compress. Then lunch in my room with Karl [Ritter], to prevent insubordination. Then an hour spent in idleness: brisk two-hour walk – alone. 4th, around 5 o'clock: another wet rub-down, and a short walk. 5th, hip-bath for a quarter of an hour around 6 o'clock, followed by a walk to warm me up. Fresh compress. Around 7 o'clock dinner: dry bread and water. 6th immediately followed by a first and then a second clyster; then a game of whist until after 9 o'clock, after which another compress, and then around 10 o'clock we all retire to bed.[2]

'Water torture' was the laconic description in his autobiographical notes, the Annals. Worse still, it did not seem to work, although on a later occasion a similar remedy did seem to clear up the erysipelas, at least, for well over two decades. A brighter note was struck by the proposal of two

The hydropathic
establishment at
Albisbrunn, just
outside Zurich, where
Wagner underwent
'water torture' in a
partially successful
attempt to rid himself
of bodily ailments.

Jessie Laussot in
later years. No earlier
pictures have survived
of the Englishwoman,
who was an attractive
23-year-old when she
and Wagner planned to
elope together.

female admirers – Frau Julie Ritter, a widow from Dresden, and Jessie Laussot (née Taylor) – to support him financially. Their joint allowance of 3,000 francs was intended to free him from the mundane business of making ends meet in order that he might devote himself to the composition of the masterpieces he and they believed it was his destiny to accomplish.

Wagner compromised his position, however, by falling in love with Jessie, who was an attractive young Englishwoman unfortunately married to a Bordeaux wine merchant. Not only was Jessie a passionate admirer of Wagner's music, she also spoke fluent German and had the intellectual capacity to discuss aesthetic matters with him. On visiting the Laussots in Bordeaux, Wagner observed that the marriage was an unhappy one – nor was he deluded in this respect, for Jessie eventually left her husband and went to live in Florence with the historian Karl Hillebrand. But Wagner's plan that they should elope to Greece or Asia Minor – to which Jessie readily agreed – came to grief when she rashly apprised her mother, Ann Taylor, of it. Jessie's husband, Eugène, was informed and, far from willingly agreeing to give up his wife, he threatened to kill his rival. Wagner set out for Bordeaux with the intention of persuading Laussot of the reasonableness of the plan, but he was intercepted by the local police and forced to leave the town, his mission unaccomplished.

Needless to say, Wagner's own marriage to Minna was not exactly helped by this escapade. But in truth it had, as he wrote to her in a reproachful letter from Paris of April 1850, already broken down irretrievably. Wagner suggested that they should live apart, and he pressed half of the allowance he had been promised on her. Whatever one's view of his behaviour, there seems little doubt that he genuinely found the prospect of such a separation painful: describing to Julie Ritter his marriage to Minna, he said that he felt himself 'bound to her by a thousand chains of old and mutual suffering'.[5] It is no coincidence that a couple of particular dramatic projects were sketched (they remained uncomposed) exactly at this time, between December 1849 and March 1850. The first, *Wieland der Schmied* (Wieland the Smith), tells the story of a smith, crippled by his enemies, who forges a pair of wings with which to soar above the world united with his lover, Schwanhilde, the swan bride. Languishing in bondage, Wieland represents on one level the oppressed German nation. But the story is also a poignant allegory of Wagner's own desire to be liberated from the shackles imposed by exile, a broken marriage and stultifying artistic conventions.

The other project, *Jesus von Nazareth*, treats events from the life and ministry of Jesus Christ, portraying him as a social revolutionary. The second of the project's three parts consists of a series of commentaries on issues arising from the narrative. The notion propounded here that true love is self-sacrificial in nature, given of free will, together with the assertion that humanity is essentially divine (God being a projection of man in his own image), owes much to Ludwig Feuerbach (see the following chapter). The influence of the French anarchist Pierre-Joseph Proudhon is also evident in Wagner's espousal of the idea that the protection of property is a crime against nature: without the evil of property there would be no crimes against property. Love, in *Jesus von Nazareth*, is afforded a status above that of the law or the institution of marriage, which is regarded as the mere establishment and perpetuation of property rights. The relevance of all this to an indigent composer thwarted in love scarcely needs underlining.

Meanwhile *Lohengrin*, though completed in 1848, still had not been performed, and Wagner prevailed upon his friend Liszt, now Kapellmeister at the court in Weimar, to mount a production there. The premiere was given at the Court Theatre on 28 August 1850. Wagner, unable of course to attend, was reduced to imagining the events unfolding in real time in Weimar from an inn (aptly named *The Swan*) in Lucerne – except that the performance in Weimar was unduly protracted, thanks probably to the stiff delivery of recitative-like passages by some of the singers.

During the years following the completion of *Lohengrin*, Wagner toyed with no fewer than four dramatic subjects in the search for one that would serve his purposes adequately. *Wieland der Schmied* and *Jesus von Nazareth* have already been mentioned; he also made sketches for works based on the figures of Friedrich Barbarossa (*Friedrich I.*) and Achilles.[4] But an idea originally mapped out as early as autumn 1848 gradually began to come into focus. *Siegfrieds Tod* (Siegfried's Death), the title of that sketch, betokens the fact that at this point Wagner's planned Nibelungen project was intended, rather like a Greek drama, to centre on the final catastrophe, preceding events dealt with in the form of sung narrative.[5] As will be seen in the section on *Der Ring des Nibelungen*, things turned out rather differently.

At this point it is interesting to note how a natural phenomenon experienced by Wagner in Switzerland may have contributed to one of the most spectacular scenes in the *Ring*. The incident took place during Wagner's first ascent of the Rigi, one day late in the August of 1850:

The Rigi in Switzerland, whose *Glorie* halo effect may have given Wagner the idea for the rainbow bridge in *Das Rheingold*.

After climbing up [the mountain], Wagner walked to the outermost edge of Rigi-Kulm, while Minna went into the house to order dinner. When she came out again and looked up at the sky, she saw Wagner's image quite clearly in it as if in a mirror, and in her surprise she called to him: 'Richard, move your arms!', and every one of his movements was mirrored, too, in the sky again. Then Minna went up to his side and both of them made movements, happily like children, enjoying their heavenly mirror image as long as this atmospheric reflection lasted (known popularly as the 'Rigi ghost', as they then found out).[6]

As is noted by Chris Walton, in his important study of Wagner's Zurich exile, the phenomenon is not exclusive to the Rigi, and the report is consistent with many others by travellers. The latter often feature the following: the observation of one's shadow projected massively onto a bank of mist or cloud, the ringing of the shadow by a rainbow-like halo (or *Glorie*), and the effect of figures walking into the air, enveloped in a rainbow.[7] A comparison of these features with the stage directions for the close of *Das Rheingold* is striking:

Froh has vanished with [Donner] in the cloud … . The cloud suddenly lifts, revealing Donner and Froh. From their feet a rainbow bridge of blinding radiance stretches out across the valley to the castle, which now glints in the glow of the evening sun.

A further discovery made in Switzerland was to have an even more profound impact on the *Ring*, and indeed on Wagner's outlook in general. It was in fact another political refugee, Georg Herwegh, who introduced him in September or October 1854 to the philosophy of Arthur Schopenhauer. The latter's magnum opus *Die Welt als Wille und Vorstellung* (The World as Will and Representation) was claimed by Wagner to be a life-changer. Certainly he never ceased reading, discussing and recommending it. The appeal was twofold. First, Schopenhauer's aesthetics, reduced rather drastically to a single formula, amounted to the elevation of music over other media. In his theoretical writings, Wagner had been grappling with the concept of total equality of text and music, but Schopenhauer's thesis afforded an intellectual justification for a more practical balance between the constituent parts of the *Gesamtkunstwerk*. Second, Schopenhauer's pessimistic philosophy of life – he opined that the suffering in the world was a consequence of the 'will to live' and that only by the denial of the will, in a state similar to that of the Buddhist nirvana, could deliverance be effected – chimed with Wagner's own state of mind in this period.

The influence of Schopenhauer should not be overstated, however. On one crucial point he and Wagner were poles apart: where the misanthropic, misogynist Schopenhauer held that love was a destructive force, for Wagner the sexual act provided the path to redemption. In the *Ring*, the Schopenhauerian notion of renunciation is counterbalanced, indeed outweighed, by the Feuerbachian principle of 'the glorious necessity of love' (the phrase is Wagner's). But Wagner had reasons for his intellectual alignment with the Sage of Frankfurt. On the one hand it suited him to suggest that he was in tune with the latest great exponent of the German Idealist tradition (following Hegel and Kant). On the other, Schopenhauer's pessimistic formulation enabled Wagner to make some sense of the lingering existential malaise to which he was prey throughout the 1850s and beyond (see also the following chapter).[8]

In March 1855 he began a four-month stay in England, where at the invitation of the Philharmonic Society he conducted eight concerts of music by, among others, Beethoven, Mendelssohn, Weber, Cipriani Potter and himself. It was not a happy visit: Wagner did not speak the language, the foggy London weather was not to his taste, and nor were the customs of the inhabitants. When he refused to pay court to the gentlemen of the press, as they expected, they took revenge in ferocious prose that throws revealing light also on the conservative outlook of the time. The *Sunday Times* excelled itself:

Either Richard Wagner is a desperate charlatan, endowed with worldly skill and vigorous purpose enough to persuade a gaping crowd that the nauseous compound he manufactures has some precious inner virtue, that they must live and ponder yet more ere they perceive; or else he is a self-deceived enthusiast, who thoroughly believes his own apostolic mission, and is too utterly destitute of any perception of musical beauty to recognize the worthlessness of his credentials.[9]

Wagner and his music were at least appreciated by one person: Queen Victoria, no less. She attended the penultimate concert on 11 June 1855 with Prince Albert, noting afterwards in her diary:

We dined early with Feodore, her girls, our Boys, and & all the Ladies and Gentlemen going to the Philharmonic where a fine concert was given, under the direction of the celebrated composer Herr Richard Wagner. He conducted in a peculiar way, taking Mozart's & Beethoven's Symphonies in quite a different time time [*sic*], to what one is accustomed. His own overture to 'Tannhäuser' is a wonderful composition, quite overpowering, so grand, & in parts wild, striking and descriptive. We spoke to him afterwards. He is short, very quiet, wears spectacles & has a very finely developed forehead, a hooked nose, & projecting chin. He must be 3 or 4 & 30.[10]

The queen's flattering estimation of Wagner's age – he was forty-two at the time – is not entirely matched by his assessment of her in a letter to his wife, though he was clearly gratified by the reception:

Gracious me, dear Minnikins, I am quite hoarse from so much talking with – the – Queen! First she asked me what Peps [the Wagners' dog] has been up to? then, if Knackerchen [the parrot] was behaving himself? then, if I was taking anything back for my wife? …

Wagner

Silhouette of Wagner conducting, by Willi Bithorn.

Queen Victoria, whose reception of Wagner was warmer than that given by the English critics.

Do not think that I am joking: I'm deadly serious – the Queen of England spoke with me at great length. And I can assure you that she is *not* fat, but very small and not at all pretty, with, I am sorry to say, a rather red nose: but there is something uncommonly friendly and confiding about her ... . Here was I, a man pursued by the police in Germany like some common thief and who has had problems obtaining a passport in France, now being received in the presence of the most aristocratic Court in the whole world by the Queen of England herself and treated with the most uninhibited friendliness: that really is quite something![11]

Wagner's visit a few years later to Paris was similarly a mixed success. Neither audience nor orchestra could come to terms with the prelude to *Tristan*, but other music of his heard at a series of three concerts at the Théâtre Italien at the beginning of 1860 was well received. The main event, however – a production of *Tannhäuser* at the Opéra – was destined to go down as one of the great scandals in the annals of opera history. Everything seemed to be stacked against Wagner: an incompetent conductor (Pierre-Louis Dietsch), a temperamental Tannhäuser (Albert Niemann), a hostile press and, above all, the clientele of the Opéra. The white-gloved aristocratic members of the Jockey Club were used to arriving late at the theatre after dining well, and were interested primarily in the performance of the ballet dancers, with whom they were intimately acquainted. Refusing to provide them with their customary second-act ballet, Wagner spiced up his Act I Venusberg Bacchanal instead, but its demonic, orgiastic frenzy predictably offended their refined tastes. Having disrupted the first performance with coordinated outbursts of shouting and catcalls, the louts returned to disrupt the second and third performances with dog whistles. The unpopularity of the Austrian Princess Pauline Metternich, who had helped to make the production possible in the first place, sealed its fate: the demonstration was as much political as anything else.

By this time, following a series of appeals, Wagner was able once again to enter German territory. It was only a partial amnesty, however: Saxony remained closed to him until March 1862. In November of that year he visited Minna, now back in Dresden, for what was to be the last time. Despite the abundance of female admirers flitting around him, the soulmate he sought had yet to present herself. A chronic inability to live within his means and the continuing lack of the large-scale funding needed to mount the *Ring* cycle, now more than half complete, did little to meliorate his views on accumulated wealth. The following May he took up residence in an upper-floor apartment in Penzing, near Vienna, where he sought emotional compensation for his problems, pecuniary and personal, in wildly extravagant décor and clothing (see Chapter 15: In the Pink). 'I must have beauty, splendour and light!', he told his friend Eliza Wille. 'The world owes me what I need!' The world was shortly to repay that debt.

A cartoon from *Charivari*, 10 March 1861, showing the claque, whom Wagner refused to employ for his fateful Paris production of *Tannhäuser*, compelled to operate outside the theatre.

10   The Rise and Fall of Valhalla: *Der Ring des Nibelungen*

The Ring *is the mirror Richard Wagner holds up to humanity.*
    Wieland Wagner

Wotan (Bryn Terfel) confronts Alberich transformed into a dragon. Carl Fillion's set for Robert Lepage's *Ring* (Metropolitan, New York, 2010–12) was an attempt to realize Wagner's stage directions through state-of-the-art technological wizardry.

Wagner's *Ring* is one of the most ambitious works of art ever conceived. The sheer scale of it is formidable: over fourteen hours of music,[1] spread out over four days, each instalment as long as many a conventional opera. The curtain-raiser, *Das Rheingold*, itself lasts two and a half hours, a similar length to, say, *The Magic Flute* or *Peter Grimes*. No doubt it is in part its colossal scale that causes the *Ring* to attract the kind of attention it does. It demands to be taken seriously. It demands our time, our attention and a disproportionate slice of any opera house budget. It is simply one of the enduring pillars of Western civilization.

The sources

By the beginning of the 19th century, the anonymous medieval epic poem the *Nibelungenlied* had already acquired a prominent position in Germany; by the 1840s it had become a potent symbol in the struggle for German unification. The *Nibelungenlied*, dating from *c.* 1200, was the only one of Wagner's main sources in German (Middle High German, in fact). His other major sources were the Poetic (or Elder) Edda, the *Völsunga Saga*, and the Prose Edda by Snorri Sturluson, all three of which were compiled in Iceland, probably in the first half of the 13th century. Also important was *Thidreks Saga af Bern*, a prose narrative written *c.* 1260–70 in Old Norse. The significance of these Icelandic sources is that they enabled Wagner to discern the structure of the myth in its entirety. As he put it in his 'Communication to my Friends':

Even if the magnificent figure of Siegfried had long since attracted me, it first really enchanted me only when I was successful in seeing it freed of all later costuming in its purest human manifestation before me. Now for the first time I recognized the possibility of making him the hero of a drama – something that had never occurred to me as long as I knew him only from the medieval Nibelungenlied.[2]

We may note the faintly pejorative use of the description 'medieval' here: Wagner was eager to emphasize the mythic, as opposed to historical, roots of the story, an aspect he considered more pronounced in the earlier Norse versions.

The genesis of the cycle

To understand how this enormous project came about, we have to go back to its origins. Wagner's initial outline for the drama dated from October 1848 and was called 'The Nibelung Myth: as Sketch for a Drama'. In this résumé the drama centres on Siegfried's death, and at its conclusion Brünnhilde purges the guilt of the gods through an act of self-immolation, allowing them to reign in glory instead of perishing. The story at this stage largely follows the order familiar from the finished work, but Wagner next, in autumn 1848, compiled a libretto for just *Siegfrieds Tod* (Siegfried's Death). A problem now arose, however, as Wagner began to address himself to the musical and stage conception of the work:

But when I turned to its musical execution and was finally obliged to fix my sights firmly on our modern stage, I felt how incomplete was the product I had planned: all that remained of the vast overall context – which alone can give the characters their enormous, striking significance – was epic narration and a retelling of events on a purely conceptual level. In order, therefore, to render 'Siegfried's death' feasible, I wrote 'Young Siegfried': but the more imposing a structure the whole thing assumed, the more it was bound to dawn on me, as I began the scenico-musical realization of 'Young Siegfried', that all I had done was to increase the need for a clearer presentation *to the senses* of the whole of the overall context. I now see that, in order to be fully understood from the stage, I must present the entire myth in visual terms.[3]

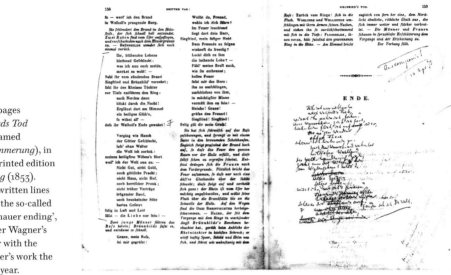

The final pages of *Siegfrieds Tod* (later renamed *Götterdämmerung*), in the first printed edition of the *Ring* (1853). The handwritten lines represent the so-called 'Schopenhauer ending', added after Wagner's encounter with the philosopher's work the following year.

In other words, by focusing initially on the death of the hero, Wagner had been compelled to tell the rest of the story in the form of back narration. Even when he prefaced *Siegfrieds Tod* with *Der junge Siegfried* (Young Siegfried, 1851) the problem remained, and he realized the need to flesh out the entire story on the stage. The process was completed by taking the story back to the start, with first *Die Walküre* and then *Das Rheingold* (1851–52). Thus the texts of the constituent parts of the cycle were actually written, more or less, in reverse order, though the music was composed, of course, in the 'correct' order.

Wagner then had to go back and revise *Siegfrieds Tod* and *Der junge Siegfried* in the light of *Walküre* and *Rheingold*. The alterations he made at this point are of some significance: essentially Siegfried was replaced as the central character by Wotan, and the ending was changed so that the gods were no longer purged and allowed to reign in glory but instead doomed and due to go up in smoke along with their home, Valhalla. *Der junge Siegfried* and *Siegfrieds Tod* were eventually renamed *Siegfried* and *Götterdämmerung*.

Problematic as the genesis of the text had been, Wagner was delighted with the result. He shared his pleasure with Theodor Uhlig, a former violinist in the Dresden orchestra and a close friend of the revolutionary years whose incendiary correspondence with Wagner was prudently censored by Cosima on publication. Wagner wrote:

I am again more than ever moved by the comprehensive grandeur and beauty of my subject: my entire philosophy of life has found its most perfect expression here ... . After this work I do not suppose I shall ever write another opera poem! It is the finest and most perfect work ever to have flowed from my pen.[4]

Theoretical essays

During the years in which the scenario and text of the *Ring* were taking shape, Wagner composed no music. Rather, he was grappling with the crucial social and aesthetic issues brought to a head by the recent revolutionary upheavals. In a series of essays, beginning with 'Art and Revolution' (1849), he addressed himself to fundamental questions of the social role of art, which most composers, whether successful or unsuccessful with their publics, had been content to ignore. 'Art and Revolution' was particularly polemical, advocating an 'artwork of the future' in which emancipated humanity would express itself through artistic structures that had at last been divorced from capitalist speculation and considerations of profit. The concept of the reunification of the arts into a comprehensive *Gesamtkunstwerk* (total work of art) on the Greek model was developed in two longer essays, 'The Artwork of the Future' (also 1849) and 'Opera and Drama' (1850–51). If in 'Art and Revolution' Wagner's perception of the worthlessness of artistic endeavour within the framework of existing social structures is influenced by Proudhon and Feuerbach, both of whom he had recently been reading, in 'The Artwork of the Future' it is Marx and other revolutionary thinkers, as well as Feuerbach (to whom the essay is dedicated), whose ideas are taken up. As part of an inevitable historical process, the new work of art was to emerge as the creation of the *Volk*. The product not of the individual genius but of a fellowship of artists, it was to be a communal response to prevailing historical conditions. 'Opera and Drama', the third and last of these major essays, is a vast tract, a whole book in itself, setting out a detailed and radical vision of the future. First it offered a critique of the genres of modern opera and analysed the nature and history of theatre; Wagner then went on to provide a kind of blueprint for the proposed music drama, detailing its linguistic, dramatic and musical ingredients.

The influence of Greek drama

During the 1840s Wagner had been increasingly fascinated by Greek drama, and this was something that would profoundly influence the *Ring* tetralogy in several important ways.

First, the notion of a tetralogy is fundamental to Greek drama. Athenian festivals in the age of Aeschylus and Euripides consisted of a series of three tragedies succeeded by the lighter entertainment of a satyr play (a pattern Wagner to some extent reversed, with *Das Rheingold* as a shorter prologue to the principal trilogy). The Greeks also regarded their drama as essentially a religious ritual, to be celebrated in a special festival, attended by all sections of society, rather than as part of the daily round. Wagner, too, wanted people of all classes to set aside time to immerse themselves in drama rather than attend the theatre in a state of exhaustion after a tiring day behind a counter or desk. No less important to him was the fearless, life-enhancing ethos of Greek culture. Under the influence of Feuerbach, Wagner celebrated that uplifting ethos, contrasting it with the craven, guilt-ridden spirit of Christianity as manifested in the modern age.

There are also some specific aspects of Greek drama that were appropriated by Wagner for his artwork of the future or music drama. In the confrontations between pairs of characters we see a central dramaturgical principle of Greek drama that Wagner frequently used. Another technique, the linking of successive episodes through the themes of guilt and a curse, would also be central to the *Ring*. It has further been suggested that Wagner's development of the leitmotif principle itself may have been influenced by Aeschylus' use of recurrent imagery.

A pair of recent studies both draw attention to a neglected aspect of Wagner's Hellenism: namely the extent to which it interlocks with the nationalistic ideology that permeates the *Ring* and the prose writings of the period. For Simon Goldhill, Wagner's celebration of the Greeks was intrinsic to the utopian vision of a racially regenerated, 'purely human' German spirit, purged of alien (especially Jewish and French) elements. 'Wagner's Hellenism and his anti-Semitism are integrally connected,' he concludes, noting the 'staggering irony' that it was to the Greeks that Wieland Wagner would turn in the 1950s to offer a supposedly depoliticized reading of the works (see Chapter 29: Regime Change).[5] Daniel H. Foster similarly sees the struggle on which Siegfried embarks as analogous to Wagner's battle for supremacy on behalf of the German spirit. Fafner symbolizes French theatre, according to Foster; the Woodbird, German lyric; and Siegfried's confrontation with Fafner 'heralds the German artwork of the future [...] in short [...] a Hellenized form of German music drama equivalent to Greek tragedy'.[6]

Das Rheingold

Called by Wagner the *Vorabend* (preliminary evening) of the *Ring*, *Das Rheingold* is one of the most generous curtain-raisers in the history of the theatre. It lasts about two and a half hours, and is in four scenes, through-composed without an interval. It begins in E flat and ends in D flat. There are thus parallels between *Das Rheingold* and the *Ring* as a whole: each is in four parts, begins in E flat and moves to a D flat peroration several hours later. The structure of *Das Rheingold* could therefore be said to pre-figure that of the *Ring*.

The opening of *Das Rheingold* is one of the most extraordinary in all music. The first thing we hear is a very low E flat, way down on the double basses (who actually have to tune their bottom E string down in order to reach it). The note should be barely audible, as though it were coming from the very depths of the earth, from the beginning of time. In fact it is, in a sense, a musical representation of the act of Creation itself. Eight horns enter one by one, sounding the fundamentals of the harmonic system in overlapping arpeggios. It is a remarkable effect, using the most basic elements of music to evoke something primeval, beyond time, beyond space. More instruments enter – cellos, woodwind, violas, finally violins – building the momentum in ever-decreasing note values until a waving, seething organism is in motion. It is 136 bars before the first voice is heard.

The orchestra dominates too in the three transitional passages that link the four scenes: indeed, these passages contain some of the work's finest music. The first transition takes us from the bottom of the Rhine to the mountain heights, though as often as not in modern productions the second scene is set inside Valhalla. The swirling of the waters and the elastic, curved motif associated with the ring itself gradually morph into the resplendent music representing Valhalla. The transition from Scene 2 to Scene 3 takes us from Valhalla down to Nibelheim, amid much chromatic flickering, presumably representing the sulphurous vapours that the stage directions tell us thicken into a black cloud. The final transition, between Scenes 3 and 4, takes us in the opposite direction, from Nibelheim back to the heights of Valhalla. Each transition is a skilful orchestral working of the various motifs, a highly coloured tapestry that provides an aural equivalent of the almost cinematic scene changes (see Chapter 27: Panning for Gold).

Stabreim

For Wagner's revolutionary artwork of the future, nothing less than a new verse form was required. He devised for the purpose an alliterative structure that makes use of *Stabreim*, an ancient verse form used in Germanic (and Anglo-Saxon) poetry. Wagner was the first composer to use *Stabreim* in an opera libretto. As developed for the *Ring*, it typically employed verse pairs, each line of which contained two (sometimes three) 'lifts' (stresses). The first and/or accented syllables were alliterated, though Wagner also liked to set up interlocking, double alliterations, as in the following example from Scene 2 of *Das Rheingold*:

Design by Charles Ricketts for the opening scene of *Das Rheingold*, showing 'the rock in the river depths with the dazzling Rhine gold guarded by the Rhine maidens'.

Valhalla and the Rainbow Bridge from *Das Rheingold*. Lithograph by Hermann Hendrich, 1906.

Trügt mich ein Nebel?
Neckt mich ein Traum?
Wie bang und bleich
verblüht ihr so bald!

What Wagner loved about *Stabreim* was the sense that he was forging a link with primitive folk culture. It was important to him to feel that he was tapping the very roots of German language and culture. This is how he expressed it in 'A Communication to my Friends':

> It was this very *alliterative verse*, accommodating itself to genuine speech accents and the most natural and lively sense of rhythm, and adaptable to endlessly varied manifestations, in which the *Volk* once expressed itself, when it was still both poet and mythmaker.[7]

Stabreim can be heard throughout the *Ring*. Wagner was much mocked for it: contemporary parodies at his expense were rife. But the fact is that the principle of *Stabreim* is fundamental to the language – and to English as much as German. German has phrases like 'Mann und Maus'; English has 'hearth and home', 'safe and sound', and many more.

Leitmotif

One of the most important devices used by Wagner in the *Ring* is the leitmotif. This is a short musical idea associated with a particular character, object, emotion or concept, which is recalled whenever that character, object, etc. reappears in the text. Wagner did not use the term 'leitmotif' himself: it was invented, or at least popularized, by one of his acolytes, Hans von Wolzogen, after which a whole motif-naming industry mushroomed. All kinds of guides to the motifs were published, naming them as 'Renunciation', 'World Inheritance', 'Siegfried's Heroism', 'Wotan's Wilful Authority', and so forth. In recent times leitmotif-naming has gone out of musicological fashion, as more emphasis has been placed on the way Wagner builds his motifs and other thematic ideas into musical paragraphs. It is nevertheless legitimate, if only for convenience' sake, to refer to some of the less conceptual motifs by their familiar names. The phallic Sword and the extended Spear, for example, seem unarguable; so do the hammering of the Nibelungs, and the Ring itself – sinuous, winding downwards in thirds and curving up again. They are all illustrative: a graphic musical representation of an object or an idea. Others are not so specifically illustrative but are still graphic, for example the Rhinegold motif, based on a pure major triad, or Valhalla, grand, stately and imperious, as befits a god and the castle he has had built for himself.

But the motifs are far more than merely illustrative: they also help create a structural framework for the cycle. Nobody had previously attempted anything so huge in music before, and Wagner had to find a way of binding together all the various strands of the music drama, of making the fourteen and a half hours of music as cohesive and thoroughly integrated as he could. Structural unity is achieved in a variety of ways, and the use of leitmotif is one. In *Das Rheingold* and *Die Walküre* the

Alberich's theft of the gold, as depicted by Franz Heigel, 1865–66.

motifs are clearly heard and easily identified. By *Siegfried* they are appearing in such profusion that it is no longer always possible to identify them all. The result is a rich fabric of allusion – sometimes six or seven leitmotifs swirling around in the space of a couple of bars.

The most comprehensive study of the leitmotif in modern times is that by Christian Thorau, who demonstrates how, in spite of changing fashions and more sophisticated analytical approaches in the post-war era, the lure of the leitmotif was too great for it ever completely to lose its appeal.[8]

Musico-poetic synthesis

No less central to the music drama than the leitmotif was a new kind of vocal line, one that was moulded explicitly to carry the nuances of the verse. There was to be no more artificial rhyme, and no more of the regular melodic construction imposed by the straitjacket of conventional four- or eight-bar phrases. Rather, the text and the melody would be blended in a line that registered the shifting nuances of the former. Wagner gives an example of what he means in 'Opera and Drama'. In a line such as 'Die

Liebe gibt Lust zum Leben' (Love gives delight to living), the mood is constant throughout, so the composer would feel no need to modulate to another key. If, however, the line were to be 'Die Liebe bringt Lust und Leid' (Love gives delight and sorrow), he would instinctively move away from the initial key to one representing a contrasting emotion; and yet the modulation would need to express the interrelationship of delight and sorrow as well as their difference.

Das Rheingold, composed 1853–54, was Wagner's first attempt to put his theories into practice – with, it has to be admitted, only partial success. The vocal line in *Das Rheingold* often perfectly mirrors the contours and accents of the verse, but it fails to make an emotional impact simply because the musical idea is not sufficiently interesting. In *Die Walküre*, by contrast, the musico-poetic synthesis is seen at its finest, especially in Act I, where word stresses are preserved and melodic lines register every nuance but remain musically interesting in their own right. Acts II and III are no less masterly, but already there are signs of a shift away from the absolute equality of poetry and music (partly under the influence of Schopenhauer, who elevated music above all other forms of art).

The poem of *Siegfried*, which was actually the first to be written after the theoretical works of 1849–51, does not display the same level of mastery of the new style of verse as *Die Walküre*: there is much alliteration, to be sure, but of a generalized sort, not highlighting parallels of meaning. The free rhythms of lines and the high proportion of root syllables conform faithfully to the precepts set out in 'Opera and Drama'. In *Götterdämmerung* there are many fine passages of musico-poetic synthesis, but there is also a tendency towards quick-fire exchanges, a form of dialogue taken over from *Die Meistersinger* (and ultimately from Greek drama) but modified in accordance with the elevated tone of *Götterdämmerung*.

A corollary of the musico-poetic synthesis is the abnegation of concerted singing in the *Ring*. For much of the cycle the principle is maintained, though of course the first scene of *Rheingold* features ensemble writing for the Rhinemaidens. They, like the Valkyries in *Die Walküre*, may perhaps be considered a single entity.

Ludwig Feuerbach

By the 1840s Ludwig Feuerbach had established himself as one of the most distinctive and controversial philosophers of the era. His *Thoughts on Death and Immortality* was published anonymously in 1830, and his most influential work, *The Essence of Christianity*, appeared in 1841. Wagner was certainly reading Feuerbach by 1849 and may well have been introduced to his ideas earlier. In any case they would profoundly influence the philosophical conception of both the essays of the Zurich years and the *Ring* itself.

The Essence of Christianity advances the revolutionary, and heretical, thesis that God was merely a projection of human fantasies, desires and needs. The conventional wisdom was that God had created man, but

Feuerbach reversed the formulation, arguing that it was in fact mankind that created God or gods. This is how Feuerbach himself put it:

Religion is the disuniting of man from himself; he sets God before him as the antithesis of himself. God is not what man is – man is not what God is. God is the infinite, man the finite being; God is perfect, man imperfect; God eternal, man temporal; God almighty, man weak; God holy, man sinful.[9]

In other words, we have created God in our own image. We have set up a divine entity that is everything we are *not* but would like to be: perfect, eternal, almighty.

One of the terms Wagner borrowed from Feuerbach is *Noth*: 'need' or 'necessity'. 'Necessity' was a concept of the Young Hegelians, indicating an overwhelming natural force that would arise in the breasts of the populace, driving them to liberation. *Noth* is frequently mentioned in the *Ring*: Siegfried's sword is actually named 'Nothung' or 'Needful'.

What Wagner responded to above all in Feuerbach's philosophy was his celebration of love – what Engels several decades later was to describe, with just a hint of disdain, as Feuerbach's 'extravagant glorification of love'. Engels, of course, like Marx, felt that Feuerbach had given too much attention to the principle of love and not enough to the emancipation of the proletariat. But it was music to Wagner's ears in the late 1840s and 1850s.

For Feuerbach the essence of human nature, and the source of its morality, is the 'I–you' relationship. Morality is inconceivable for the solitary being; only in conjunction with another, by creating a mutual drive to happiness, does an individual develop any consciousness of social responsibility. The love affairs of Siegmund and Sieglinde in *Die Walküre,* and of Siegfried and Brünnhilde later in the cycle, embody this kind of life-affirming philosophy.

Die Walküre

It is in *Die Walküre* that Wagner's enthusiasm for Feuerbach can be discerned at its clearest. For Feuerbach there was an underlying harmony between the laws of nature and human conduct. That harmony was disrupted by what Wagner, following Feuerbach, calls *Willkür* – the arbitrary, as opposed to the necessary. The dictates of religion, for example, are arbitrary, in this view, as are those of nationality or state.

In the *Ring*, Wagner repeatedly celebrates the necessary over the arbitrary. The sword Nothung is a constant, symbolic reminder of the power of necessity. Wotan disrupted that harmony by his crimes against nature, tearing off the branch of the World Ash Tree in the pursuit of wisdom. In Feuerbach's terms, he represents the conflict between the arbitrary and the natural. But Wotan's grandson Siegfried will make all well again. That at least was the plan, though he, too, falls prey to forces beyond his control.

In the chronology of the mythical world in which the *Ring* takes place, Wotan, the ruler of the gods, is a pagan god, but of course he is also the God of the modern world. In *Das Rheingold* he endeavours to shore up his power by resorting to devious tactics: stealing the ring from Alberich in order to pay the bill for his grand new fortress, Valhalla, he sinks deeper and deeper into the mire of compromises and deception. In *Die Walküre*, his wife Fricka exposes his self-deception and he caves in, as he must, to her demand that Siegmund, Wotan's son, be punished for his illicit, incestuous love.

Remarkably, Wotan's abdication of power is voluntary: although under pressure from Fricka, he comes to realize the error of his ways and of human existence. In a celebrated letter to his friend August Röckel, Wagner points to the source of the tragedy, locating it in the loveless relationship of Wotan (referred to here as 'Wodan') and Fricka:

The firm bond which binds them both, sprung from the involuntary error of a love that seeks to prolong itself beyond the stage of necessary change and to obtain mutual guarantees in contravention of what is eternally new and subject to change in the phenomenal world – this bond constrains them both to the mutual torment of a loveless union. As a result, the remainder of the poem is concerned to show how necessary it is to acknowledge change, variety, multiplicity and the eternal newness of reality and of life, and to yield to that necessity. Wodan rises to the tragic heights of *willing* his own destruction. This is all that we need to learn from the history of mankind: *to will what is necessary* and to bring it about ourselves.[10]

Political leaders and gods do not normally give up their power without a struggle, but Wagner is saying here that the god-centred universe has had its day: it is time for a new era, in which human beings decide things for themselves. Later in the century, Nietzsche was famously to declare 'God is dead', but in fact he had, for some time, been seriously unwell. Feuerbach was a leading force in undermining the hegemony of Christianity, though there were many other key figures too, including David Friedrich Strauss, Bruno Bauer, Max Stirner and others. This, then, is the philosophical core of the *Ring*: it concerns the end of a world order governed by God or gods, and its transformation into a new humanistic world order, one in which individual men and women take responsibility for their own actions; one, too, in which love and compassion are prized more than power and material possessions.

The opening of *Die Walküre* succeeds in trumping even the extraordinary opening of *Das Rheingold*. An exhilarating tremolo on unison strings, sustained for no fewer than 60 bars, underneath which cellos and basses rampage about in stormy fury, serves as an electrifying setting of the scene – though, as with *Rheingold*, there is also a striking touch of minimalism.

Act I of *Die Walküre*, and especially the long scene for Siegmund and Sieglinde, is particularly rich in the musico-poetic synthesis described earlier: the melding of word and note, verse and line. Sieglinde's Narration is the classic demonstration of this synthesis: almost every nuance of the verse seems to be reflected in the vocal line. More conventional, at least superficially, is Siegmund's 'Winterstürme', also in the first act, while the long duet for the lovers that follows comes close to an infraction of the rules Wagner laid down for himself in 'Opera and Drama', even if in fact the voices barely overlap.

If Act I of *Die Walküre* is notable for the perfection of its musico-poetic synthesis, Act II is remarkable for two scenes each of considerable length and immense emotional weight. In Scene 2 Wotan bares his soul to his favourite daughter, Brünnhilde, apprising her (and us, the audience) of his earlier deeds and misdeeds, longing for the end and instructing her to allow Siegmund to fall in battle. As Wotan unfolds his narrative, more and more motifs appear – the Ring, Valhalla, Erda, etc. – gradually building up the texture into a frenzy of violence. The double climax of this scene, described by Wagner as 'the most important

The sibling lovers Siegmund and Sieglinde throw caution to the winds in Mariano Fortuny's painting of 1928.

Brünnhilde expresses her compassionate love for Siegmund in Hans Makart's painting *The Kiss of the Valkyrie*.

scene for the development of the whole of the great four-part drama', is appropriately overwhelming. At one point even Wagner had misgivings about its length, but he put them to rest by singing the scene through to himself.

His concerns about the act were expressed in a letter to Liszt:

I am worried that the second act contains so much material; there are two crises here of such import and such power that there is really enough material for two acts; but they are both so interdependent, and the one follows so immediately upon the other that it would be quite impossible to keep them apart. If it is presented as I require – and if all my intentions are fully understood – it is bound to produce a sense of shock beyond anything previously experienced.[11]

The second of the two scenes to which he refers, in which Brünnhilde appears to Siegmund to tell him he has to follow her to Valhalla, is Act II Scene 4, known as the 'Annunciation of Death'. More expansive than Scene 2, the Annunciation of Death evokes sublimity and heroism by turning the belligerent Wagner tubas that announced the arrival of Hunding in his hut into velvet-toned harbingers of destiny.

The final act also contains a momentous scene, that for Wotan and Brünnhilde. The tussle between them – Brünnhilde appealing to Wotan's finer feelings but provoking his guilty anger in the process – is enacted in page after page of emotionally heightened arioso, accompanied by richly scored orchestral textures that mark a new maturity in Wagner's virtuoso deployment of thematic material.

The Sage of Frankfurt, in a photograph of 1850. Schopenhauer's influence on Wagner and the *Ring* was considerable, if exaggerated, not least by Wagner himself.

Arthur Schopenhauer

Schopenhauer is generally cited as the philosopher whose ideas shaped the *Ring* and other works by Wagner, but, as already explained in the previous chapter, he in actual fact maintained a position fundamentally opposed to that held by the composer. For the Sage of Frankfurt, the sexual impulse was the expression of 'the will' or 'the will-to-live' (his terms for the blind force that constitutes the inner nature of things and that, in his view, had to be transcended). Sexual activity, for the misogynistic Schopenhauer – who seems to have expended a good deal of effort repressing homosexual inclinations[12] – was the root source of life's pain and suffering. For Wagner, on the other hand, love – and specifically sexual love – was a life-enhancing, redeeming force. It is true that Wagner felt himself, or claimed to be, indebted to Schopenhauer. But he appears to have been deluding himself – at least with regard to many of the fundamentals of that philosophical system. Certainly Wotan's renunciation of his rule has less to do with Schopenhauer's denial of the will than with Feuerbach's transformation of human values.

Siegfried

Siegfried, the archetypal hero, represents a set of macho values, a concept of heroism, with which it is sometimes difficult to identify these days. As Thomas Mann pointed out, there is an element of Punch and Judy in Siegfried. Mann reminds us that Wagner was delighted by a puppet show he witnessed one day. 'That delight,' Mann says,

is hardly surprising in the director of the theatre in Bayreuth, the man who staged *The Ring of the Nibelung*, that quintessential piece of puppet theatre with its mindless hero! Is the marked similarity of this Siegfried to the little chap who wields the slapstick in the fairground not evident to everybody?[13]

T. W. Adorno similarly described 'Siegfried, the man of the future', as

a bully boy, incorrigible in his naivety, imperialistic in his bearing, equipped at best with the dubious merits of big-bourgeois self-confidence as contrasted with petty bourgeois pusillanimity.[14]

A loutish bully is bad enough, but Wagner's characterization is overlaid with racial stereotyping that makes Siegfried's behaviour difficult to stomach. The overtones of racial supremacy are hard to ignore, and the sympathy we are invited to feel for the upstanding virile hero at the expense of the cowering, underdog outsider is a worrying aspect of the work.

There are, however, redeeming features to the character. We should remember that Wagner conceived of Siegfried as a *free* hero, one who would be untrammelled by the compromises made by his grandfather, Wotan. Brave, fearless and with a boundless capacity to love, he was described by Wagner himself as 'the most perfect human being'.[15] Elsewhere Wagner called him 'man in the most natural, sunny fullness of his physical manifestation'.[16] In similar vein, Thomas Mann described him as

The gold shimmers
behind a wall of water
in Michael Scott-
Mitchell's arresting
design for the first
scene of *Das Rheingold*
for the State Opera
of South Australia
(2004), directed by
Elke Neidhardt.

the mythical figure of light, bounded and restricted by nothing, man unprotected, totally self-reliant and self-sufficient, resplendent in freedom, the fearlessly innocent doer of deeds and fulfiller of destiny, who through the sublime natural phenomenon of his death heralds the twilight of old and outmoded world forces and redeems the world by raising it to a new plane of knowledge and morality.[17]

This is the more positive side to Siegfried. But we are left with the chasm dividing the type of a bronzed 19th-century hero from our own post-Vietnam, post-feminist consciousness. How can we reach across that divide? Wotan, we should remember, has finally had to accept that Siegmund cannot repair the harm that he, Wotan, has done: he is not a free hero. Hence the need for Siegfried, who is truly free and who embodies that long-lost harmony between nature and human conduct – the idea Wagner got from Feuerbach, and ultimately from Rousseau. Naïve and innocent, in the sense of Rousseau's 'noble savage', Siegfried seems to be congenitally incapable of doing harm. Admittedly he is none too gentle with his foster father, but that is just an excess of adolescent high spirits. And it goes with the territory: heroes are hardly known for their sensitivity and benevolence.

Siegfried's role is to restore the unity of humanity and nature, to reunite heaven and earth. As a sun god – which is what the legendary Siegfried was – he is endowed with the aura of immortality. Courage, fearlessness and pure love are the qualities he possesses, and are all that is needed to usher in this new era.

The first scene of *Siegfried* consists of an allusive network of motivic ideas recalled from *Das Rheingold* and *Die Walküre*. If we reduce it to its essentials, however, we have a thematic idea for each of the characters on stage, Mime and Siegfried, both much repeated and altered, yet always retaining a kernel so representative of the character in question that there is never a moment's doubt as to whose music we are hearing.

Mime's idea is heard, in its most complete form, in a little song, 'Als zullendes Kind', in which he retells the story of how he brought up the young Siegfried from a baby, clothed and fed him, acting as father and mother in one. Siegfried's music, on the other hand, is by turns lyrical and virile, the embodiment of the sunny, resplendent hero Wagner conceived him to be. Interwoven are motifs from *Die Walküre* associated with spring, love, heroism, and Siegfried's parents, Siegmund and Sieglinde. The character of the music changes markedly for the Riddle Scene (Act I Scene 2), with the arrival of the magisterial Wanderer. His music has a chorale-like nobility, contrasting effectively with Mime's excitable jabbering. The third scene of the first act is dominated by Siegfried's two forging songs, their testosterone-filled energy very much a matter of taste.

The second act shows us more nuanced aspects of Siegfried, however. Brought by Mime to the dragon's cave at Neidhöhle, Siegfried may not

Siegfried as a child of nature communing with the Woodbird, in a gouache by Franz Stassen.

(quite) yet learn to experience fear, but we do at least find him communing with nature in the music of the Forest Murmurs: voluptuous, multiple divisions of the instruments in idyllic E major, rooted over a sustained, rustic-style pedal note with pentatonic colouring.

In the third act, started in 1869 after a twelve-year break, during which Wagner had composed *Tristan* and *Die Meistersinger*, the renewed vigour of the writing, and the compositional virtuosity, are evident right from the first bar. The prelude to Act III is one of Wagner's finest achievements: a quasi-symphonic development of no fewer than nine motifs summoned from the repository of the cycle, just as Erda is summoned from her subterranean resting-place.

The scene for the Wanderer and Erda that follows is breathtaking in its sublimity, with longer, more expansive themes that impart a marvellous lyrical sweep to the music. The final scene charts the erotic encounter of Siegfried and Brünnhilde, finally, after much hesitation on both sides, pledging themselves one to the other with high-flown images that foreshadow the end of the gods in *Götterdämmerung*.

Much of the imagery is aquatic, and the music, too, surges like a series of unstoppable tidal waves. Clearly the imagery is intended to be sexual: submitting to each other with wild abandon, the lovers sweep on to their ecstatic C major climax: nothing can hold them back now. We share the thrill of the delirious passion they are experiencing, although something tells us it cannot last.

Rousseau and Proudhon

Both names have been mentioned briefly in the preceding sections. Jean-Jacques Rousseau is not a name commonly bracketed with Wagner's, but his ideas underpinned so much of the German Romantic idealism of the 19th century that a closer examination is called for, especially in light of the recent discovery, made when the library at Wahnfried was catalogued, that the shelves supported his complete works.

Rousseau held that men and women were essentially good, but that they were corrupted by institutions and contracts. His concept of the 'noble savage' articulated the belief that 'man' (women were either implicitly embraced by, or excluded from, Rousseau's theory) enjoyed a natural and noble existence until he became slave to the demands and temptations of civilization, whereupon he lost his fundamental freedom. Rousseau additionally maintained that the rich and powerful contrived to persuade the poor and powerless to police the status quo for them. The result of this egregious deception was that 'all ran to meet their chains in the belief that they were securing their freedom'. Thus civil society was based on a fraud

which bound new fetters on the poor, and gave new powers to the rich; which irretrievably destroyed natural liberty, eternally fixed the law of property and inequality, converted clever usurpation into unalterable right, and, for the advantage of a few ambitious individuals, subjected all mankind to perpetual labour, slavery and wretchedness.[18]

The relevance of this to the *Ring* is self-evident. First Wotan and then Alberich bend subjects to their will, the latter condemning the Nibelungs to 'labour, slavery and wretchedness'. Wotan's tragedy is the loss of his personal freedom and his recognition of the fact. Siegfried, of course, is the noble savage, brought up in the forest, far from the material goods and trappings of society. He, too, is corrupted by institutions and contracts. His encounter with the Gibichung court ensnares him in a web of social aspiration and advancement. Promising to secure a good match for his new-found friend Gunther, he abandons his true love, and with her his freedom.

Rousseau further argued, it should be noted, that the savage *needs* society if he is to be truly free: the pure state of nature had, he recognized, to be superseded. It is surely something of this sort that Wagner had in mind when he had Brünnhilde send Siegfried off into the world in search of glorious deeds to perform. She knew that he could not remain in a state of nature, though she did not foresee the deception and betrayal his education would involve. Rousseau claimed that man everywhere thinks he is free but is really in chains. This is how we may see Siegfried, as he makes his journey down the Rhine, hastening towards his chains. In a similar way, Wotan himself, compromised by his own deceitful bargains, finds in the course of the tetralogy that he is bound in chains, though at first he assumed he was free.

One further influence on the philosophical content of the *Ring* needs to be mentioned. From the French writer and anarchist Pierre-Joseph Proudhon, Wagner inherited a deep and undying suspicion of laws, contracts and anything that came between human beings and their instincts. The blood brotherhood sworn between Siegfried and Gunther, and the oaths sworn by Siegfried and Brünnhilde in the presence of the vassals, are both examples of the love-abnegating contracts that Wagner, following Proudhon, believed soured human relations.

Orchestration

In order to give expression to his complex dramatic conception, Wagner massively expanded the orchestral forces at his disposal. In the *Ring* he used quadruple woodwind (e.g. 3 clarinets and 1 bass clarinet), and enlarged his brass section so that it could divide into four independent families: 8 horns (4 alternating as Wagner tubas); 3 trumpets and a bass trumpet; and 3 trombones and a contrabass trombone. The bass trumpet (often used for the Sword motif) was introduced to the orchestra by Wagner himself. The contrabass trombone, rescued from obscurity by Wagner, provides a bass for an independent trombone family (a role usually performed by the tuba). Unprecedented melodic demands were made of the trombones, for example to announce the motifs of Wotan's Spear and the Curse. The Wagner tubas, again made specially for the *Ring* but this time based on instruments Wagner had seen in the Paris workshop of Adolphe Sax, have horn mouthpieces and are played by members of the horn section. Their distinctive, velvety tone colour can be heard at the announcement of the Valhalla theme (*Rheingold*, beginning of Scene 2).

For all the immense scale of his orchestral forces, it is the expressivity of Wagner's deployment that is notable. The bass clarinet, like the various brass instruments, is liberated in order to exploit its characteristic doleful quality, while oboe, clarinet and bassoon solos are ubiquitous in Wagner's subtly calibrated chamber textures.

Similarly Wagner calls for a huge body of strings – 16 first violins, 16 second violins, 12 violas, 12 cellos, 8 double basses – but divides it into many parts, creating intricate webs of figuration. The first appearance of the gold under the waters and Donner's 'Heda! Hedo!' in *Das Rheingold* are just two fine examples.

Götterdämmerung

There is a curious paradox about *Götterdämmerung*. On the one hand, the opera marks the culmination of Wagner's monumental *Ring* cycle, a magnificent finale to the project initiated a quarter of a century earlier. On the other hand, this final instalment appears, at first sight, to be characterized by some of Wagner's most stylistically regressive writing in the entire tetralogy.

George Bernard Shaw is only one of many critics to have pointed this out, but he did so particularly trenchantly, commenting on what he saw as 'the loss of all simplicity and dignity' in *Götterdämmerung*, 'the extreme staginess of the conventions', the disappointing collapse of the political allegory that he, Shaw, had discerned in the cycle, and the generally old-fashioned operatic nature of the final work.[19] For all his hyperbole – Shaw's disappointment with Wagner's political equivocation seems to have blinded him to the glories of the music – his fundamental observation has a kernel of truth that has to be confronted.

In his theoretical essays of 1849–51, Wagner had rigorously expunged self-contained numbers, such as arias, duets and choruses, from the so-called 'artwork of the future' (i.e. the music drama). Yet *Götterdämmerung* features some good old-fashioned, blood-and-thunder ensembles – Hagen's Summoning of the Vassals and the so-called Conspirators' Trio of Act II in particular. They do not appear in previous instalments of the tetralogy. Why now in *Götterdämmerung*?

Part of the answer lies in the fact that, as explained earlier (see p. 88), *Götterdämmerung* was the last opera to be composed, but its libretto came first: *Siegfrieds Tod*, as it was originally called, was the starting point of the whole cycle in 1848, and Wagner gradually worked backwards in order to dramatize more of that tragedy's pre-history. Given the chronology, it is hardly surprising that the dramatic conception of *Siegfrieds Tod* should be closer to that of *Lohengrin* (completed in April 1848) than *Das Rheingold* (the music for which was not begun until November 1853). And, indeed, a glance at the poem for *Siegfrieds Tod* is enough to confirm that the form of the big ensembles of Act II of *Götterdämmerung* is adumbrated there.[20] The text for Gunther, Brünnhilde and Hagen in the Conspirators' Trio

On the post-war resumption of the Bayreuth Festival in 1924, Siegfried Wagner commissioned Kurt Söhnlein and Friedrich Kranich to replace the conventional flat, painted scenery with solid three-dimensional sets. This model for *Götterdämmerung* dates from 1925.

is set out much as in the final poem (though it is extended in the latter), while the text for the Summoning of the Vassals also seems to demand ensemble treatment.

But Wagner's apparent lapse into conventional opera mode also touches on a more fundamental aesthetic issue. The precise balance of purely musical and dramatic aspects in the 'artwork of the future' was a question that engaged him throughout his life. In the theoretical essays of the Zurich years, he advocated an equal status for the various art forms in a grand reunification of the arts: the so-called *Gesamtkunstwerk*. But his experience of actually writing the *Ring*, and his encounter with the philosophy of Schopenhauer, who elevated music above the other arts, effected a change of perspective.

By the time he came to compose the music for *Götterdämmerung* (the first composition draft was begun in October 1869) Wagner's theoretical position had shifted considerably. And it was continuing to shift: a comparison of the prologue and Act I of *Götterdämmerung* with Act II reveals a marked penchant in the latter for ensemble numbers of a more conventional kind. It is surely no coincidence, therefore, that in the year that elapsed between the completion of the second complete draft of Act I (2 July 1870) and the commencement of the first complete draft for Act II (24 June 1871) Wagner was engaged on another theoretical essay, 'Beethoven', in which he now proclaimed (to oversimplify drastically) that music was the ultimate vehicle of expression and that words should occupy a subordinate position. Of course, the music drama remained for Wagner a more potent form, precisely because of its composite nature, than 'mere' music. But there is a sense in which Wagner needed to rationalize the direction his music had been taking – the choral numbers of *Die Meistersinger* are an example of this – before proceeding with the culminatory opera of the *Ring* cycle.

Right from the start of *Götterdämmerung* we know we are inhabiting a very different world from that of the sun-filled end of *Siegfried*. The prologue begins in the sombre but numinous key of E flat minor for the Norns' Scene. As their wisdom is unfolded, and the rope of fate is passed from hand to hand, earlier stages of the narrative are filled in with an abundance of leitmotifs now familiar from previous operas. This is no ensemble scene, however: the Norns sing one after the other, until the very end when they have half a dozen bars in unison. The dusky atmosphere subsides as dawn breaks (a wonderful evocation moving from low cellos via horn fanfares to the radiant heights). The following love duet for Siegfried and Brünnhilde is highly impassioned – some of the most glorious music in the *Ring* is heard here – but Wagner allows the voices to overlap only in the climactic final bars. It is therefore not a duet in the

The Norns weaving the rope of destiny. Wagner commissioned costume designs for the *Ring* from Carl Emil Doepler, asking him to evoke the timelessness of myth. Doepler's impeccably researched pseudo-historical designs caused dismay at Wahnfried.

'Siegfried's Journey down the Rhine'; linocut by Phil Redford, 2005.

conventional operatic sense. The link to Act I is made via a purely instrumental interlude known as 'Siegfried's Journey down the Rhine'. This, too, paints a picture through a flood of motifs relating to Siegfried and his heroic exploits.

As the curtain goes up on Act I, there is once again a darkening of tonal coloration for the first scene in the Gibichung Hall, though Gutrune's presence lightens up the proceedings. Hagen's music is, as one would expect, more abrasively masculine, as when he hails Siegfried down on the river. The swearing of blood brotherhood by Siegfried and Gunther in the following scene is similarly extrovert and energetic, but includes some subtle colouring on Wagner tubas as well.

Remarkable scoring is also to be heard in the interlude that joins the second and third scenes, known as 'Hagen's Watch', which contains a passage where the strings sound as if they had been 'spun from ravens' feathers', to quote Cosima Wagner's vivid description. Also notable is the seamless transition from this interlude to the following scene, Waltraute's visit to Brünnhilde (Act II Scene 3). Wagner begins by introducing fragmentary figures associated with the Valkyries – chiefly the dotted rhythm of the riding motif – and gradually the canvas is built up until Waltraute's imminent arrival is depicted in a texture brimming with animated detail. As the exchange between the half-sisters unfolds, we are aware of how much richer the texture is than in *Das Rheingold*. Here in *Götterdämmerung* the motifs are compressed so that often two or three, or even more, are sounding together. Having now worked through his theoretical reforms, Wagner has the confidence to write what he likes, and it is powerful, heady stuff: vibrant, with densely associative orchestral textures topped by soaring vocal lines.

Brünnhilde on her rock refuses to give up the ring, in spite of the pleading of her sister Valkyrie Waltraute. Drawing by Franz Stassen, *c.* 1910.

The Ride of the Valkyries by William T. Maud (1890). The trumpet is not authentic, but Wotan's two ravens, seen in the foreground, are.

Compared with the complex textures of this and other scenes, the Summoning of the Vassals (Act II Scene 3) is quite different. Here Wagner is obviously aiming for the broad gesture, with the kinsmen breaking into a hearty C major drinking song. Shaw believed that such ensemble numbers were a retrograde step, but there is more to it than that. In the first place, they resulted from Wagner's recognition that the time had come for the 'artwork of the future' to be able to embrace ensemble singing; in this sense, they mark a step forward rather than one back. Moreover, it is no coincidence that it was this scene that so inspired Schoenberg in his depiction of the Wild Hunt in *Gurrelieder*. The latter comes close to quoting the choral scene of *Götterdämmerung*, whose augmented harmonies, disruptive of the tonal system, Schoenberg evidently relished. Not as backward-looking as they might first appear, then.

The great Immolation Scene that closes the entire cycle, though often extrapolated from the opera and performed in concert, is a far cry from a number like the Ride of the Valkyries, with its relatively self-contained thematic material. The Immolation Scene, by contrast, is, as one would expect, a wide-ranging deployment of motifs from the whole tetralogy (Loge's fire music from *Das Rheingold* unsurprisingly looms large). The motifs are woven together in a masterly symphonic synthesis that satisfies both musically and dramaturgically.

What we have in *Götterdämmerung*, therefore, is a stylistic chasm between intimate dialogue and vast choruses, between the complexity of Wagner's late style and the more blatant, but dramatically highly effective, style rooted in Romantic opera. The chasm looms large, but such is the power and sweep of Wagner's grand peroration that reservations are drowned along with everything else in the flood that engulfs the world.

Interpretations

The *Ring* was begun at a time when Wagner was in the throes of revolutionary utopianism. By the time he completed it, both he and Germany were in a very different state. Wagner himself was older, if not necessarily wiser, certainly less fired with revolutionary zeal, and more prone to bouts of depression and a world view embracing an acceptance of the inevitable. Unsurprisingly, therefore, the *Ring* has been subjected to a bracingly varied, even contradictory, range of interpretations.

The first attempt to interpret the *Ring* in symbolic or allegorical terms was George Bernard Shaw's commentary *The Perfect Wagnerite* (1898). For Shaw the *Ring* was a political allegory exposing the oppression and injustice brought about by rampant capitalism. The plutocrat Alberich enslaves the Nibelungs with the 'whip of starvation'; lovelessness and greed, the inevitable result of exploitation for profit, pervert the natural order of things. Siegfried is the naïve anarchist hero who will overturn religion, law and order to free humanity from its fetters. This interpretation, while clearly reflecting Shaw's own socialist outlook, was also consistent with the genesis of the work in the revolutionary period of 1848–49.

Alberich tries on the magic Tarnhelm, forged by Mime. Fritz Friedrichs and Hans Breuer, 1899.

In Germany, meanwhile, Wagner had, by the end of the 19th century, been appropriated by the political right, notably the nationalists; for them Bayreuth was to become not just a shrine, but a powerhouse for idealism of a reactionary, Aryan supremacist kind. The key figure in the ideological transition from the Wilhelminian era (1888–1918) to Nazism was Houston Stewart Chamberlain, an Englishman who married Wagner's daughter Eva. Wilhelm II willingly accepted Chamberlain's designation of his role as that of Siegfried the dragon-slayer, whose divine mission it was to restore the former glory of the fatherland. At an extraordinary performance of *Siegfried* at Bayreuth in 1914, the entire audience, sensing the moment of destiny, leapt to its feet at Siegfried's cry 'Nothung! Nothung! Neidliches Schwert!'

In the years leading up to World War I, the festival's house journal, the *Bayreuther Blätter*, generally attempted to depoliticize the *Ring* – just as both Wagner and his whole oeuvre were depoliticized by Chamberlain, with all references to revolutionary activity airbrushed out – giving it a spiritual/religious, and specifically Christian, connotation. After the Great War, the *Ring* was often interpreted as a parable of the decline of the German Empire: the spirit of Siegfried was required to fulfil the noble destiny of the Germans.[21] Curiously, however, the *Ring* was hardly discussed at all, from an interpretative point of view, in the *Bayreuther Blätter* during the 1920s and 1930s.

From a very different perspective, the critics of the Frankfurt School in the 1920s and 1930s also sought to interpret Wagner's work as a parable of decline. Walter Benjamin discussed Wagner in terms of 'bourgeois false consciousness' that separated art from man's social existence, while T. W. Adorno anatomized Wagner as reactionary rather than revolutionary: a terrorist but a bourgeois one. He experienced the *Ring*, rather like Shaw, as something of a betrayal: the harnessing of 'a failed insurrection and nihilistic metaphysics'.

In the aftermath of World War II and the Holocaust, further attempts were made to depoliticize Wagner's work. Wieland Wagner's first *Ring* at Bayreuth (1951) consciously eschewed its Teutonic and Nordic associations in favour of more universalized, archetypal forms (see Chapter 29: Regime Change). Dispensing with conventional props (picture-book castles, fairytale dragons, naturalistic trees), he attempted to penetrate to the irreducible core represented by the familiar symbols.

Of the left-wing intellectuals who surrounded Wieland in Bayreuth – Adorno, Ernst Bloch and Hans Mayer among them – it was notably Adorno who provided the theoretical basis for his explorations into depth psychology. In other respects, the influence of these Marxists was less visible: liberating Wagner's works from their dubious legacy was, of course, in itself a political gesture, though the world was not yet ready for the explicitly political productions of the decades to follow.

More directly analogous to Wieland's conception, in as much as it deals in mythic archetypes, was the unapologetically apolitical interpretation of Robert Donington, expounded in *Wagner's 'Ring' and its Symbols* (1963). Donington drew his inspiration from Jungian psychology and its notion of a collective unconscious inhabited by archetypes, reading the mythological elements – dragon, bear, heroes, World Ash Tree – in terms of Jung's archetypal symbols, while the characters and their motivations are seen as externalizations of the composite human psyche: ego, persona, shadow, anima, animus. Thus Wotan's actions are the ego's assertion of wilful authority; Brünnhilde fulfils the role of anima (inner femininity) for both Wotan and Siegfried; Siegfried's fight with the dragon represents an archetypal confrontation with mother-longing; and the final death and ritual purgation (cremation) undergone by the main characters signifies transformation in the psyche.

Donington's analysis attracted a certain amount of adverse criticism, some of the most stringent from Deryck Cooke in his book *I Saw the World End* (1979). Attempting his own, somewhat fundamentalist, interpretation – endeavouring to uncover the 'manifest' meaning of the *Ring*, asserting Wagner's insistence on the 'purely human', and reclaiming love as the paramount social force – Cooke lambasted Donington for his interiorization of human relations that renders the *Ring* an allegory of 'everyman's psychological development' instead of the broader parable of social relations Cooke believed it to be.

A more sympathetic confrontation with Donington, launched by a Jungian fellow traveller, is Jean-Jacques Nattiez's *Wagner Androgyne* (1990). Nattiez rejected what he regarded as the straitjacket of the conventional psychoanalytical model – be it Freudian or Jungian – elaborating instead his own brilliant thesis, which employed psychoanalytical insights drawn from Freud, Jung, Lévi-Strauss and others. Essentially his thesis is as follows: just as Wagner perceived art as the union of feminine and masculine principles (the music was feminine for Wagner, the poetry the masculine seed that fertilized it), so the *Ring* should be understood, according to Nattiez, as an androgynous symbolic union in which Brünnhilde and Siegfried, representing, respectively, music and poetry, merge their individual identities, achieving a primal state of unity through the oblivion of death. The strength of Nattiez's exegesis is that it is rooted in Wagner's own aesthetic and theoretical oeuvre.

Meanwhile, the face of Wagner opera production was radically transformed over the final three decades of the 20th century. Landmark productions included those of Joachim Herz (Leipzig, 1973–76) and Patrice Chéreau (Bayreuth, 1976), which both addressed the social and political issues of the *Ring* in a direct, confrontational fashion. Harry Kupfer (Bayreuth, 1988) investigated further the work's environmental issues, viewing the desecration of nature as leading inexorably to global (nuclear) catastrophe.

Less explicitly political, yet no less iconoclastic, was Ruth Berghaus's surreal, image-rich commentary on the Wagnerian legacy (Frankfurt, 1985–87). Her development of a non-naturalistic style, charged with potent references to the Theatre of the Absurd, influenced the work of many subsequent directors, not least Richard Jones (Covent Garden, 1994–95) and Peter Konwitschny (*Götterdämmerung*, Stuttgart, 2002). Other important productions of this era include those of Ulrich Melchinger (Kassel, 1970–74), Götz Friedrich (Covent Garden, 1974–76),

The final tableau of Patrice Chéreau's landmark production of the *Ring* (1976), in which ordinary men and women looked out into the audience, challenging us to act on what we had seen.

Siegfried (John Treleaven) and Mime (Gerhard Siegel) amid the wreckage of technological aspirations in Keith Warner's production for Covent Garden, designed by Stefanos Lazaridis (2005).

Nikolaus Lehnhoff (Munich, 1987), Herbert Wernicke (Brussels, 1991) and a multi-director staging in Stuttgart (1999–2000). Further notable productions since the turn of the century include those of Robert Carsen (Cologne, 2000), Keith Warner (Covent Garden, 2004–6), Kasper Bech Holten (Copenhagen, 2003–6), Ivo van Hove (Antwerp, 2006–8), Günter Krämer (Paris, 2010–11), Vera Nemirova (Frankfurt, 2010–12), Robert Lepage (New York, 2010–12) and Francesca Zambello (San Francisco, 2011). What most, if not all, of these productions share is a scepticism with regard to the Wagnerian tradition, and towards the ethos of the sublime and the cult of the hero.

In the best of these contemporary postmodernist productions, the deliberate anachronisms – settings, costumes and props refracting the modern world to their audience – are combined with a mythic or otherwise universalizing dimension. In this sense, Wagner's aim to set forth, in allegorical form, the potentially catastrophic degradation of values he perceived in contemporary society is accomplished with all the emotional force and immediacy the modern theatre can command.

11 'Most Excellent Friend': Franz Liszt

Everything that I am and that I have achieved I owe to one man.
   Wagner on Franz Liszt in a speech following the first
   performance of the *Ring*

Given that they were two of the greatest artistic innovators of the 19th century, it is hardly surprising that Wagner and Liszt were drawn to each other as fellow toilers in the field, ploughing their adjoining furrows. But their friendship was far more than that: it was a deep and generous love that survived – just about – the vicissitudes of four decades. When they had their first encounter, in Paris in April 1840, Liszt was already established as one of the most dazzling executants of his generation: his glittering career as a touring virtuoso had begun the previous year. On neither that occasion nor their second meeting, in 1841, was there a meeting of minds, but a friendship blossomed over the following decade and ripened further in the 1850s when Wagner was in exile in Zurich and Liszt ensconced in Weimar as Kapellmeister at the ducal court. This was the period during which their creative endeavours meshed most productively: both were pushing the boundaries of their art, and the impatience of each to examine, hear and discuss the works of the other as they were set down is palpable from their impassioned correspondence. In later years the friendship was to be tested to breaking point, not least over

Watercolour of
Weimar, *c.* 1810.

Wagner's initially illicit relationship with Liszt's daughter, Cosima von Bülow. But when the musical world was gathered at a reception the day after the completion of the first *Ring* cycle at Bayreuth, Wagner proposed a toast to his now father-in-law with the following effusive words:

For everything I am and have achieved I have one man to thank, without whom not a single note of mine would be known, a dear friend who, when I was banned from Germany, with incomparable devotion and self-sacrifice drew me to the light and first recognized me. To this dear friend is due the highest honour. It is my noble friend and master, Franz Liszt!![1]

The correspondence between Wagner and Liszt in the 1840s was warm rather than voluminous ('Most Excellent Friend' was a typical salutation), and what set the seal on their relationship was Liszt's support for Wagner as he was driven into exile, and his enthusiasm for *Tannhäuser* and *Lohengrin*. Liszt provided Wagner with money to leave Dresden in 1849 and helped him obtain a false passport. The following year he mounted the world premiere of *Lohengrin* in Weimar, conducting and reviewing the performance into the bargain (see Chapter 7: Swansong to Traditional Opera). His subsequent essay about *Lohengrin* gave greater weight to the work's supposedly religious significance than Wagner would have wished but praised the 'advanced' compositional technique and orchestration in glowing terms.[2]

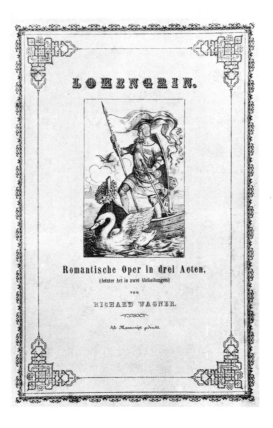

Title page of the first edition of the *Lohengrin* text, published in Weimar in 1850 in conjunction with the work's premiere there under Liszt.

In due course Wagner was at pains to put the record straight on the work's content, but his first response was an outpouring of gratitude:

Your rare friendship, the energetic love you feel for my works, your untiring eagerness to propagate those works, and, above all, the glorious intensity, the spirit, the delicacy and the boldness with which you express yourself in your eagerness to help me, – these qualities of yours moved me far too deeply and far too violently for me to be able to address you earlier to express my thanks, at a time when I was already in so agitated a state; I had to postpone doing so until such time as I had recovered my health and collected my thoughts sufficiently to be able to communicate my feelings more fully. I hope that I have now reached that point, and my first words to you therefore are to say that the sacrifice which you have once more made for me in the name of our most beautiful and loving friendship has stirred me to the very depths of my being, bringing me joy and great happiness.[3]

In the following years, letters and enclosed scores flew back and forth between Zurich and Weimar. Occasionally the correspondents were able to meet, as in July 1853 – a particularly rewarding occasion for them both. Wagner declaimed his newly completed *Ring* poems, and such was the 'storm of conversation' in this 'wild, exciting – and yet tremendously beautiful week'[4] that he lost his voice after a few days. But he was thrilled to hear his friend's most recent compositions, which were on another level entirely from the virtuoso piano works of the previous decades. Liszt played him several of his symphonic poems, various new piano compositions and possibly introduced him to material sketched for the *Faust* Symphony, the main composition of which took place between August and October 1854.

It has generally been assumed that Wagner's autobiographical account of this visit, which mentions the *Faust* Symphony, erroneously elides it with one made in October 1856, but it is equally possible that Liszt was sharing with him an inspiration that had been obsessing him for many years (sporadic sketches for a *Faust* Symphony were actually made during the 1840s). Moreover, this hypothesis gains greater credibility when one takes into account striking parallels between the symphony and Act II of Wagner's *Die Walküre*, the main composition of which (i.e. the 'complete draft') was made between 4 September and 18 November 1854. The *Faust* Symphony opens with two themes associated with Faust the thinker. The first is an enigmatically sinuous theme on muted lower strings that remarkably contains all the notes of the chromatic scale: in other words, it is one of the first twelve-note rows in musical history. The second is a pensive theme characterized by a falling 7th. Now Act II Scene 5 of *Die Walküre*, in which Sieglinde gradually wakes from a bad dream about the torching of her family home, contains a theme too similar to this to be a coincidence. It is important to point out, however, that Wagner appropriates it by adjusting the harmonic language to his purpose: unlike Liszt's theme, which is built on augmented chords, Wagner's is based on major, minor and a single diminished chord. Yet the pungent effect of the augmented triad – and Liszt's deployment of it is markedly avant garde – *is* heard elsewhere in the *Ring*. It is particularly rife in Act II of *Die Walküre*, because it is associated with the Valkyries, who make their first appearance in that act; but augmented triads are also used to invoke the terrors of the forest by which Mime's imagination is haunted in Act I Scene 3 of *Siegfried*.

Another work of Liszt's that stalks the undergrowth of the *Ring* is the Piano Sonata in B minor, whose descending main theme bears an uncanny resemblance to the stepwise, similarly dotted themes associated with the spear of Wotan and more generally with the authority with which he bestrides the stage. Other intriguing parallels between Wagner's works and Liszt's have been discussed elsewhere, notably Liszt's songs 'Ich möchte hingehn' and 'Die Lorelei', and his symphonic poem *Hamlet*, all of which contain intimations of *Tristan und Isolde*,[5] but it is worth pointing out that the falling 7ths of Liszt's *Faust* Symphony, mentioned above, occur frequently in Romantic music. A particularly notable use, however, is in a work by the Liszt pupil and Wagner protégé Hans von Bülow. Falling 7ths are ubiquitous in the latter's orchestral fantasy *Nirwana* (see Chapter 20: Creative Spark), the score of which Wagner was examining, on Liszt's recommendation, in the autumn of 1854. He was also affected by the brooding melancholy of *Nirwana*, but he hardly needed models for Faustian introspection: he had, after all, written his own *Faust* Overture in 1839–40 – revised, significantly enough, in January 1855 – the wide-spaced, arching main theme of which evokes the questing spirit of *Faust*. And indeed the temporal proximity of work on the revised *Faust* Overture and *Die Walküre* is underlined by the fact that the beginning of Act III of the latter was outlined on the same page and on the reverse of sketches of the former.[6]

Nor was the influence all one way, by any means. Liszt's conducting of Wagner's *Faust* Overture in a concert of May 1852 may well have given him the inspiration to proceed with his own symphony on the subject. The meeting of October 1856 gave Liszt the opportunity to hear some of the music for the *Ring* – Wagner had by this time got as far as the first act of *Siegfried* – by which he was enthralled. Wagner was equally transported by Liszt's playthrough of his *Dante* Symphony and by the symphonic poems *Les Préludes* and *Orpheus*, which Liszt conducted in St Gallen the following month at a concert in which he shared the podium with Wagner.

In fact it is often difficult to determine who was the greater beneficiary of this creative exchange, Wagner or Liszt, so closely does the work on their respective scores overlap.[7] At the same time, it needs to be emphasized that, for all their common enthusiasms, a handful of close thematic associations in no way dilutes the stylistic identity of either. Liszt's penchant for quasi-atonal experimentation was not shared by Wagner, whose most extreme chromaticism was always rooted in traditional functional harmony. It is certainly true, though, that Liszt's technique of thematic transformation has much in common with the Wagnerian leitmotif: in each case a core melodic motif evolves to form numerous independent motifs. Thematic transformation is seen in its exemplary form in both the

Faust Symphony and the Piano Sonata. In the former it is able to suggest the conflicting aspects of Faust's personality, while the Love motif (for example) is a lyrical transformation of one associated with doubt. At the same time, the metamorphosis of themes binds the work together into a cohesive whole. Thus Liszt's method has both a programmatic and a structural function. The same is true of Wagner's leitmotifs: the dozens of motifs in the *Ring*, each associated with a different character, object or emotion, can all in theory be traced back to the simple rising arpeggio that opens the cycle. The system is a way of imposing a measure of structural unity over a vast canvas, at the same time forging a link between textual/dramatic and musical elements.

The allegation that Wagner was incapable of showing gratitude or appreciation of other people's talents was never less justified than in his relationship with Liszt. His letters to his friend abound in generous expressions of indebtedness, of which the following – written from a French hydropathic establishment at Mornex, and making appropriate use of aquatic metaphor – is one of many examples:

Your symphonic poems are now much more familiar to me: they are the only music that occupies me at present, since I myself am not allowed to think of work during the course of my treatment here. Every day I read through one or other of the scores, just as I would read through a poem, fluently and uninhibitedly. On each occasion I feel as though I were diving down into some crystal flood, in order to be quite alone there, to leave behind the whole of this world, and to live my own life for an hour. Refreshed and fortified I then swim back to the surface and long for your presence.[8]

Wagner gives his friend Liszt an early taste of one of his works. Painting by Hermann Torggler.

Wagner was all too well aware, however, of how frank expressions of indebtedness could be portrayed by hostile commentators. In an article on *Tristan* the young critic and composer Richard Pohl committed what Wagner regarded as a faux pas:

There are many things we willingly admit to between ourselves – for ex., that I have become a totally different fellow in matters of harmony as a result of getting to know Liszt's compositions; but when friend Pohl blurts out this secret for the whole world to hear, right at the head of a short notice on the Tristan Prelude, it is indiscreet to say the least, and am I not supposed to assume that he was authorized to commit such an indiscretion? Liszt, for ex., may well write in ink on the dedication page of his Dante [Symphony] that he thinks he owes me a great deal; I can accept that as an excess of friendship. But it would be foolish of me to insist that something of the kind should be printed and added to the dedication for all the world to read.[9]

By coincidence or otherwise, it was about this time, 1856, that tensions began to creep into the relationship. The antipathy towards Wagner of Liszt's mistress, the Princess Carolyne von Sayn-Wittgenstein, was reciprocated, but there were also problems of a pecuniary nature. Then, in the 1860s, Liszt took profound exception, on moral grounds, to Wagner's liaison with Cosima von Bülow: Liszt himself had had girlfriends and

Photograph of Carolyne von Sayn-Wittgenstein in Rome. The formidable princess was the companion of Liszt, but no friend of Wagner.

Wagner holds court at Wahnfried. W. Beckmann's oil painting of 1882 imagines Cosima, Liszt and Wagner's disciple Hans von Wolzogen all appropriately enraptured by the Master's reading.

mistresses aplenty all his adult life, but somehow it was different when his own daughter was involved. He was eventually reconciled to Cosima's relationship with Wagner when it was sanctified by marriage in 1870, albeit in a Protestant church (Liszt and the princess were devout Catholics), but the friendship was never restored to its pristine splendour. Numerous entries in Cosima Wagner's diaries allude to quiet sulking and exploding tempers at Wahnfried even in the later years.

And yet, even then Wagner was able to refer to his friendship with Liszt as 'his only genuine relationship',[10] while the toast at the Bayreuth banquet, quoted earlier, speaks for itself. This was, by any standards, one of the most remarkable friendships between two composers of any era, sustained by deep mutual admiration and understanding. The effects on their respective oeuvres are incalculable.

12   Muses, Mistresses and Mother-Figures: Wagner's Women

All my women are now passing before my eyes.
Wagner, two days before his death

Carl Friedrich Sohn's portrait of Mathilde Wesendonck, painted in 1850, portrays her much as Wagner regarded her: as an angelic muse.

You would scarcely know it from the conventional, stereotypical accounts of the subject, but for a 19th-century Romantic artist Wagner's sexual appetites were hardly exceptional. The tally of his serious and casual affairs taken together barely exceeds a dozen, and yet the received image of Wagner is that of an unscrupulous wife-stealer congenitally incapable of doing the decent thing in matters of the heart. That the image is a grotesque distortion is evident from even a superficial knowledge of the facts, but such is the apparent need in the human psyche for scapegoat figures that the comforting canards continue to be recycled.

Exhibits A and B for the prosecution are Mathilde Wesendonck, the wife of Wagner's benefactor, Otto Wesendonck, and Cosima von Bülow, the wife of Wagner's loyal friend and the conductor of *Tristan und Isolde*.

Otto Wesendonck, in a chalk lithograph by Franz Hickmann, *c*. 1848–49. Wesendonck had his own reasons, psychological and social, for supporting Wagner as assiduously as he did.

In the former case, the hackneyed version of the scenario runs something like this: 'opportunistic, manipulative composer sponges off generous patron and steals his wife into the bargain'. This has never sounded truly convincing, but recent research by the South African scholar Chris Walton has thrown fascinating new light on the triangular relationship.[1] Otto emerges as a complex character, and his financial support of Wagner may not have been quite as disinterested as it first appears. Certainly Otto, whose social status stood to gain from association with the leading German composer of the day, took a commercial view of the various loans he extended to Wagner. But he also had an extraordinary penchant for clandestine incestuous identifications, which may well have drawn him to Wagner's works: Mathilde was not his wife's real name, but it was the name of Otto's previous, deceased wife, which his second wife was obliged to take in her place; and it was also the name of an elder sister who had played the role of surrogate mother.

Nor was Mathilde the passive sex object of biographical myth: as Walton shows, she was remarkably adept at manipulating the menfolk around her and getting her own way. She handled the intricacies of the Zurich ménage (Wagner and his wife, Minna, lived in the house next door, and Mathilde visited his first-floor workroom on a regular basis as the composition of *Tristan* got under way) with a firm hand, allowing Wagner (as far as we can tell) just as much licence as was acceptable to her husband. She was by no means a dumb muse (in any sense) either. Not only did she write the five poems set by Wagner in his *Wesendonck Lieder* – a unique occurrence in his oeuvre, and one that he would hardly have countenanced had he not felt the texts were of adequate quality – but she went on in later life to write further poems, folksongs, stories and dramas. While not exactly works of genius, they are nevertheless of a higher calibre than often credited.

The earliest known photograph of the Wesendoncks' villa (1865), including a very rare view of the Asyl (to the right) – the little house placed at the disposal of Wagner and his wife.

All the evidence suggests that the 'love affair' – if that is not a mis-nomer – between Mathilde and Wagner remained unconsummated. The fact that Wagner's rampant passion for Mathilde supplied a kind of emotional matrix for the upthrust of libidinal urges in *Tristan und Isolde* – a story of unquenchable yearning and unfulfilled desire – is further evidence of a sort (see Chapter 17: Fatal Attraction). Wagner's own account of the affair, in a letter to his sister Clara Wolfram, will to some seem self-serving hypocritical cant; to others it may have the ring of truth:

What has sustained and comforted me during the last six years and what, more especially, has given me the strength to endure living with Minna [his wife], in spite of the enormous differences in our character and nature, has been the love of that young woman [Mathilde Wesendonck] whose initial response to me was one of diffidence, doubt, hesitation and shyness, but who later approached me with increasing certainty and self-confidence. Since there could never be any question of union between us, our deep and mutual affection assumed that sadly melancholic character that banished all vulgarity and baseness, and recognizes the source of all joy in the other's well-being. Since first we came to know each other, she has shown the most untiring and tender concern for me, and, in the most courageous manner, obtained from her husband all that could ease my life's burden. Faced with his wife's open candour, the latter could not but fall prey to increasing jealousy. Her greatness lay in the fact that she kept her husband constantly informed of the state of her heart, and gradually persuaded him to resign her completely.[2]

Wagner goes on to say that Otto, despite his jealousy, was obliged to concur with his wife's whims: her weapon was her children. Rather than lose both his wife and his children, he 'accepted his renunciatory role' and put on a smiling face ('not a single black look' was allowed to betray his real feelings). Wagner's own marriage, to Minna, had long since broken down irretrievably, but on grounds of incompatibility rather than infidelity. The romance leading to their marriage had been an infatuation based on physical attraction. Cracks began to appear in the relationship from the time of the wedding (see Chapter 3: Earning his Keep) and in the years to come it became evident that Minna, for all her qualities, lacked both the temperament and the education to measure up to the inordinately high demands of consort to a man who believed himself to be worthy of adoration.

That was a role better suited to Exhibit B, Cosima von Bülow. Here the conventional script reads that Wagner stole the wife of his protégé, callously putting his own emotional and physical needs before those of others. But this is to reckon without the powerful force of nature that was Cosima, and without the predictable disaster that was her marriage to Bülow. For all the agonies of guilt she suffered throughout her life, Cosima had a steely, ruthless determination to get her own way (see Chapter 21: The Silent Sufferer). That she had made a disastrous mistake in marrying Bülow soon became as evident to her as it had been to her father Liszt ('Bülow lacks the talent to be a husband,' he opined[3]). A wife-beater and prey to crippling neuralgic pains and black moods of despair,

Photograph of Cosima von Bülow taken *c.* 1865, the year in which Isolde, her first child with Wagner, was born.

when he would lash out with sharp tongue, subjecting all around him to humiliating sarcasm, Bülow was a bully who had long since buried any affectionate impulses deep inside him. He was in particular a monstrously insensitive husband and father, barely aware of Cosima's grief at losing her brother, Daniel, or of the fact that she was entering the agonizing final stages of labour with their second daughter, Blandine, while he was busying himself in another part of the house.

Cosima's masochistic propensity for suffering (her Catholic upbringing had a lot to answer for) might have permitted her to tolerate this living nightmare indefinitely had she not encountered the man for whose happiness she believed destiny had made her responsible. It rapidly became apparent to all parties concerned – including Bülow himself – that Cosima belonged not with him, but with Wagner. 'Wife-stealing' is hardly an appropriate term to describe what all the participants themselves regarded as a rational reordering of an anomalous situation.

Two decades earlier a different set of circumstances had obtained. Barely had the signatures on Wagner and Minna's wedding certificate dried when Minna was seeking solace elsewhere (see Chapter 3: Earning his Keep). The marriage was patched over but it was never one based on the ideal love Wagner was endlessly seeking, in his real life as much as in his works. By 1850, if not earlier, the marriage had irretrievably broken down, as Wagner acknowledged in a letter to Minna:

The fundamental differences between us have proved, to a greater or lesser extent, to be a torment both for me and, more especially, for you, ever since the time we first became acquainted. *I* at least have no need to remind you of the countless scenes which have passed between us since the earliest days of our marriage, – for I have no doubt but that you have a livelier memory of them than I do. Yet what bound me so irresistibly to you then was love, a love which was blind to all the differences between us, – a love, however, which you did not share ... the one emotion which really mattered, and which enabled us to bear all our sufferings with a smile – unconditional love, the love with which we love the other person as he is and love him, moreover, for *the man he is*, – this love was something you could never feel.[4]

The letter just quoted was sent from France, where Wagner was, it has to be said, hot in pursuit of a 23-year-old Englishwoman who at first appeared to offer precisely that elusive unconditional love. Jessie Laussot (née Taylor) was fluent in German and intimately acquainted with

Minna Wagner and Peps as painted by Clementine Stockar-Escher in 1853. Resembling more of a *Hausfrau* by this time, Minna nevertheless retains a bright-eyed charm.

Wagner's works to date.[5] Like Wagner and like Cosima many years later, Jessie was trapped in an unhappy marriage. The pair conceived a plan to elope to Greece or Asia Minor, a romantic adventure aborted by Jessie's husband and mother (see Chapter 9: The Zurich Years). As Wagner put it, shortly after the episode, in a letter to a sympathetic benefactress, Julie Ritter:

If only you could have witnessed this triumph of love as it burst forth from every sinew of this rich and blessed woman, when she revealed to me that she was mine – not through any spoken confession – but entirely through her own self, through the involuntary, radiant and naked manifestation of love! If only you could have seen this joy, this rapturous delight which animated every fibre of her being, from the movement of her fingertips to the most subtle workings of her mind, when this youthful woman cast her lustrous radiance on me.[6]

And so on. But, as Wagner also admitted, he had been acting 'in utter indifference to the risk I was running of being shot through the head by her injured husband'.[7] Eugène Laussot had indeed been threatening to

Judith Gautier: orientalist, intellectual, translator and legendary beauty. Her many male admirers included Victor Hugo, Wagner and John Singer Sargent, who sketched and painted her on a number of occasions.

kill Wagner: evidently he did not hold him in such reverence as did Bülow two decades later.

The only other affair of any consequence in Wagner's life was that with the French writer Judith Gautier, who visited Wagner and Cosima with her husband, Catulle Mendès, and the poet Villiers de l'Isle-Adam, at Tribschen in 1869 and then again the following year (see Chapter 22: Tribschen Idyll). By the time of the first Bayreuth Festival, in 1876, Judith had separated from Mendès and was allowing herself to be courted by an obscure composer called Louis Benedictus. (She did not return his passion, though it was not until later in her life that she discovered her latent bisexuality.[8]) But that did not deter Wagner from attempting to claim her favours too. Judith certainly pandered to his somewhat fetishistic bodily needs (see Chapter 15: In the Pink), though whether she surrendered herself to him entirely is less clear. They did sustain an intimate and clandestine correspondence, facilitated by the local barber, until Cosima brought it to a swift end in February 1878. Given Cosima's devotion to Wagner, and indeed his to her, the dalliance with Judith may seem perplexing. In the first place, however, it needs to be borne in mind that it was only five or six years into their relationship that Cosima began to withdraw her sexual favours – a challenge for a man as testerone-filled as Wagner. Second, the fetishism to which Judith pandered was an essential part of Wagner's psycho-sexual make-up, but one to which the puritanical Cosima was never likely to be sympathetic.

There is surely an element of the exotic Judith in Wagner's characterization of Kundry in *Parsifal*, and certainly the stolen kisses and glances he exchanged with her at the time of its composition stoked the creative fires just as the caresses of Mathilde Wesendonck had done at the time of *Tristan*. He imagined Judith lying on the chaise longue (christened 'Judith' in her honour) adjacent to his writing desk and looking at him with her large, dark eyes. But Kundry's sexual allure encompasses long-suppressed maternal longings too. Wagner's problematic, much-analysed relationship with his mother, Johanna, may or may not have worked its way out in his music dramas, but absent and ersatz mothers of various kinds indubitably loom large in both his life and his works.[9]

We can probably discount the gossip about a late-blossoming affair with the Flowermaiden Carrie Pringle as just that (see Chapter 25: Death in Venice), and evidence that Wagner's relationship with his faithful housekeeper Verena ('Vreneli') Weidmann involved the rumpling of bedsheets is also lacking, despite the profiles of Vreneli's daughter and first son bearing a similarity to Wagner's. The most persuasive case for such an affair is made by Eva Rieger,[10] in her compelling recent study of the momentous impact on Wagner of his various inamoratas, but it hinges largely on Vreneli's three pregnancies, which occurred between 1868 and 1872 – a period that coincided not only with Vreneli's marriage to Jacob Stocker, who also entered Wagner's service, but also with the most sexually satisfying years of Wagner's relationship with Cosima. All of which leaves just a handful of liaisons to mention: a few pre-marital diversions

Mathilde Maier

Mathilde Maier, the daughter of a notary. Wagner felt a great attraction for her, but she was reluctant to get involved with him on account of her incipient deafness.

in Wagner's youth (reported in *Mein Leben*), and his close friendships with Mathilde Maier, Friederike Meyer and Blandine Ollivier in the early 1860s, when Wagner was between partners, none of which appears to have developed into undue intimacy. From the same time dates a brief fling with the adorable Seraphine Mauro, inconveniently attached to Peter Cornelius. And then, of course, there is the 'sweet-tempered, obliging'[11] seventeen-year-old pork butcher's daughter, Lisbeth Völkl, who did for Wagner in his apartment in Penzing, and her sister, Marie, whose duties involved a famous pair of pink drawers (see Chapter 15: In the Pink).

13   The Behemoth of Bayreuth: Wagner's Personality

No man is a hero to his valet.
> George Wilhelm Friedrich Hegel

An inveterate scrounger and irredeemable philanderer who, not content with fleecing his friends, also helped himself to their wives; a man who was thoroughly loathsome and untrustworthy in his personal dealings. In sum, an utterly monstrous human being: the Behemoth of Bayreuth. This is the conventional image of Wagner, and while, like much received opinion about him, it contains a grain of truth, it is actually so risible that one wonders how it has held sway for so long. The reality is more complex and far more interesting.

Pecuniary matters and Wagner's notorious anti-Semitism are dealt with in more detail elsewhere in this book (see the following chapter, and Chapter 19: Grit in the Oyster). Here we will attempt to draw a more rounded portrait of Wagner the man. There is, at least, no lack of contemporary testimony: basking in reflected glory, almost everybody who encountered him was pleased to record their impressions.[1] A young composer called Robert von Hornstein, for example, describes both the unbearable and the charismatic aspects of Wagner's character. Wagner hated to be ignored, especially by Mathilde Wesendonck; and at supper one evening in Zurich, when he felt he was not getting enough attention, he suddenly uttered a piercing scream, followed by an announcement that he wished to read a tale by E. T. A. Hoffmann, which he did from start to finish. He then proceeded to pick an argument with Otto Wesendonck and finally complained volubly that he was being persecuted by creditors.

'Conversely,' Von Hornstein continues, Wagner

was enchanting whenever he went walking with Ritter and me. Witty insights flew through the air. He regaled us with tales from the rich storehouse of his experiences. Many a word of wisdom there was to be heard. Idiosyncratic views on people, relationships, art and politics were aired. His whole good-naturedness, of which he had a plentiful supply, came to the fore.[2]

The artist Friedrich Pecht got to know Wagner in Paris, but here records his reminiscences of later years:

There can be no doubt that, of all the artists of genius whom I have known, Wagner was by far the most gifted and richly talented. In the first place, none of

them possessed his indomitable courage and tremendous will-power. Yet he was the most good-natured and benevolent master towards his servants and, in spite of his feverish impatience, invariably showed them forbearance, doing everything in his power to see to their needs. For his musicians and singers, he was quite literally an inspiration, and they would do anything for him.[3]

Is it possible that Wagner, therefore, provides an antithesis to Hegel's epigrammatic thesis cited at the head of this chapter? The French writer Edouard Schuré came under Wagner's spell in the 1860s but writes perceptively about his nature:

His manner was no less surprising than his physical appearance, changing, as it did, between reserve and absolute coldness on the one hand and, on the other, a familiarity and unceremoniousness that could hardly have been more complete. There was no trace of the poseur about him, not a vestige of affected solemnity, no sense of deliberation or calculation. As soon as he appeared, he burst forth like a floodtide that nothing can stem. One was left dazzled by his exuberance and protean nature, a nature, moreover, that was passionate, private, extreme in everything and yet marvellously balanced by his all-consuming intellect. The frankness and extreme daring of a character whose qualities and faults were plain for all to see had the effect of a spell on some, but served only to repulse others.[4]

Viennese caricature
by Karl Klic (1873),
turning the tables
on Wagner and his
anti-Semitism.

Wagner entertaining his friends on New Year's Eve, 1840. The impoverished company – which included Minna Wagner, the librarian Gottfried Anders, the philologist Samuel Lehrs, the painter Friedrich Pecht and wife, and Ernst Benedikt Kietz, who drew the picture – were regaled with champagne and a crazy speech on the absurdity of life.

That volcanic energy is well attested by all Wagner's contemporaries. Combined with an incorrigible self-centredness, the result was no doubt as repellent to some as it was intoxicating to others – not that it was necessarily one or the other exclusively. Budding composers such as Peter Cornelius found the situation particularly oppressive:

Our great friend has to talk about *himself*, he has to sing and read from his *own* works, or he is unhappy. That's why he always wants to be surrounded by a small, intimate circle, because he can't have what he wants with other people. From the moment I dine with him – 2 o'clock in the afternoon – I cannot hope to get away, except on very exceptional occasions, and the situation is killing me.[5]

Solipsistic behaviour of this type, however unattractive, is hardly unusual, though. Indeed, for a creative artist or other exceptional genius of the 19th century it was almost part of the job description. One of Wagner's female friends, Malwida von Meysenbug, diagnosed the situation acutely:

A man so dominated by his elemental spirit should from the beginning have had a high-minded and understanding woman at his side – a woman who understood how to mediate between the genius and the world by realizing that the two were bound to be eternally poles apart. Frau Wagner never realized this. She tried to mediate by demanding concessions towards the world from the genius, which the latter could not and must not make.[6]

Another female friend, the novelist Eliza Wille, attributed Wagner's mood swings to the 'terrible experiences' he had had as a result of the uprising and subsequent exile. Those experiences, coupled with his congenital 'nervous irritability' and 'the powerful workings of his imagination', made life frankly intolerable for him at times – though his frequent visits to the Wille household had happier moments too:

On the days when Wagner felt like joining us the sun seemed to enter our lives. All who knew him know how warm-hearted and kind he could be. He paid the friendliest heed to sons and mother alike … . But his good moods soon passed. Letters arrived that depressed him. He withdrew to the solitude of his room, and whenever he found me alone, he would break into a flood of words that rarely boded well for the future.[7]

It is often stated that Wagner's arrogance made it impossible for him to acknowledge the merits of others. It would be truer to say that he found it impossible to give praise where he felt it was not due. His autobiographical writings and letters are indeed peppered with derogatory comments about contemporaries whose work he did not admire. On the other hand, he could be effusive about others' achievements. His letters to Liszt, which overflow with genuine expressions of gratitude and admiration, are just one example. His warm encouragement of Hans von Bülow, a composition student when he first encountered Wagner, helped to set the young man on a musical rather than a legal path. At a soirée at Wagner's apartment in Penzing in 1864 the thirty-year-old Brahms was invited to play the piano. After performing Bach's organ Toccata in F major and a number of other pieces, he then played, at Wagner's express wish, his Variations on a Theme of Handel. 'None of us who was present on that occasion will ever forget the unfeigned warmth with which Wagner, who always found

Wagner regularly visited the home of François and Eliza Wille at Mariafeld in the 1850s. Here he found both intellectual stimulation and spiritual solace.

Aus Bayreuth.

Aeschylus und Shakespeare, nach Porges die beiden einzigen Bühnendichter, welche Wagner an die Seite gestellt werden können, machen im vorschriftsmäßigen Frack dem Meister ihre Aufwartung.

Aeschylus and Shakespeare pay humble obeisance to Wagner – the only dramatic poets (according to Heinrich Porges's original caption in the *Berliner Ulk*, 1876) whom Wagner considered his equals.

it impossible to praise a work that had nothing to say to him, commended the young composer and how convincingly he discussed every detail of the piece,' reported a witness to the event.[8] It is true that Wagner's perception of Brahms was not always so positive – they were, after all, on opposite sides of the great 19th-century divide between absolute music and that of the New German School – but the unstinting admiration he expressed on this occasion is one of countless examples that could be adduced with respect to his contemporaries.

The question of Wagner's relationships with women is another that has fallen prey to ill-informed cliché. While it is true that Wagner's eye was no less roving than that of the average man, it is also the case that he was far more loyal to each of his two wives than the typical man of his generation (or indeed ours). The statement requires elucidation. In the case of Minna, there is no evidence or suggestion that he was unfaithful to her before the time their marriage had irretrievably broken down (and even after they were living apart, he insisted on maintaining her). His marriage to Cosima was briefly shaken by his infatuation with Judith Gautier, but the 'affair', such as it was, came to a swift conclusion.

In between those two marriages there was an extended period during which Wagner took advantage of the fact that he was a free agent. But even then his serious liaisons hardly amount to anything out of the ordinary. The abortive affair with Jessie Laussot in 1850 (see Chapter 9: The Zurich Years) was but a further nail in the coffin of a marriage that was already in a terminal condition. A handful of other close friendships are described in the previous chapter. Wagner's intimacy with Mathilde Wesendonck is a special case, but the relationship was almost certainly not consummated.

It is therefore difficult to avoid the impression that Wagner's amours have been greatly exaggerated. Why should that be? Could it be that Wagner has become the classic figure of the scapegoat or whipping-boy: the one made to take the blame for a common human failing? By creating a stereotype of outrageous behaviour we salve our consciences about our own. This, it seems to me, is true of other aspects of Wagner's behaviour too – not least his anti-Semitism.

One of a series of eight photographs of Wagner taken by the photographers Elliott & Fry on 24 May 1877, during his English visit that year.

WAGNER.

ELLIOTT & FRY   Copyright.   55, BAKER STREET. W.
AND AT 7, GLOUCESTER TERRACE. S.W.

Quite apart from the grotesque unfairness of the stereotypical misrepresentation of Wagner, there is an aspect of it that is even more dangerously misleading. An all-too-common gambit is to invest Wagner's personality with every flaw in the catalogue, the better to enjoy the music with a clear conscience. With the character of the man blackened, the works are able to shine more brightly. As Barry Emslie suggests in his admirable study *Richard Wagner and the Centrality of Love*, 'You cannot put a firewall around the music dramas.'[9] Rarely has there been such a continuity, in fact, between the social character and ideological outlook of a composer and his works as with Wagner. And, indeed, it is that often murky ideological subtext that makes the operas the fascinating, perplexing, endlessly thought-provoking works they are.

Reassuring as one-dimensional cartoon images of the Behemoth of Bayreuth may be, it is time to turn the page to a more sophisticated, nuanced and frankly honest picture. The result may be a revelation.

14 Always Short: Wagner and Money

What makes you think I could ever have enough money?
Wagner to Theodor Uhlig

While vainly trying to seek his fame and fortune in Paris in the early 1840s, the young Wagner and his wife, Minna, were forced to live on the breadline. Often they did not know where the next meal was coming from, and Wagner came close to being jailed as a debtor. Less than a quarter of a century later he was sashaying through luxury apartments in Vienna and Munich dressed in satin dressing gowns with flounces, his own body draped in silk, with expensive perfumes scenting the air. It was not exactly a story of 'rags to riches', since he was never really wealthy, though in the latter years he was undoubtedly comfortably off.

Having failed to take Paris by storm, Wagner had earned his keep for six years as a liveried Kapellmeister at the Saxon court before going into exile, where he relied on the generosity of friends and patrons. His famous 'rescue' by King Ludwig in 1864 delivered him at last from financial embarrassment. In truth, however, it was not responsible for his change of lifestyle, for just days before the royal rescue, while he was pondering his lack of means to bring the *Ring* project to fruition, Wagner had been inhabiting one of his luxury apartments.

The fact is that Wagner had a penchant for living beyond his means, with the result that he always needed to be bailed out. It is this that has given him the indelible reputation of a scrounger, despite the over-simplification. In order to see the matter in its true perspective, a number of factors need to be taken into account. First, new forms of patronage were opening up in 19th-century Germany. In Wagner's city of birth, Leipzig, a new bourgeois musical culture had established itself, with sub-scription concerts at the Gewandhaus and elsewhere. In Dresden, where Wagner was in the royal service, the court still subsidized its theatre, but box-office revenue was now vital too. The shoestring provincial operations he was involved with in Magdeburg and Riga were typical of the time.

Second, composers in Germany in Wagner's day received no royal-ties on their works as a right. Until the German copyright law of 1870, a composer would expect to receive a single, flat fee, any profits reverting to the publisher and the theatre. Had he chosen to plough the furrow of popular success, as exemplified by Offenbach or Meyerbeer, or even continued to write in the vein of *Rienzi* and *Tannhäuser*, Wagner might

One of a series of five photographs taken by Ludwig Angerer in Vienna in the winter of 1862–63.

The Leipzig Gewandhaus, one of the more prestigious venues for the burgeoning bourgeois musical culture of the early 19th century. Several of Wagner's early works were performed there.

well have made enough money to stock a wardrobe of silk dressing gowns. But given the expansive, impracticable nature of his music dramas, he was condemning himself to the role of perpetual mendicant. No project as radical, as ambitious as the *Ring* could hope to succeed in existing 19th-century conditions.

The money for which Wagner continually cajoled his friends and patrons was intended to create a new art form to replace one he regarded as meretricious and vacuous. Whatever the accuracy of that diagnosis, there is no denying the huge and enduring influence Wagner's art had on not only opera, but all the arts over succeeding generations (see Chapter 26: Perfect and Imperfect Wagnerites). From that perspective, one might have thought that awe and gratitude would have been more appropriate reactions than the mean-spirited cavilling and stereotypical opprobrium to which Wagner is normally subject.

Of course Wagner did not help his own cause by his spendthrift tendencies or the arrogance of his expectations. Some of his letters of supplication take on a hectoring quality. 'Dear Hornstein!', he wrote to an acquaintance in December 1861:

I hear you have become rich. Just how wretched I have become you may easily infer from my failures. I am hoping to rescue myself by isolation and a new work. In order to make possible such a restoration in this way, i.e. to free myself from the most distressing commitments, cares and necessities that deprive me of all peace of mind, I need an immediate advance of ten thousand francs. With this I can put my life in order once more and start working again … . So show us now whether you are a real man![1]

At the same time Wagner is clearly aware of his own weakness:

My Franz, when you see the second act of Tristan, you'll admit that I need a lot of money. I'm a great spend-thrift; but, really, it does produce results.[2]

And when he evokes the harsh reality of artistic creation, it is difficult not to empathize:

But it is really only out of utter despair that I take up my art again: when this happens, and I again have to renounce, – if I am obliged once more to plunge into the waves of an artist's imagination in order to find satisfaction in an imaginary world, I must at least help out my imagination and find means of encouraging my imaginative faculties. I cannot then live like a dog, I cannot sleep on straw and drink common gin: mine is an intensely irritable, acute, and hugely voracious, yet uncommonly tender and delicate sensuality which, one way or another, must be flattered if I am to accomplish the cruelly difficult task of creating in my mind a non-existent world.[3]

In order to create the conditions in which that art could be brought into being, Wagner needed, or felt he needed, a certain level of material well-being, which in his more mature years tended towards luxury (see the following chapter). In the early years of his exile he was offered an unsolicited annual allowance of 3,000 francs by two wealthy female admirers, Julie Ritter (mother of the musician and poet Karl Ritter, who was shortly to join his circle) and Jessie Laussot. Proposing to liberate the cultured Jessie from her unfulfilling marriage by eloping with her, Wagner had to kiss goodbye to the allowance, along with Jessie, when their little plan was uncovered. Julie Ritter, however, did continue her support, to the tune of 800 thalers a year, from 1851 to 1859.

Other generous friends at this time were Liszt, now resident in Weimar, the recipient of innumerable *cris de coeur*, and Jakob Sulzer, one of the two cantonal secretaries in Zurich. But it was the retired silk merchant Otto Wesendonck who did most in the Zurich years to keep Wagner and his ambitious projects afloat. By means of loans and other financial support Wesendonck made his Zurich exile far more endurable than it might otherwise have been. In particular he made available to Wagner the small house and garden (named by the composer the 'Asyl', or 'Refuge') adjoining the luxury villa built for himself in the suburb of Enge. Magnanimous to the point of self-sacrifice as this was, given that his wife was more than just a landlady to Wagner (see Chapter 12: Muses, Mistresses and Mother-Figures), it should be noted that Wesendonck charged him a commercial rent of 800 francs per annum, the same as Wagner had been paying in his previous lodging in the Zeltweg.

As the *Ring* took shape – Wagner began work on the composition of *Siegfried* in 1856–57, but then abandoned it in part for financial reasons – his need for pecuniary assistance became ever more pressing. But in August 1859, when the wind had blown over following Wagner's enforced departure from the Asyl in the wake of marital dissension, Wesendonck made an unsolicited offer of financial help to enable him to finish the

Julie Ritter, a widow from Dresden who made an annual allowance to Wagner from 1851 to 1859.

Otto Wesendonck, like Wagner a lover of silk, from which he made his fortune. Portrait by Julius Roeting, 1860.

Ring. Wagner's response is somewhat surprising:

My dearest friend, for God's sake do not interpret it as an insult if I entreat you to take back the money you have offered me! –

I cannot, in all honesty, accept a loan when I know my own situation and constitution as well as I do, and that neither of them can ever be expected to change.

Even less can I accept a gift, and this, you may rest assured, from *no one*, not just because it is you, to whom I already owe so many notable sacrifices.

Please accept my warmest thanks for your kind sentiment and my most sincere good wishes.[4]

What he suggested to Wesendonck instead was a business proposition, calculated to appeal to his commercial instincts. The deal stipulated that Wesendonck would enjoy any proceeds from his purchase of the copyright in the four scores of the *Ring*, which he would buy for 6,000 francs each. For his part, Wagner would receive any revenues from public performances. Later that year, when Wagner's publisher, Schott, indicated a willingness to publish a score of his, Wagner offered him *Das Rheingold* for 10,000 francs, with which he intended to reimburse Wesendonck; his hope proved unrealistic, however, in the light of the deficit sustained by his recent series of concerts in Paris. It was at this point that Wagner hit on the ingenious idea of asking Wesendonck to regard the 6,000 francs he had paid for *Das Rheingold* as an advance payment for the fourth work in the tetralogy, as yet unwritten. With Schott trying to beat him down, the publisher's intermediary, Heinrich Esser, insisting on his cut ('I shall then claim the usual fee of a successful matchmaker') and even Wesendonck paying less for the works than Wagner was able to secure from his stingy publisher, one can but smile at the composer's resourcefulness.

Wesendonck in any case agreed, perhaps realizing, as a good capitalist, that this fraction of his fortune was scarcely being risked on a nonentity. In non-financial terms, too, it could be argued that Wesendonck did as well out of his patronage of Wagner as did the composer himself. Having made his money in business and retired to Zurich to enjoy it, the *nouveau riche* Wesendonck and his wife were able to buy social esteem by their proximity to Wagner. The concerts at their villa were glittering occasions that enabled them to rub shoulders with some of the leading artists and intellectuals in Zurich. Who would remember Otto the silk importer and Mathilde the dilettante poet today were it not for their association with Wagner?

It is also the case, of course, that King Ludwig, for all his generosity, received something from Wagner beyond price: the chance to befriend a boyhood hero and to enable him to conjure in dramatic form that fantasy world to which the king loved to retreat. The support he gave (see Chapter 16: 'My Adored and Angelic Friend') inevitably had political repercussions, and indeed the conduct of Wagner's personal life would also compromise their relationship. But in an age where innovative forms of art could in general be achieved only with the support of private patronage, King Ludwig played his role (almost) to perfection.

View from the salon through the boudoir to the conservatory of the Wesendonck villa. The carpets, portieres, silk wall-coverings and most of the furniture probably date from after the time of the Wesendoncks' occupation.

Against the image of Wagner as incorrigible mendicant, one has to set the fact that he was also a man of effusive generosity. He liked to keep the champagne flowing, and his Christmas presents demonstrated a largesse he could ill afford. It is not, of course, difficult to reconcile lavish, arguably excessive, generosity with lack of money: so little regard for money *per se* did Wagner have that, as soon as he had some, he spent it either on himself or on friends. Nor should it be forgotten that he maintained his support of his estranged wife Minna right up to the time of her death in 1866. Thereafter he also continued maintenance payments to Minna's daughter, Natalie, even though she was unrelated to him by blood.

The avaricious acquisition of wealth and casino speculation were not vices in which Wagner indulged. Money for him was only a means to improve the existence of himself and others – and of course to improve the world by endowing it with the 'artwork of the future'.

15 In the Pink: The Role of Silks and Satins in Wagner's Life

But who could fail to notice the rustle of satin in Wagner's work?
Thomas Mann

Hubris, in the Greek dramas so admired by Wagner, invites catastrophe. Just a year after he had reached the pinnacle of his success with the premiere of the *Ring* at the newly established Bayreuth Festival, Wagner suffered a humiliating reversal. In 1877 a Viennese journalist and satirist by the name of Daniel Spitzer published a cache of letters written by Wagner to a woman called Bertha Goldwag. Though described as a *Putzmacherin*, or milliner, Goldwag served Wagner in the dual roles of a

Caricature dating from the time of the *Putzmacherin* revelations. The rose garland around his head, the fetishized clothes and the footwear all satirize Wagner's effeminacy.

costumier and what we would today call an interior designer. The letters, written over a number of years, itemize in titillating detail Wagner's requirements in both departments, revealing to the world that this high-minded composer of monumental music dramas was also a sybarite on a grand scale, with a particular penchant for silks and satins. From his violet velvet drapes to his pink silk underwear, his tastes became the stuff of the gossip sheets and satirical cartoons. Self-publicist as he was, Wagner drew the line at having his linen aired in public, and it is no coincidence that it was precisely at this time that he toyed seriously with the idea of emigrating to America.

'Frou-Frou-Wagner' from *Der Floh*, 24 June 1877. Caricature depicting Wagner acquiring pink satin by the yard and being shafted by the journalist Daniel Spitzer, who published the letters to his milliner.

The apartments in Penzing, near Vienna, for which Wagner commissioned his silk-lined luxury suite from Bertha Goldwag.

Plan of the Penzing apartment drawn by Wagner. The private boudoir described by Bertha Goldwag is the 'Kleiner Salon' marked 'e'.

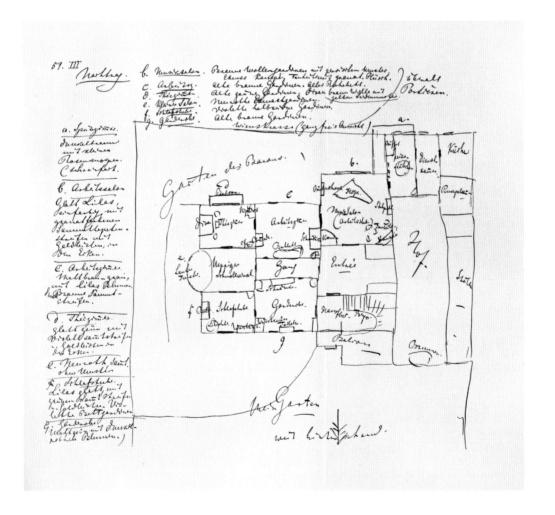

Bertha Goldwag's first major assignment was the fitting out of the upper-floor apartment Wagner rented in Penzing, near Vienna, in May 1863. The illustration opposite shows Wagner's own plan of the apartment, together with the description of a décor that would raise eyebrows in a millionaire's luxury executive suite, let alone a near-destitute composer's bachelor pad. Every room is a riot of silk, velvet or damask, but on one room – an inner sanctum to which very few were admitted – particular care has been lavished. Here is Goldwag's own description of this sensual haven:

The walls were lined in silk, with relievo garlands all the way round. From the ceiling hung a wonderful lamp with a gentle beam. The whole of the floor was covered in heavy and exceptionally soft rugs in which your feet literally sank. The furnishings of this boudoir – as I should like to call this room – consisted of a small sofa, a number of armchairs and a small table.[1]

The following year, shortly after his rescue from penury by Ludwig, Wagner moved into a more spacious house at 21 Briennerstrasse in Munich. Here, too, a small room (dubbed the 'Grail Room' by Peter Cornelius) was set aside for sensual indulgence and creative activity of one sort or another:

The walls were covered with fine yellow satin, finished off with yellow valances of the same material … . The white curtains and their draperies were also adorned with delicate artificial roses. The room was lighted by a window in the narrow wall at the left of the entrance. The curtains of this window were of pink satin, interlaced with pink and white satin draperies. In the middle of the broad wall was a mirror, and on the narrow wall opposite the window a reproduction of Murillo's Madonna. The cornice of the window curtains, the frame of the mirror and that of the picture were puffed out with pink satin and tied back with white satin bows. The ceiling was also bordered on all four sides with similar pearl-grey ruches strewn with artificial roses. The centre of the ceiling was adorned with a rosette of white satin about 12 inches in circumference and 10 inches in depth, trimmed with narrow blond lace and with roses like those on the ceiling. The floor was covered with a soft Smyrna carpet.[2]

Rear view of the house in the Briennerstrasse, Munich, to which Wagner moved on his 'rescue' by King Ludwig.

But the extravagant décor was only part of the story. When it came to cosseting his own body, Wagner's imagination was not to be found lacking either. In addition to the velvet drapes and portières, Goldwag provided him with an extended wardrobe of satin dressing gowns with flounces, suits in silk lined with fur (in various colours, with matching slippers and neckties), and shirts and underclothes in silk and satin, as well as delicate scents with which to perfume the atmosphere. Pink was a favourite colour, as were rose-scented fragrances. A famous letter to a local Viennese girl by the name of Marie Völkl throws intriguing light on his predilections:

Now, my darling, prepare the house for my return, so that I can relax there in comfort, as I long very much to do. Everything must be clean and tidy, and well-heated. See that the best room is really welcoming for me: when you have heated the stove, open the door, so that the temperature in the room warms up. *And plenty of perfume: buy the best bottles, so that it smells really sweet.* Heavens! how I'm looking forward to relaxing with you again at last! *(I hope the pink drawers are ready, too???)*[3]

Photograph by Jules Bonnet (1867) depicting Wagner clad and seated in the velvet-lined comfort to which he had become accustomed.

Wagner's own designs for a beribboned satin housecoat and breeches.

That the garments in question (*Rosa-Höschen*) were to pamper his own nether quarters rather than Marie's can scarcely be doubted. In the words of Joachim Köhler:

For reasons known only to himself, he wore tailor-made silk underwear and elegant indoor clothing decorated with all manner of ruches, tassels and rosettes that seem more in keeping with a woman's wardrobe than a man's. He also had negligees made to his own designs, dressing gowns of a kind that Madame de Pompadour might well have worn, and even in Bayreuth he read Paris fashion magazines in order to keep abreast of the latest trends.[4]

We also have no less an authority than Nietzsche for the fact that the Wagnerian undercarriage liked to be encased in silk. A student of the philosopher's reported the following encounter:

One day just as he had returned from his usual Sunday visit to Wagner, Nietzsche asked me most casually where he might find a good silk shop in Basel. Eventually he admitted he had undertaken to shop for a pair of silk underpants for Wagner, and this important matter filled him with anxiety; for – added the smiling iconoclast – 'once you've chosen a God, you've got to adorn him!'[5]

Evidently the post of professor of classical philology at Basel University brought its fair share of headaches.

In his seminal study of Wagner's erotics, Laurence Dreyfus does not shirk from using the 'f' word. Wagner's predilection for silks and satins, together with a penchant for cross-dressing, amounts to a fetish, Dreyfus says,[6] and it is one that continued into his old age. In the Bayreuth years, when Wagner was engaged in a mild flirtation with the fragrant Judith Gautier, the French writer supplied from Paris items that could not easily be obtained locally. They included silk garments, pink satin, rose water, ambergris bath oils and aromatic powders. As he related to Judith, there was a creative component to this fetish: his bathtub was positioned strategically below his studio in order that he might be stimulated by the rising perfumes.

After Cosima had brought his *affaire* with Judith to an abrupt conclusion – having caught her husband burning some incriminating correspondence – Wagner was obliged to look elsewhere for a supplier. To his rescue came a leading light in the English Wagner Society, Julius Cyriax, who gamely fielded regular requests for silk nightshirts, copious quantities of rose oil and specially fine lavatory paper for the Wagnerian derrière. One challenging commission from Cosima, who was well

LES MODES PARISIENNES

Parisian fashion magazine of the kind Wagner plundered for sartorial inspiration.

acquainted with her husband's penchant for pink luxury items, was for 'a carpet made exclusively from the breast feathers of flamingos, with a border of peacock feathers'.[7] That Cyriax was persuaded to believe in the inspirational efficacy of a magic carpet is clear from his expressed wish that 'this charming artwork, worthy to lie in the Master's composing studio, might help him orchestrate Klingsor's magic garden'.[8]

An earlier correspondence that recently came to light is suggestive on the matter of Wagner's propensity for cross-dressing. Between 1869 and 1874 he wrote a dozen or so letters to a Milanese tailor by the name of Gaetano Ghezzi. Ghezzi and his wife, a couturière called Charlotte (or Carlotta) Chaillon, supplied Wagner with a number of items of women's clothing, including 'a cazavoika (or polonaise) [a dress or over-dress consisting of a bodice with a skirt open from the waist down] in black velvet, lined and richly furnished with a fine pelisse' (a cloak or mantle that was often fur-lined or padded); a 'black satin costume' of flexible use 'even as a negligee'; and a pair of satin underdresses to go with a jacket, one in pink, one in white.[9] Not surprisingly, Wagner was reluctant to admit, even to his tailor, that these pieces of women's clothing were for himself, claiming that they were a present for his wife. Some items were indeed given to Cosima as presents, but, as Dreyfus points out, a pink satin dress was unlikely to be for her, 'since there is no evidence that Cosima ever dressed in pink'.[10]

An episode in March 1864, when Wagner escaped his creditors in Vienna wearing women's clothes, may be evidence of theatrical ingenuity rather than a bent for cross-dressing *per se*, but the Ghezzi correspondence has a strong whiff of bodily self-indulgence about it. What is clear is that Cosima, though initially disapproving of his silk fetishism, came to accept it and pass it off as a family joke.[11] Less amusing was the fact that Wagner was wearing a pink dressing gown – doubtless one from his satin collection – at the time of his death, as was reported by an obituary syndicated in the Italian press.[12] At least Wagner was spared the humiliation of this revelation broadcast to posterity.

It has often been pointed out, not least by Wagner himself, that the skin condition erysipelas, from which he suffered, made it unbearable for him to wear rough fabrics adjacent to his skin. This may be a partial justification but hardly accounts for the sheer volume of soft materials in question. In any case Wagner himself told Nietzsche's doctor, Otto Eiser, in 1877 that he had been completely cured of his erysipelas many years back by a hydropathist (one Dr Vaillant, whom Wagner visited at his establishment at Mornex, near Geneva, in 1856, and who diagnosed the condition as a nervous allergy).[13] Between 1856 and 1877, according to Wagner, he had been free of the complaint, though it seemed to recur towards the end of his life.

But whatever the physiology, and irrespective of all the sensationalist aspects of Wagner being dragged out of his silk-lined closet, there is an element in his fetishism that is of profound significance in the understanding of his music. One has only to think of the prominent role played

The rosy delights
of the Venusberg
in a watercolour by
Heinrich Breling
(1881) of the Venus
grotto built for
Ludwig II in Linderhof
(left), and in a souvenir
postcard (above).

in Wagner's operas by sensory (as well as sensual) experience: indeed, his music often seems to swathe us in seductive luxuriance just as its composer liked to be cosseted by strokable fabrics and alluring fragrances. *Tannhäuser* is perhaps the most egregious example: 'a magical rosy light', 'an even denser rosy mist' and 'rosy scents' are evoked in Act I, while in Act III Tannhäuser senses the proximity of the ravishing fragrances of Venus and her realm. Wagner conjures up this paradise of the senses with all the technical means in his Romantic armoury: sumptuously enriched harmonies, voluptuous chromaticism, succulent doublings in the orchestral texture.

In *Tristan und Isolde* the lovers sink down onto a flowery bank; and the Liebestod is a hymn to the senses: waves of gentle breezes and clouds of blissful scents swirl around Isolde, who knows not whether to breathe or to listen, to sip them or to dive below them to expire in their sweet aroma. It is difficult to imagine this total abandonment to the senses being more ravishingly evoked than it is here by Wagner in some of the most sublime music he ever wrote. In Hans Sachs's Flieder Monologue ('Was duftet doch der Flieder' – How the scent of the elder wafts around me) in *Die Meistersinger*, the delights of summer blossom are linked associatively with the spirit of creativity, while Klingsor's Magic Garden in *Parsifal* merges visual and olfactory stimuli with erotic desire. The callow Parsifal hardly knows whether to gaze on, to smell or to pluck the blooms paraded for his pleasure.

Laurence Dreyfus, who in recent times has done more than any other commentator to determine how Wagner's erotics are given expression in

The sensual extravagance of the Magic Garden in *Parsifal*, as conceived by Paul von Joukowsky and executed by the Brückner brothers (1882).

his music, points out the curious disjunction in the *Ring* between the virile heroics of Siegfried (the two forging songs and his heroic musical character generally, not to mention his rough forest clothing) on the one hand and Wagner's feminized tendencies on the other.[14] His conclusion is that Siegfried, in his uncomplicated masculinity, is an anomaly in Wagner's oeuvre: the love he experiences is not the sweet, effeminate sensuality that Wagner himself enjoyed, and that characterizes several other of his male heroes.

In the final analysis, then, Wagner's fetish for silks and satins, his obsessive desire to be surrounded by soft materials and sweet fragrances, is not an embarrassment to be swept under one of his deep-pile Smyrna carpets. On the contrary, these tendencies provide a key to the music, which would not be what it is had its composer been a model of ascetic Calvinist rigour. It is entirely appropriate that such a man should take his leave of the world in a pink satin dressing gown.

16 'My Adored and Angelic Friend': Ludwig II

The man who seems to have been sent to me from heaven!
Wagner describing Ludwig II to Judith Gautier

The story of Wagner's 'rescue' from penury by King Ludwig is well known: the eighteen-year-old romantic dreamer comes to the throne, summons Wagner, whose works he adores, and settles on him an annuity so generous that the composer is able to complete and stage his massive *Ring* tetralogy. And yet there is an element of the story that has not always been adequately understood, perhaps because of its essentially indefinable, mystical quality.

But first, here is an eyewitness account of what happened, provided by Wendelin Weissheimer, a friend and fellow composer:

It was around evening when the waiter brought in a visitor's card bearing the inscription: 'Von Pfistermeister, Secrétaire aulique de S. M. le roi de Bavière.' Wagner was feeling so disheartened and assumed that, whatever it was, it boded no good, with the result that he could not initially bring himself to receive Herr von Pfistermeister, and it was only when the latter insisted that he had come on the supreme orders of King Ludwig II and begged most insistently for an audience that Wagner agreed to admit him. In order not to disturb him during what was bound to be an extremely important meeting, I made my excuses and left. The meeting went on and on – a good sign! When the gentleman in question finally took his leave and I was able to return to the room, Wagner, who was completely overcome by his sudden change of fortune, showed me a valuable diamond ring of the king's and, on the table, a photograph of His Majesty shining with a wonderful sheen. 'That *this* should have happened to me – and that it should have happened *now*!' And, beside himself with happiness, he threw himself around my neck, weeping uncontrollably.[1]

Weissheimer assumes that the new king's dramatic intervention was entirely unexpected by Wagner. And so, on the level of everyday practicalities, it was. And yet, at some deeper, psychic level, it was not quite the surprise it seemed. In a letter of 8 April 1864, less than a month before the fateful visit from Pfistermeister, Wagner wrote a letter to Peter Cornelius lamenting his woes, chiefly pecuniary, and ending: 'As I say: *some good* and truly helpful miracle must now befall me, otherwise it will all be over!'

Julius Fröbel, a journalist friend of Wagner's, relates how the following year there occurred 'a curious incident with a mysterious old woman' named Frau Dangl,

LUDOVICUS II.
BAVARIAE REX
MDCCCLXV.

Portrait of Ludwig II
in general's uniform
painted by Ferdinand
Piloty in 1865, the
year after the king's
accession.

who came to him one evening and told him that she had to speak to him about the young king and his calling. She had already advised Ludwig I and Max II, but neither of them had followed her advice. But the young king, she went on, was destined for greatness, it was written in the stars. 'Do you believe in the stars?' she had asked Wagner in a loud and solemn voice. 'It is written in the stars that this young king has been singled out for great deeds. I want my king to have peace of mind, and you, Herr Wagner, must protect him and guard him against the machinations of evil men who seek to destroy him just as they destroyed his father and grandfather.' Wagner became extraordinarily agitated when he told me about this encounter, which appears to have left a deep impression on him.[2]

And indeed it did. As he wrote to his friend Mathilde Maier, he felt that his fate was profoundly linked to that of the young king by 'a mystical magic': the meaning of his duty to the king had been revealed to him 'through an almost supernatural experience'.[3] Ludwig was, according to Wagner, 'the man who seems to have been sent to me from heaven!'[4] There is undeniably a strain of mysticism in Wagner's philosophical outlook, as his enthusiasm for the medieval mystics Hafiz and Meister Eckhart bears witness. And, clearly, he liked to see his rescue by Ludwig II as a phenomenon of cosmic significance, one that was written in the stars. Historical events such as the death of Maximilian II and the ascent to the throne of his son Ludwig take second place to 'mystical magic' as an explanation of what happened in the early days of May 1864.

That first encounter between the composer and his regal benefactor was described by Wagner himself in a letter to Eliza Wille:

You know that the young king of Bavaria sent for me. Today I was taken to him. He is so handsome, so great in spirit and in soul, so glorious that, alas, I fear that his life will evanesce in this mean world like a fleeting dream of godhood. He loves me with the intensity and fire of first love: he knows everything about me and all my works, and understands me like my own soul. He wants me to stay near him always, to work, to rest, to have my works performed.[5]

Model of the grandiose (but unrealized) project for a festival theatre in Munich commissioned by Ludwig II from Gottfried Semper. The approach road, via a new bridge over the Isar, would have cut a swathe through the Bavarian capital.

Ludwig's first act was to install Wagner in the Villa Pellet, overlooking Lake Starnberg (just outside Munich) and opposite the royal castle Schloss Berg, presenting him with 4,000 gulden to relieve his most pressing debts. Then in October 1864 Wagner took up residence in Munich itself, in an imposing house at 21 Briennerstrasse, made available to him by the king. Ludwig had already followed up his initial gift with an annual stipend of 4,000 gulden (comparable to that of a ministerial councillor) and a further gift of 16,000 gulden in June, to which he now added another 4,000 gulden for removal expenses.

The king's largesse permitted Wagner to deck out his Munich residence with luxury on an eye-watering scale. Plans were put in hand for a festival theatre to produce the *Ring*, and for a music school to produce singers of a requisite standard to perform in it. Only the latter project ever came to anything, under the directorship of Hans von Bülow. Further annual stipends were negotiated, and the strain on the royal exchequer, coupled with Wagner's penchant for offering Ludwig advice on matters of state, led to a campaign by the king's ministers and the press to have the composer banished from Bavaria. Subjected to enormous pressure from all sides, Ludwig was finally forced to concede, and Wagner was given his marching orders at the beginning of December 1865. The king, of course, continued to offer his patronage and even turned up at the door of Wagner's new house at Tribschen, Lucerne, announcing himself as Walther von Stolzing. The presence there of Cosima, who by then was a somewhat regular visitor, had to be accounted for with the explanation that she was the composer's amanuensis.

While it is true that Wagner exploited his royal association shamelessly, both to promote the cause of his art and to enable himself to enjoy

The Villa Pellet, overlooking Lake Starnberg, where Wagner was installed by Ludwig.

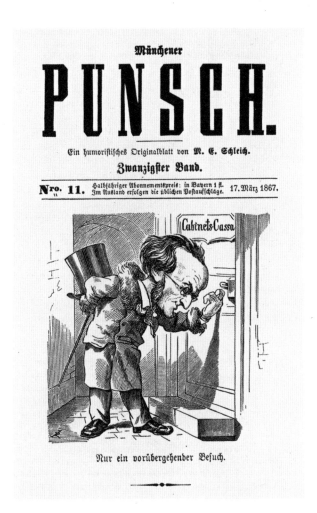

Münchener

PUNSCH.

Ein humoriſtiſches Originalblatt von M. E. Schleich.

Zwanzigſter Band.

Nro. 11. Halbjähriger Abonnementspreis: in Bayern 1 fl. 17. März 1867.
Im Ausland erfolgen die üblichen Poftaufſchläge.

Nur ein vorübergehender Beſuch.

'Just a passing visit' (to the royal treasury): one of numerous hostile cartoons and articles published in the Munich press. This example is from *Punsch*, 17 March 1867.

a lifestyle commensurate with his hedonistic instincts, the figures should be kept in proportion. The total amount Wagner received over the nineteen years of his relationship with Ludwig – including stipend, rent and the cash value of presents – was 562,914 marks. This amount, which is less than one-seventh of the yearly Civil List (4.2 million marks), may be compared with the 652,000 marks Ludwig spent on just the bedchamber of Herrenchiemsee, or with the 1.7 million marks spent on the bridal carriage for the royal wedding that never took place. It remains, however, a substantial sum of money. One recent commentator has calculated that 'Ludwig paid four million euros at today's prices to subsidize his early passion for Wagner' – half of that sum going on Wagner's private household, including servants, and the rest on promoting his music.[6]

The relationship between Ludwig and Wagner was both flamboyantly operatic and tragically flawed. On the one hand their expressions of mutual admiration – 'My adored and angelic friend', 'My most beautiful, supreme and only consolation' are typical salutations – scale the heights of hyperbole to the point of self-parody. On the other, there was from the

Regal extravagance Ludwig-style. The king's gold-encrusted bedchamber at Herrenchiemsee.

start a worm in the bud of their reciprocal infatuation, anatomized thus by the painter Friedrich Pecht:

Wagner's influence on the young king was certainly not a good one, if only because it encouraged his tendency to cocoon himself in a world of dreams and fantasies. The composer himself was only too ready to believe that the world existed solely in order to listen to Wagner's music and to despise everything else. Egoism of this order is perhaps natural in a genius, but it was the last thing to wield a beneficial influence on a character like the king's, whose own egoism could only be fed by it.[7]

Joachim Köhler astutely observes that Wagner 'got everything he wanted' – financial support, social advancement, the resources to complete the *Ring* – but only at a price: the 'loss of self'.[8] When Wagner prostrated himself before his generous benefactor and told him what he wanted to hear, it could of course be construed simply as a strategic accommodation to the king's outlook: mere words that cost nothing but reaped a rich return. However, that is not to reckon with the lies and subterfuges to which he and Cosima were reduced in order to keep their liaison a secret from the king, and which exerted a severe psychological toll.

It was also the case that Wagner found himself denying his relationship with Ludwig to Cosima. So demanding was her love and adoration that Cosima could only regard a third party as an intruder on the relationship. Wagner realized what was required of him and began to malign the king to his own lover. Again, one could perhaps regard this as purely tactical, and yet there is force in Köhler's pithy summary: 'The man who had reinvented the essence of love in his works betrayed that love in real life and in the process betrayed himself, too.'[9]

The betrayal was all the more painful in that Wagner evidently held Ludwig in some affection. He could hardly fail to be gratified by the lavish praise and munificence showered on him, but there was more to it than that: for all their differences of breeding and temperament, there existed between them a bond based on a shared cultural outlook.

Ludwig survived Wagner by just over three years, dying in Lake Starnberg in mysterious circumstances (suicide, assassination and natural causes are all possible explanations for his death). Homosexual, eccentric if not mentally unbalanced (no proper diagnosis was made), and ill-suited for kingship, he led a tortured and controversial life. His wish 'to remain', paraphrasing Schiller, 'an eternal enigma to myself and to others' was amply fulfilled.

Imaginary reconstruction of a nocturnal serenade for Ludwig, who is shown being conveyed by swan-drawn skiff.

17 Fatal Attraction: *Tristan und Isolde*

To this day I am still looking for a work of such dangerous fascination,
of such shivery and sweet infinity, as Tristan.
Friedrich Nietzsche

Reduced to its essentials, *Tristan und Isolde* is but another riff on a time-less theme – love and death – that has nourished opera handsomely since its origins over four hundred years ago. And yet *Tristan* is different, for Wagner's opera transcends its scenario of a conventional love story to offer a profound meditation on the nature of the material world, on the metaphysics of subjectivity and on the mysteries of human existence itself.

Production of *Tristan und Isolde* (2008) at the Teatro Real, Madrid, with Waltraud Meier as Isolde.

Wagner's primary source was the version of the Tristan and Isolde legend by the German poet Gottfried von Strassburg, who was active during the first twenty years of the 13th century. As was his habit, Wagner

King Mark exiles
Tristan and Isolde
(above), and King
Mark finds Tristan
and Isolde sleeping
in a cave (below):
a miniature from a
manuscript of *Tristan*
by Gottfried von
Strassburg.

rigorously excluded all events and characters superfluous to his narrative. The figure of Melot, for example, the friend who betrays Tristan, was moulded from three separate characters in Gottfried's poem. Each act has one central, dramatic happening – Tristan and Isolde's drinking of the love potion; the entry of king and courtiers surprising the lovers; Isolde's arrival – a crisis towards which the action leads.

It was in 1854 that Wagner felt the first stirrings of a desire to set forth the Tristan legend in music. One of the spurs to his imagination was the flawed attempt of his young friend Karl Ritter to dramatize it himself (see Chapter 20: Creative Spark). Wagner's own pared-down version of the story was intended at that stage to be a drama about the vicissitudes of love in all its intoxicating glory, a state that Wagner claimed he had never experienced in his own life. In fact, it turned out to be more about desire, that unquenchable yearning for satisfaction, than about the real enjoyment of love. Not coincidentally, it was precisely at this time that his infatuation with Mathilde Wesendonck began: a 'love affair' that was almost certainly not consummated (see Chapter 12: Muses, Mistresses and Mother-Figures), but that provided the artist with the authentic throbbing of emotion he needed to capture this state of heightened awareness. And, as is well known, the scenario of passionate lovers and cuckolded husband replicates the situation in which Wagner found himself at the time of composition: the obstacle to his love for Mathilde was not a king but his benefactor, Mathilde's husband, Otto. This is how Wagner, in a letter to his sister in 1858, described the connection between his relationship and *Tristan*:

Such was the unheard-of success brought about by the glorious love of the purest and most noble of women; and it was this love, to which we never gave expression, that was bound at last to reveal itself when I wrote the Tristan poem a year ago and gave it to her. Then, for the first time, her strength failed her, and she told me she would die![1]

However, Wagner's simultaneous encounter with the abnegatory philosophy of Schopenhauer helped to ensure that by the time he came to write the actual music drama it had already taken on considerably more metaphysical baggage. The prose scenario was begun on 20 August 1857, and the poem completed on 18 September. Unlike all the other music dramas with the exception of *Siegfried*, each act of *Tristan* was drafted and elaborated in sequence, the full score being reached before the next act was embarked on in sketch. In fact, Wagner's publisher, Breitkopf & Härtel, was even able to begin engraving the score for each act before the previous ones were written – an extraordinary tribute to Wagner's command of large-scale structure. The fair copy of the full score of Act I was completed on 3 April 1858 in Zurich, Act II on 18 March 1859 in Venice, and Act III on 6 August 1859 in Lucerne.

Wagner's muse and helpmeet Mathilde Wesendonck, photographed probably in the 1850s.

King Mark boards the ship at the end of Act I. David Hockney's set for the Chicago Lyric Opera production (1985, revived 2009) renders the vessel symbolically. Bold colours and iconographical details evoke medievalism in modernist abstract terms.

One of the most treasurable moments in the whole opera is a quiet passage towards the end of Act II. The lovers have been discovered *in flagrante*, King Mark has delivered his more-in-sorrow-than-in-anger monologue, and he asks Tristan what he has done to deserve such treatment by his friend and loyal servant. By way of reply, Tristan says that, in fact, there is no answer to the king's question. The opening phrases of the opera return, but the rising chromatic line that previously resolved, in the seventeenth bar of the prelude, into an exquisite dissonance now simply melts into a new tonality (A flat major), reprising a beautiful melody from the love duet, heard over a ravishing background of muted strings. Tristan now turns to Isolde and invites her to join him in the 'wonderful realm of night', an invitation accepted by Isolde in music of equal tenderness and inner peace.

In reality this is nothing less than a suicide pact, though so lofty is the philosophical language in which it is framed, and so rarefied the music, that the real-life significance of the moment may easily be overlooked. But it is also the moment at which the lovers acknowledge that death is the only possible resolution of their predicament. It is a moment of the most intense privacy that should be witnessed by no outsider. And yet it *is* witnessed, by the king, his courtiers and Tristan's traitorous friend Melot, who eventually springs forward to jolt the lovers, and us, out of our reverie.

This conflict between the public and private worlds is at the philosophical heart of the work. The lovers characterize the two spheres as Day and Night, which correspond to the categories of 'phenomenon' (the

outer, material world) and 'noumenon' (the domain of inner consciousness, the ultimate 'reality') as elucidated by Schopenhauer. Throughout the opera Tristan and Isolde seek refuge from that external, public world: the intrusion of the king and courtiers at the height of their nocturnal idyll seems to the sympathetic observer all the more of an outrage because of the way it shatters the invisible glass walls that surrounded the lovers. Just as in *Die Walküre*, where Wagner succeeds in winning our sympathies for a couple engaged in incestuous adultery, so here his emotional manipulation is so skilful that our hearts are guaranteed to be with the adulterous lovers rather than the cuckolded husband or shocked courtiers.

That is in part because there is no hypocrisy in the lovers' behaviour. Tristan and Isolde barely attempt to conceal or deny their relationship (even if that were possible): indeed, the sealing of their suicide pact described above is witnessed, as few such pacts are, by all and sundry.

A word is necessary on the philosophical underpinning of *Tristan und Isolde*. The name of Schopenhauer has been much invoked, and indeed Wagner claimed to have been profoundly influenced by the Sage of Frankfurt from the time of his first encounter in 1854. There is a good deal of mythification at work here, however, and Wagner's real debt to Schopenhauer has been much overstated.

For Schopenhauer, the sexual impulse and man's inability to master it were the root cause of all human misery. What we think of as happiness, asserts Schopenhauer in *The World as Will and Representation*, is essentially a negative quality – not so much a freely willed gratification as the satisfaction of a desire:

All satisfaction, or what is commonly called happiness, is really and essentially always *negative* only, and never positive. It is not a gratification which comes to us originally and of itself, but it must always be the satisfaction of a wish. For desire, that is to say, want, is the precedent condition of every pleasure; but with the satisfaction, the desire and therefore the pleasure cease; and so the satisfaction or gratification can never be more than deliverance from a pain, from a want.[2]

We inevitably think here of *Tristan und Isolde*, where the chief characters are ever striving for satisfaction – a striving expressed in chromaticism of unrelenting intensity. And it is that striving rather than any satisfaction (deemed to be impossible, in this life at least) that provides the motor of the work.

Sex for Schopenhauer was tantamount to suffering. The sexual impulse was the expression of the 'will to live', he claimed, but that will had to be denied. The egoism that, for him, was implicit in the sex act was an unalterable law of human life. Wagner's philosophical outlook was close to this, but he departed from Schopenhauer in two fundamental respects. He did not agree that sexual love was egoistic, inclining more to the Feuerbachian view that it was the distillation of the 'I–you' relationship between two individuals. But he went further, in the process turning Schopenhauer's thesis on its head. Where the misogynistic philosopher denigrated the loving impulse and advocated denial of the will, Wagner suggested that denial of the will and the self-knowledge that flowed from it could be achieved through the very act of sex itself. Excited by his discovery that he could square the circle of Schopenhauerian renunciation and Wagnerian self-indulgence, he even drafted a letter to the philosopher to inform him where he had gone wrong. The letter was never sent.

The Schopenhauer/Feuerbach polarity is just one of many dichotomies central to the conception of *Tristan und Isolde*. The intersection of the intensely private world of the lovers with the outer world of everyday reality (be it medieval court or 19th-century society) is another. The interweaving of life and art, of autobiographical and dramatic elements, is a third. In fact, these dichotomies are all closely related. Together they constitute one of the most intriguing transformations of subjectivity into the aesthetic sphere that art has to offer.

The influence of Schopenhauer is more consistently evident in another aspect of *Tristan und Isolde*: namely the ascendancy of music over text. Schopenhauer's elevation of music over all the other arts presented something of a challenge to Wagner, according to whose concept of the *Gesamtkunstwerk* the various arts were equal. But Wagner had already begun to reassess the hierarchy of words and music, and with *Tristan und Isolde* we see a marked shift in favour of the latter. In the Act II love duet, for example, the text is frequently rendered inaudible by the many long-held notes, and the overlapping and simultaneous declamation of the lovers – not to mention the overwhelming impact of the orchestra.

At the same time, there are many notable examples of the kind of musico-poetic synthesis advocated in Wagner's theoretical essays and exemplified to perfection in *Die Walküre*. Among these are Isolde's narrative (Act I Scene 3) and Tristan's demented monologue (Act III Scene 1), in both of which the network of leitmotifs is developed with a symphonic mastery arguably excelled not even by Wagner himself.

The preludes to those two acts are also particularly worthy of note. That to Act I introduces and develops the chief thematic material of the opera in a superbly constructed arc, which so perfectly reflects the drama's trajectory of passion aroused and stilled that Wagner himself called it (rather than the music that ends the opera) the 'Liebestod' (love-death). The spiritual desolation of the prelude to Act III, which introduces the mortally wounded Tristan in his castle, Kareol, in Brittany, is enhanced by the plangency of the raw open G strings that sound the opening notes on the violins. That prelude leads directly into a long solo for cor anglais, played by a shepherd; Tristan recognizes it as 'die alte Weise' (the old tune), associated in his memory with the death of his parents.

At the centre of the second act is the great love duet. This second scene is introduced by an orchestral passage that graphically depicts the lovers' mounting excitement, culminating in Tristan's irruption into the garden where Isolde is waiting. Falling ecstatically into each other's arms, they conduct a breathless exchange, snatching phrases from each other's lips. A calmer section at the centre of the duet, 'O sink' hernieder, Nacht der Liebe' (O sink down, night of love), is approached by a masterly transition – a gradual reduction in tension by dynamic, harmonic and rhythmic means – of the kind that Wagner so proudly draws attention to in a famous letter to Mathilde Wesendonck:

I should now like to call my most delicate and profound art the art of transition, for the whole fabric of my art is made up of such transitions: all that is abrupt and sudden is now repugnant to me; it is often unavoidable and necessary, but even then it may not occur unless the mood has been clearly prepared in advance, so that the suddenness of the transition appears to come as a matter of course. My greatest masterpiece in the art of the most delicate and gradual transition is without doubt the great scene in the second act of Tristan and Isolde. The opening of this scene presents a life overflowing with all the most violent emotions, – its ending the most solemn and heartfelt longing for death. These are the pillars: and now you see, child, how I have joined these pillars together, and how one of them leads over into the other.[3]

Some of the music heard in this calmer section of the duet, including the so-called Slumber or Love's Peace motif, is among the earliest Wagner conceived for the work (see Chapter 20: Creative Spark). The lovers' tender raptures are twice interrupted by the warning voice of Brangäne sounding from the watchtower. The syllables of her mellifluous vocal line are so distended that, contrary to Wagner's theoretical principles, it no longer conveys the semantic meaning of the text. Few experiencing this exquisitely scored passage in the opera house are likely to complain.

Ernst Gutzeit's set design for a 1916 production of *Tristan und Isolde* in London drew on the radical ideas of Adolph Appia. Tristan's castle in Act III is here suggested in abstract terms.

The final part of the love duet features the couple singing in harmony (again in breach of Wagner's theoretical principles) and developing a thematic idea first heard to the words 'So starben wir' (Thus we died). That music is built to a graphic climax, though just as the point of no return has been reached the lovers' ecstasy is cruelly interrupted by a savage discord on the full orchestra (topped by shrieking piccolo), as King Mark, Melot and the courtiers burst in on the scene.

It is this same thematic idea ('So starben wir') that launches the Liebestod, with which the opera ends. This time, however, it is developed into a radiant apotheosis for Isolde, who sinks, as if transfigured, onto the dead body of Tristan, mystically united with him at last.

Isolde, consoled by King Mark, grieves over the body of Tristan; illustration by Franz Stassen.

18 'Art is What Matters Here':
Die Meistersinger von Nürnberg

All is not German that does not glitter.
  Ludwig Marcuse

Not the least of the ironies concerning *Die Meistersinger von Nürnberg* is that this colossal work of art should have been conceived essentially as a displacement activity. It happened during the summer holiday-cum-rest cure Wagner took at the Marienbad spa in 1845 (see Chapter 4: Under the Yoke), and Wagner was under strict instructions from his doctors to desist from engaging in creative activity. His bathtime reading, however, proved to be more than usually stimulating, and to pacify his doctors he 'struggled manfully against the temptation' to flesh out the scenario for *Lohengrin* that had taken shape in his mind, occupying himself instead with a completely different subject:

From a few remarks in Gervinus's *History of German Literature* I had fashioned for myself a vivid picture of the mastersingers of Nuremberg and of Hans Sachs. I was particularly intrigued by the institution of the 'Marker' and by his function vis-à-vis the mastersingers in general. Without knowing anything more about Sachs or the other poets of his period, I invented during one of my walks an amusing scene in which the cobbler, as popular artisan poet, teaches the Marker a lesson, with blows of his hammer on the last, by making him sing, thereby wreaking revenge on him for his pedantic misdeeds. For me everything was concentrated on two points: on the one hand the presentation by the Marker of the slate covered with chalk marks, and on the other, the image of Sachs holding aloft the shoes completed by his own marking of the Marker. Each in this way delivers his own verdict on the singing.[1]

There is a tender moment in the fourth scene of Act II of *Die Meistersinger* as Eva and Sachs are discussing the possible candidates for the song competition the following day. Though hoping that her beloved Walther will take the prize, and with it her hand, she and the widower Sachs briefly entertain the possibility that they could have been joined in matrimony, despite the gap in their ages. When Sachs suggests that he is too old for her, Eva delphically remarks that 'art is what matters here' ('Hier gilt's der Kunst'). The teasing implication is that she would happily consent to Sachs if he were to win by the rules: their evident affection for each other is clear from the A flat tonality of this passage(a key frequently associated in Wagner's works with the blossoming of love) and the markings *sehr zart* (very tender), *dolce* and *dolcissimo*.

Die Meistersinger

Eva crowns Hans Sachs with a wreath of myrtle and laurel at the conclusion of *Die Meistersinger*; illustration by Franz Stassen.

'Hier gilt's der Kunst' also happens, however, to be the phrase the composer's son Siegfried Wagner displayed on a large notice on the Festspielhaus in 1924, when Bayreuth was in danger of being commandeered by the National Socialists. 'Art is what matters here' now served, in the words of the Bayreuth historian Frederic Spotts, as 'a massive fig leaf',[2] one that was to be plucked often in the future (notably when the festival reopened after the war, in 1951) to conceal truths deemed offensive. It was a subterfuge that was maintained right through the century, in fact, until it was finally blown away in the epoch-making production of the composer's great-granddaughter Katharina in 2007.[3] In this single resonant phrase is therefore encapsulated the triangulation of love, art and politics that characterizes *Die Meistersinger*.

Wagner's original idea for the opera, as confided to his publisher, Schott, in late October 1861, was something very different from the protracted masterpiece we know today:

The Muse with Hans Sachs, watercolour by F. W. Wanderer, 1870. Like Wagner's, it is an idealized representation of Nuremberg.

The opera is called 'the Mastersingers of Nuremberg', and the main hero is the – jovially poetic – 'Hans Sachs'. The subject is exceptionally rich in good-natured drollery, and I pride myself that with this original plan, which is entirely my own invention, I have hit upon something quite unexpected and singular. The style of the piece, both in the poem and the music, shall be thoroughly light and popular, and a guarantee of its rapid diffusion to all the other theatres is the fact that on this occasion I need neither a so-called leading tenor nor a great tragic soprano.[4]

Dem Meister der Töne, dem hochherzigen Förderer des Hans Sachs Denkmals

Dr. Hans v. Bülow

Nürnberg 1870.   der dankbare Ausschuß.

Der Meistersinger silbern Ehrengehänge

(above) Title page of a satirical drama (1872) aimed jointly at *Die Meistersinger* and Social Democracy. The action of the drama is summarized as 'qualified Jew-hatred of the third degree'.

(above right) Wagenseil's *Nuremberg Chronicle* (1697), from which Wagner drew much of the historical detail relating to the practice of the masters and their guilds in medieval Nuremberg.

While it is true that the finished work is actually a four-and-a-quarter-hour epic that stretches the resources of most opera houses even today, it is also the case that the scoring is only for double wind, as opposed to the triple wind of *Tristan und Isolde* or the quadruple of the *Ring*.

In addition to the Gervinus volume he imbibed along with the waters at Marienbad, Wagner almost certainly also drew for his poem on volumes by Jacob Grimm, J. G. Büsching (an edition of Hans Sachs's plays) and Friedrich Furchau (a life of Sachs), all of which were in his impressive personal library in Dresden. At this stage his main idea was to play off the rule-book pedantry of the mastersingers – personified by the Marker, who noted breaches in the rules – against the less affected artistic instincts of the people, championed by Sachs. Sachs in this first sketch is more cynical, less trustworthy than the benevolent, worldly-wise cobbler-poet he was to become.

The sketch was then put aside for sixteen years, and Wagner retrieved it from the bottom drawer only in 1861, thinking to pacify Schott with something more manageable than the *Ring* tetralogy in which he had been embroiled since 1848. Now he studied Grimm again, and also Johann Christoph Wagenseil's *Nuremberg Chronicle*, which contained copious information on the ancient crafts and guilds and on other aspects of the city. Of other possible sources on which Wagner may or may not have drawn, E. T. A. Hoffmann's story *Meister Martin der Küfner und seine Gesellen* (Master Martin the Cooper and his Journeymen), which is set in 16th-century Nuremberg, is perhaps the most important.

Wagner forthwith produced a second and third prose draft in the middle of November 1861, fleshing out the character of Sachs and placing him very much at the centre of the drama, rather as Wotan gradually replaced Siegfried as the moral fulcrum of the *Ring* over the course of its composition. In part this had to do with the fact that Wagner came increasingly to identify with Sachs. The latter is a skilled artisan, but also a creative artist who perceives the need for the best of German tradition to be allied with the music of the future – that is the lesson the impulsive, youthful Walther learns in the workshop of the cobbler-poet. And just as Wagner was fascinated by dreams, so the Schopenhauer-inspired Sachs tells Walther: 'Believe me, man's truest illusion is disclosed to him in dreams: the whole art of poetry and verse is nothing but the true interpretation of dreams.'[5]

Interwoven with this idea of the renewal of art is the love interest. There is never much doubt that Walther is the one who will get the girl,

One of a series of advertisements for Liebig's beef extract illustrated with scenes from Wagner's operas.

humiliating the pedantic Marker, Beckmesser, in the process. And yet the mildly incestuous flirtation between Sachs and Eva (we learn that when she was young she was cradled in his arms, Sachs having lost his own wife and child, and apparently the thought had occurred to both that she might be 'wife and child in one') adds a frisson.

If art and love form two sides of the triangle, the third is politics, and here we enter yet more controversial territory. The appropriation of *Die Meistersinger* by the Nazis has already been alluded to, and although many would like to exculpate Wagner he cannot be let off the hook quite so easily. That Wagner's anti-Semitic outlook pervades the work is scarcely surprising, given the all-consuming nature of his obsession at the time of its composition. As Barry Emslie's important new study makes clear, Wagner anathematized the Jews as incapable of both genuine creativity and love.[6] The Marker, Beckmesser, embodies this double lack: on the one hand he invites humiliation on account of his own risible Serenade (Act II) and his botched attempt to render Walther's Prize Song (Act III). On the other, the very idea of the crabby old critic providing a soulmate for Eva does not bear thinking about. Beckmesser, then, fails on both counts, art and love. His inability to match words and music (the test of a true composer in Wagner's world view) results in a hilarious debacle (if one can overlook the inherent cruelty) on the festival meadow in Act III. But his artistic sterility is, for Wagner, part and parcel of his lovelessness.

The scene on the Festival Meadow in David McVicar's 2011 production for Glyndebourne Opera.

What appealed to the Nazis about *Die Meistersinger*, however, was primarily the representation of an *echt* German society, in the idyllic, pre-capitalist, cobbled streets of medieval Nuremberg. Here lay the only

The historically realist set by Max and Gotthold Brückner for Act II of the first Bayreuth Festival production (1888) of *Die Meistersinger*. Cosima modelled it on the original 1868 Munich production.

hope for a modern Germany besieged by the horrors of industrial 'progress', foreign domination and racial assimilation. Only 'holy German art', as espoused by Sachs in his tub-thumping final address to the populace (Act III), could offer this broken society the redemption it so desperately craved.

If Sachs's address, 'Verachtet mir die Meisterlied' (Do not disdain the Masters) – and especially its peroration, 'Habt Acht!' (Beware!) – show him in almost belligerently defensive mood, a more philosophical quality is evident in his two great monologues earlier: 'Was duftet doch der Flieder' (How the scent of the elder wafts around me) of Act II, where he muses on the wonder of Walther's Act I Spring Song that 'sounded so old, yet was so new'; and the 'Wahn' monologue of Act III, a poignant reflection on the madness that grips ordinary civilized people at times – a madness, however, that may be harnessed in the cause of art.

Other passages particularly worthy of note are: Walther's Act III Prize Song, the number with which, having learnt to temper the effusive spontaneity of his Act I Trial Song with the discipline of structure, he sweeps judges and audience alike off their feet, staking his claim to the ultimate prize, Eva; the Riot Scene that ends Act II in a virtuoso display of counterpoint (formidably difficult to bring off in performance because of the number of voices); and the celebrated quintet of Act III, a sublime moment of calm reverie that slips voluptuously into G flat major for the main characters to reflect on their personal situation and the likely resolution of present vexations at the coming song contest.

Some may find the work occasionally overbearing or even tedious (one thinks in particular of David's recitation of the Masters' rules in Act I, and of Sachs's heavy-handed marking of Beckmesser's Serenade with blows of his hammer). But this is a score that juxtaposes exquisite expressive detail with solid, self-confident diatonicism, just as it contains both a profound meditation on the mysteries of art and love and a darker side that needs to be understood rather than magicked away. Art is certainly not 'all that matters here', except on a superficial view of things. But that is always the case with Wagner, and never more so than in this problematic but glorious work.

19 Grit in the Oyster: The Role of Anti-Semitism in Wagner's Life and Work

Forces struggling out of dark confusion to find deliverance in beauty
    Thomas Mann on Wagner's music

No aspect of Wagner has caused more controversy either in his own lifetime or in the century and more since his death than the composer's anti-Semitism. Largely because of the way Wagner and his works were appropriated by the Nazis, this element of his world view has become distorted and often misunderstood. Yet the desire to exculpate Wagner from the inhuman excesses of the Third Reich has in turn too often led to the untenable position that there is no connection between Wagner's anti-Semitism and the fanatical eruption of racial prejudice that ended in Auschwitz. It has also led to the misapprehension that Wagner's anti-Semitism is like a superfluous integument that can be peeled away from his oeuvre without leaving a trace, when in fact it is so intrinsic to his aesthetic that it is no exaggeration to say that without it, Wagner would not have been the composer he was – and his works would certainly not have taken the form they did.

The most notorious expression of Wagner's anti-Semitism is his essay 'Jewishness in Music' (1850, revised 1869) but, rabidly offensive as it is to modern sensibilities, its publication was not an idiosyncratic gesture on Wagner's part. Much of the essay is a polemic against Jewish artists who were motivated, according to Wagner, solely by commercial instincts; lacking a culture of their own, they could only imitate the art produced by the host culture:

It is entirely natural that song, being the liveliest and most indisputably authentic expression of the individual's emotional life, should reveal the peculiar offensiveness of the Jewish nature in a particularly acute form; and we might well, in accord with a natural assumption, consider the Jew to be capable of artistic expression in every branch of art save that which is rooted in song.[1]

From the traditional armoury of anti-Semitic rhetoric, Wagner draws the following insulting barbs:

What strikes our ear as particularly odd and unpleasant is a hissing, buzzing, humming and growling sound that is typical of the Jewish way of speaking.[2]

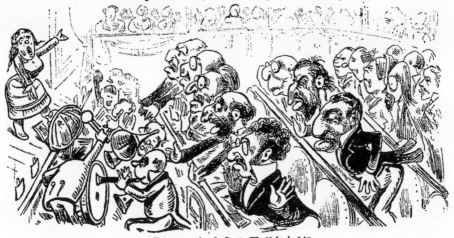

Das Judenthum in der Musik
hat über Wagner's neuestes Werk folgendes Urtheil gefällt:

„Es war ein festes Waibspiel!"

A predominantly Jewish audience delivers its judgment on Wagner's latest work in a cartoon from *Kikeriki*, Vienna 1882.

and of the sounds emanating from a synagogue:

Who has not been overcome by feelings of the most utter revulsion, mixed with horror and ridicule, on hearing that gurgling, yodelling and babbling which throws both sense and mind into utter confusion and which no attempt at caricature can ever make more repulsively distorted.[3]

The essence of Wagner's argument, then, is that the rootlessness of Jewish artists prevents them from speaking in a natural, instinctive voice and thus articulating the inner feelings and emotions of the German people. Their art could not, therefore, penetrate the depths of the soul in the way Wagner believed true art should; instead it dealt merely in surface appearances.

This racialist invective – parroted as much of it is from Wagner's Dresden friend Theodor Uhlig[4] – has an intellectual basis, the more so since it reflects the revolutionary ideas of Young Hegelians such as Bruno Bauer and Karl Marx. The Jewish consciousness needed to be overthrown, they maintained, if the society of the future was to come into being. The emancipation of the Jews – and, indeed, of mankind itself – could only come about, according to this revolutionary view, if and when Jewish identity was nullified. As Marx himself put it: 'The social emancipation of the Jews is the emancipation of society from Judaism.'[5] It is within this ideological framework that the essay's notorious final appeal to Jews should be understood:

Take part recklessly in this work of redemption so that being reborn through the process of self-annihilation we shall be united and indistinguishable! But remember that one thing alone can bring you redemption from the curse which weighs upon you: the redemption of Ahasuerus – *downfall!*[6]

The temptation to read such an injunction through the prism of subsequent history as a call for a genocidal annihilation of the Jews must be resisted. For one thing, the act is intended to be a voluntary one undertaken by Jews themselves; for another, it is clear, taking the full cultural and historical context into account, that it is a symbolic act that is proposed. In some mystic process, never quite defined, the Jew would be 'redeemed', that is become a true human being, at the same time helping to bring about the spiritual renewal of humankind as a whole.

While Wagner's remarks were framed against the ideological background of anti-capitalistic rhetoric of the late 1840s, it is also the case that there is an element of personal animus in them. As Wagner admitted in a letter to Liszt,

I harboured a long suppressed resentment against this Jewish business, and this resentment is as necessary to my nature as gall is to the blood. The immediate cause of my intense annoyance was their damned scribblings, so that I finally let fly.[7]

And he goes on, in that letter, to explain why Meyerbeer was singled out in his essay – though not by name – as the paradigmatic Jewish composer of trivial diversions, put on solely to entertain a bored public:

Meyerbeer is a special case, as far as I am concerned: it is not that I hate him, but that I find him infinitely repugnant. This perpetually kind and obliging man reminds me of the darkest – I might almost say the most wicked – period of my life, when he still made a show of protecting me; it was a period of connections and back-staircases, when we were treated like fools by patrons whom we inwardly deeply despised.[8]

Lithograph of
Wagner's *bête noire*,
Giacomo Meyerbeer,
c. 1840.

This is an astonishing admission. Whether or not Wagner was justified in blaming Meyerbeer for failing to advance his career, first during his unhappy visit to Paris in 1839–42 and then again in the late 1840s – and there is little evidence that he actively obstructed it – it does not take a trained psychologist to see that Wagner was mortified by his own earlier shameless obsequiousness. (In letters from the Paris period he had thrown himself metaphorically at Meyerbeer's feet, calling him 'Master', 'your property' and 'your slave'.) 'Jewishness in Music' was thus in part an act of exorcism.

The essay also, however, needs to be read in the context of Wagner's other Zurich writings. Central to those theoretical counterparts to the *Ring* is the notion that only the 'artwork of the future' could bring humanity the redemption it so badly needed. People had become divorced from their true nature by the meretricious values of contemporary society, he argued – Meyerbeerian grand opera being, of course, an egregious exemplar of such values. And it was the grand Wagnerian project – essentially what was to become *Der Ring des Nibelungen* – that was to liberate both Jews and humanity itself from their debased existence.

This redemptive aspect of the Wagnerian work of art was to assume ever greater significance in the decades to come, reaching its culmination with *Parsifal* and the so-called 'regeneration essays' of the late years. In general terms the evolution of Wagner's ideas over these decades can be seen to coincide with the shift in 19th-century Germany from what may be called cultural anti-Semitism (though the term itself had not yet been coined) to a more specifically racial ideology. In Wagner's case this modified form of anti-Semitism took on theological and biological characteristics.

In one sense the more 'scientific' nature of Wagner's late anti-Semitism tended to depersonalize his hostility towards the Jews. Where previously Meyerbeer and Mendelssohn had been the prime targets, now it was merely as representatives of 'Jewishness' that Semites were branded as second-class citizens. This relative objectivity, taken with the phenomenon of Jewish self-hatred, as a result of which guilt-obsessed Jews came to Wagner for something resembling redemption, helps to explain the oft-remarked paradox of Wagner's having many Jewish friends and colleagues (Joseph Rubinstein, Hermann Levi and Heinrich Porges prominent among them). The sense of not belonging, of alienation, induced by their historical and cultural situation caused them to embrace the sort of common folk culture, based on mythology and on a revival of the German spirit, that was epitomized by Wagner.

The rhetoric of the period centred on two opposing but complementary concepts: Germanness and Jewishness. Germanness was defined most comprehensively in the essay 'What is German?' (1865, rev. 1878). There Wagner salutes the German spirit as the quest for the beautiful and the noble rather than the profitable and the superficial. In a further essay, 'German Art and German Politics' (1867), he expands on some of his favourite themes: the debasement of art, and of culture generally,

Hermann Levi, the son
of a Jewish rabbi held in
high regard by Wagner
as a conductor of his
works, notably *Parsifal*,
of which he gave the
first performance.
Photograph 1893.

by materialism; the need for a revival of the folk spirit; and the responsibility of the German people to bring about such a regeneration. In an
intriguing letter to Nietzsche of October 1872 Wagner discourses further
on the matter:

I have been thinking more and more about 'what is German', and, on the basis of
a number of more recent studies, have succumbed to a curious scepticism which
leaves me thinking of 'Germanness' as a purely metaphysical concept; but, as
such, it is of immense interest to me, and certainly something that is unique in
the history of the world, its only possible counterpart being Jewishness, since
Hellenism, for example, does not really fit in here.[9]

Germanness, in other words, is not so much a question of national identity: more a Germany of the mind. But Judaism is also capable of inspiring
something like envy. The Catholics may consider themselves superior
to the Protestants, Wagner once told Levi, but 'the Jews are the most
superior of all, being the eldest'.[10] Moreover, as Wagner (reported by
Cosima) once told Ludwig, the Jews 'have preserved a feeling for genuineness which the Germans have entirely lost, and that is why many of them
cling to him'.[11]

And it is this polarity of Germanness and Jewishness that has to
be grasped if Wagner's anti-Semitism is properly to be understood. For

Wagner, Jewishness was a necessary evil, for without it one would be unable to define Germanness. In much the same way, without the loathing of all things Jewish, the elevation of love as the central concept in Wagner's epistemology would never have gained the traction it did. In other words, it can be argued that Wagner's output acquired its distinctive characteristics precisely because of his anti-Semitism. Far from the latter being an unfortunate aberration, as many would like to believe, it should actually be regarded, in Wagner's case, as grist to the mill, or, to vary the metaphor, the grit in the oyster.[12] The protectionists are happy to see Wagner the man vilified as an obnoxious racist, provided the works themselves come up smelling of roses. But the notion of such a firewall between the man and the works is a nonsense: few composers' oeuvres are as ideologically motivated as Wagner's.

Once this essential point has been grasped, the whole vexed question as to the presence or otherwise of anti-Semitism in the works themselves is clarified to a remarkable extent. Over the last couple of decades a powerful case for the prosecution has been made out, centring on the town clerk, Beckmesser, in *Die Meistersinger von Nürnberg* and on the Nibelung brothers in the *Ring* (especially Mime in *Siegfried*). The characterization of Beckmesser, according to the thesis I first advanced in 1991, draws directly on the stereotypical description of Jews in 'Jewishness in Music'. Just as in the conventional image the Jew shuffles and blinks, and is scheming, argumentative and untrustworthy, so Beckmesser slinks up the alley behind the Nightwatchman in Act II, and limps and stumbles about the stage in Act III, blinking with embarrassment when Eva turns away from his ingratiating bow at the song contest. Not only is Beckmesser unscrupulous, a plagiarist and a thief, he is also scheming, and excessively pedantic and argumentative. In his essay Wagner anathematizes the Jew as incapable of mastering idiomatic German (his language is 'an intolerably confused babble of sounds') and of true creativity (he can only imitate others). Beckmesser similarly lacks artistic sensitivity and is profoundly unmusical, incapable of matching text to music. His mangled speech patterns evoke *Mauscheln*, the bizarre travesty language attributed by Germans to Jews. His tessitura, absurdly high for a bass, forces him into falsetto screeching, recalling the nonsensical 'gurgling, yodelling and babbling' that, according to Wagner, emanated from every synagogue.[13]

Mime in the *Ring* likewise conforms to the 19th-century anti-Semitic stereotype: he is ugly and crooked, with hanging ears and dripping eyes. He, too, shuffles and blinks, jabbers excitedly and screeches at the top of his vocal range. In Act I Scene 1 of *Siegfried*, the hero refers scornfully to Mime's song about acting as both his father and mother as a 'Staarenlied', literally 'starling song', meaning an endlessly repeated squawking. Mime is directed to sing it 'in a pitifully screeching voice', and its self-pitying nature is emphasized by the many acciaccaturas, or crushed notes – a traditional trope used to depict not only whining, but more specifically Jewishness. Siegfried's motif, by contrast, strides in virile 4ths and 5ths.

These are the poles around which the scene, with its unmistakable overtones of racial supremacy, is constructed.

The case for the defence argues that there is no specifically Jewish character in any of the music dramas, no clear statement by Wagner that any such characterization was intended to be anti-Semitic, and no evidence that even the Nazis picked up any such resonances. These counter-arguments can be swiftly dealt with, however. Wagner himself discounts the possibility of a Jew appearing on the stage:

We cannot imagine a single classical or contemporary character, be he hero or lover, being played on stage by a Jew, without instinctively feeling how inappropriate to the point of absurdity such a notion must be. *This is very important*: a person who, by dint of his very appearance – not as this or that character but,

Overtones of Aryan supremacy and anti-Semitism in Arthur Rackham's depiction of a scene from the *Ring* are unmistakable.

An early representation of the dwarf Mime at Bayreuth. Hans Breuer took the role there regularly between 1896 and 1914.

collectively, in terms of his race – we must consider incapable of any artistic expression must be deemed equally incapable of the artistic presentation of pure humanity in general.[14]

No one claims that Beckmesser and Mime *are* Jews per se. Patently, a Jew in 16th-century Nuremberg could never have held the post of town clerk. That would be to introduce an absurd level of literalism, however. What can be argued is that Beckmesser, like Mime, incorporates negative traits that are stereotypically anti-Semitic. Moreover, Wagner's allegorical intentions are not restricted to anti-Semitism. In the figure of Beckmesser, Wagner was also satirizing self-important, pompous critics, reactionary cultural philistines, old lechers, shallow, creative Latins, and much more besides. Wagner's characterization may be anti-Semitic, but he is generous with his invective.

Furthermore, allegories, as Wagner was well aware, are all the more powerful for not being spelt out. Whereas 'superficial' French grand opera merely reproduced material reality on the stage, idealist German art reflected the true essence of things.[15] Thus Wagner would never have compromised his idealistic aspiration by placing a 'real' Jew on the stage; neither would he publicly draw attention to any such references, preferring to let allusive signification and metaphor achieve their own effect. Nor is it true, as it happens, that the Nazis did not interpret Wagner's works as vehicles of anti-Semitism. Goebbels, Rosenberg and others were explicit about what they regarded as the anti-Semitic content of the *Ring* and *Die Meistersinger*.[16]

And yet in general it is true that much of this went unsaid – by Wagner himself and his friends and contemporaries, as well as by the Nazis. There seems to have been a recognition that Wagner's idealism would in some way be betrayed were the vulgar anti-Semitic content to be accentuated, with the result that a 'conspiracy of silence' obtained.[17] Mahler, for example, who was in no doubt about the Jewish characterization of Mime – 'I am convinced that this figure is the true embodiment of a Jew, intended by Wagner in the spirit of persiflage (in every trait with which he has imbued him: the petty cleverness, the greed, the whole *Jargon* so perfectly suggested by both music and text)'[18] – considered it highly unwise for the tenor Julius Spielmann to emphasize that aspect in his performance at the Vienna Opera.

It is perhaps understandable that this debate should have been so heated. There is a widely held perception that one could no longer enjoy Wagner's works with a clear conscience if it were admitted that they carried an anti-Semitic subtext. But those who hold this view worry unnecessarily. Wagner was merely expressing sentiments widely held in his time. While he cannot be acquitted entirely of historical responsibility – the ideological continuum linking Wagner and the Nazis is not imaginary – neither is it reasonable to hang the indictment of Nazi atrocities round his neck. Anti-Semitism is an intrinsic element of the Wagnerian world view that gave us some of the greatest masterpieces of Western civilization – the *Ring, Die Meistersinger, Parsifal*.[19] So rich and multi-layered are these works that it would be foolish to limit their content to an ideological obsession. Rather, we should embrace them for all their infelicities, accepting that it was precisely that ideological obsession that drove Wagner to such inspired heights.

20 Creative Spark:
Sources of Inspiration in Wagner's Work

It is indeed difficult not to believe that the work of art has a metaphysical will of its own as it strives to come into being.
    Thomas Mann

Every artist has repeatedly to confront the tyranny of the empty page – that tormenting limbo immediately prior to the setting down of the first ideas.

In Wagner's case the gestation period – particularly of the later works – was often long: years, even decades. What did it take, then, to get the creative juices finally flowing? By looking at three of the late, great works – the *Ring*, *Tristan und Isolde* and *Parsifal* – we can see that the initial creative spark was often not so much a single musical idea as a conceptual nucleus of some kind. That nucleus might well have included a musical idea, but it was likely also to have embraced a creative cell that might be mythological, philosophical or existential in nature.

The initial inspiration does not necessarily correspond to the opening bars of the work in question. Intriguingly, too, there may be a borrowing involved: Wagner is not unique in seizing on a musical idea from elsewhere and making it his own, modifying and transfiguring it in the process.

Der Ring des Nibelungen

As befits a work that deals with gods and heroes, there is more than a hint of mythmaking in Wagner's autobiographical account of the *Ring*'s inception. He tells us there how he succumbed to an attack of dysentery, supposedly caused by over-indulgence in ice cream, while on holiday in La Spezia. Lying on a couch in a kind of half-sleep,

> I suddenly got the feeling that I was sinking in swiftly flowing water. Its rushing soon developed into the musical sound of a chord of E flat major, surging continually in broken chords; these presented themselves as melodic figurations of increasing motion, but the pure chord of E flat major never altered …. With the sensation that the waves were now flowing high above me I woke with a violent start from my half-sleep. I recognized immediately that the orchestral prelude to *Das Rheingold*, as it was already within me but without any definite form, had come to me …. I decided at once to return to Zurich in order to begin the composition of my great poem.[1]

Musicologists have long thrown cold water, so to speak, on the La Spezia 'vision'. But before discounting it we first need to be aware of the chronological facts, in so far as they are known. Wagner's first recorded musical ideas for the *Ring* were notated in late July or early August 1850, and consisted of a setting of the Norns' scene for *Siegfrieds Tod* (later to become *Götterdämmerung*). The setting is quite extensive, beginning with darkly brooding Norn music in E flat minor (the key in which *Götterdämmerung* was to begin) and moving on to a duet for Siegfried and Brünnhilde. While some characteristic motifs and phrases are adumbrated here, the setting would be entirely recast. From probably the following year, 1851, date some vestigial sketches for *Der junge Siegfried* (later to be renamed *Siegfried*), consisting of motifs relating to Fafner, the Woodbird and the Forging Song. A further undated sketch sheet includes a setting of some words for a Rhinemaiden ('Weia! Waga!') and probably dates from 1852. Then came the 'vision' of La Spezia on 5 September 1853, followed by the complete draft for *Das Rheingold*, begun on 1 November.

Doubt was first cast on the genuineness of Wagner's account by John Deathridge, who pointed out: (a) the gap of two months between the supposed vision and the start of work on the complete draft, and (b) that the similarity of the beginning of the draft to the swirling music that opens the work as we know it lacks the 'clarity and exactness' that Wagner alludes to in a letter to Emilie Ritter of 29 December 1854, in which he first describes his 'vision'. In particular, the deep E flat that opens the prelude is missing.[2] Warren Darcy, however, in a comprehensive study of the *Rheingold* sketches, takes a different view, suggesting that the available evidence neither supports nor contradicts the possibility of a 'vision' at La Spezia. As Darcy points out, the 1854 draft prefigures an important aspect of the *Rheingold* prelude. The prelude's structure is actually a strophic design in which a sixteen-bar statement is continually repeated and elaborated, gradually acquiring momentum until the climactic moment of Woglinde's entry 'Weia! Waga!' That structure is clearly evident from the draft, in which Wagner saves himself time by writing '16' and similar annotations to signify the repetitions. Also evident is the principle of accelerating motion, of swirling string figurations and of increasing arpeggiation – all growing out of a simple E flat major chord. Composers often speak of the inspiration for a work arriving in the form of a creative epiphany: a single, sonorous image that simply has to be fleshed out. Might Wagner, indeed, not have experienced some such creative epiphany at La Spezia? He certainly set out for home immediately, telegraphing his wife to ask her to have his work-room ready, though once home he was subject to various delays – including a promised rendezvous with Liszt in Basel, which somehow expanded into a visit to Paris. Healthy scepticism remains in order where Wagner's mythologizing fantasies are concerned,[3] but it may just be that he did indeed have some hallucinatory experience on that couch in La Spezia, which gathered together the various shards of inspiration accumulating in his mind into a concretized sound-image that was then to be elaborated and refined.

Tristan und Isolde

It was in the autumn of 1854 that Wagner conceived a plan to develop a musical stagework based on the legendary love story of Tristan and Isolde. The inspiration behind the project at this stage was memorably expressed in a letter to Liszt:

Since I have never in my life enjoyed the true happiness of love, I intend to erect a further monument to this most beautiful of dreams, a monument in which this love will be properly sated from beginning to end: I have planned in my head a *Tristan* and *Isolde*, the simplest, but most full-blooded musical conception; with the 'black flag' which flutters at the end, I shall then cover myself over, in order – to die.[4]

No musical sketches from this time have survived, and in all probability none were made. The first that have survived date from the winter of 1856–57 and include a group of ten in a notebook catalogued in the Bayreuth archive as B II a 5, later described by Cosima as the 'very first sketches for *Tristan*'.[5] These are mostly fragments of text, with occasional dialogue, but two of the sketches contain music for Act II: the so-called Slumber or Love's Peace motif, but here setting the words 'Sink' hernieder Nacht der Liebe', later to be associated with quite different music. These sketches, however, were apparently preceded by a page of sketch material, dated 19 December 1856, almost entirely relating to the love scene of Act II (see illustration). Headed 'Liebesscene. Tristan u. Isolde', the page essays various textless versions of the Slumber motif.

A close examination of these and other fragmentary sketches suggests a shift of emphasis in Wagner's conception at this crucial period. The last entry in his Annals for 1855 reads: 'Tristan conceived in more definite form: Act III point of departure of mood for whole.'[6] As Egon Voss points out,[7] Act III may indeed have been crucial for the piece as eventually written, for it is there that its lead characters' existential crisis reaches its apogee. But Wagner's original conception was for a 'monument' to the never-enjoyed 'true happiness of love' – in other words, a conventional tragedy brought about by social circumstances. The shift from that to a deepened, Schopenhauer-influenced perspective probably began, according to Voss, around the summer of 1856.

The ideas Wagner found in Schopenhauer's philosophy – notably the essential worthlessness of human existence, and renunciation of the 'will to live' as the only liberation from the endless round of suffering – clearly formed a part of the conceptual nexus of *Tristan*, even if they took some time to mature. A more immediate influence was a dramatization of the subject (unfortunately no longer extant) by Karl Ritter, one of Wagner's young protégés. As Wagner records in *Mein Leben*:

I had at the time pointed out to my young friend the defects of his draft. He had concerned himself with the spirited scenes of the romance, while I had been immediately drawn by the deep tragedy itself and was determined to keep all irrelevant inessentials separate from this central theme.[8]

Page of early sketches for the Act II love scene of *Tristan und Isolde* dating from 1856, together with a realization by Egon Voss.

Hans von Bülow's gestural style is caricatured in an unsigned cartoon sequence (*c.* 1890) of him conducting *Tristan und Isolde*.

Majestoso

Wer wagt, mich zu höhnen?

crescendo

Herr Tristan trete nah.

pianissimo

Heiliger Dämm'rung
Hehres Ahnen
Löscht des Wähnens Graus
Welt-erlösend aus.

decrescendo

Mund an Mund
Eines Athems
Einiger Bund.

Fermat-Pause-

Mir — dies — dies — Tristan mir?

fortissimo

In der Duftwellen tönendem Schall
In des Weltathems wehendem All —
Ertrinken — versinken — unbewußt —
höchste Lust.

Karl Ritter, whose drama on the subject inspired Wagner's own *Tristan und Isolde*.

Hans von Bülow's *Nirwana*, originally intended as an overture to the drama by Ritter, to whom it was dedicated.

Ritter's dramatization was nevertheless clearly of vital importance in stimulating Wagner's creative instincts, and there was a fascinating corollary. In the autumn of 1854 the 24-year-old Hans von Bülow sent Wagner an orchestral fantasy called *Nirwana*, originally conceived as an overture to a tragedy on the same subject by Ritter. Bülow's fantasy, a sombre meditation on the subject of death and the hereafter, on the futility and suffering of life as compared with the quiescence of the Buddhist nirvana (the work was also known familiarly as the 'Suicide Fantasia'), made a significant impact on Wagner. Acknowledging the score, Wagner compared it with Bülow's slightly earlier Overture and March for *Julius Caesar* in the following glowing terms:

If ever a piece had *atmosphere*, this is it; that it is a quite dreadful atmosphere is a different matter. You are certainly much more independent in this work, everything about it is unmistakable. But in both pieces I admire your technique where, as regards difficulties of form both in detail and in the overall design, it would – in my opinion – be hard to surpass you. I cannot deny your mastery, indeed, I believe you could accomplish anything you set out to achieve.[9]

What impressed Wagner about *Nirwana*, then, was its gloomy mood as much as its technical accomplishment. Both Bülow and Wagner had suicidal tendencies. So, too, did Cosima, who married first one man then the

The final bars of Bülow's *Nirwana* (top) and of Wagner's *Tristan* (bottom), showing Wagner's debt to the young composer.

other. An abortive suicide pact concluded between Cosima and Ritter has long been common knowledge. What was not known until comparatively recently is that Cosima made repeated attempts to kill herself shortly after marrying Bülow in 1857. That information was contained in a passage of a letter Wagner wrote to his confidante Eliza Wille; it was suppressed in the printed edition and published in full only in 1987.[10]

Even more intriguing is the fact that Wagner borrowed material from Bülow's *Nirwana* for his *Tristan*. The rising chromatic phrase of bars 2–3 of *Tristan* (mentioned by Wagner, incidentally, in the context of nirvana, in a letter to Mathilde Wesendonck),[11] is clearly derived from *Nirwana*. More extraordinary still is the way Wagner's sublimation of that motif at the very end of his opera (where it rises to settle calmly on a chord of B major) is prefigured by the conclusion of *Nirwana*, where an almost identical rising chromatic phrase settles on a chord of B minor (see musical example). The radiant glow imparted by Wagner's version, enhanced as it is by his luminous scoring, absolves him from any charge of plagiarism: the debt is repaid with generous interest. But the circle of associations (*Tristan* – Ritter – *Nirwana*/suicide – Bülow – *Tristan*) provides a resonant conceptual nexus that needs to be considered alongside the earliest musical sketches as the creative spark that ignited *Tristan*.

Parsifal

As is well known, Wagner first familiarized himself with the Parsifal legend during a summer holiday in Marienbad in 1845 (see Chapter 7: Swansong to Traditional Opera). It was not until August 1877 that he began sustained composition of the music, but musical ideas actually began to occur to him in February of the previous year, oddly enough while he was struggling to find inspiration for a commission he had undertaken for a march to celebrate the American centennial. As Cosima recorded in her diary on 9 February 1876:

No dictation today, R. works on his composition for the Americans (opening of the World's fair, Centennial of Independence); he has asked for 5,000 dollars for it – we wonder whether the promoters will agree to this. When I go to lunch, he is playing a gentle, rocking theme – he says nothing occurs to him to represent American pomp.

A week later, there is a further entry:

After lunch he shows me his latest album leaf, 'an attempt to be American,' and says it is the chorus the women will sing to Parzival: '*Komm, schöner Knabe!*' ... He is thinking a lot about *Parzival* and is grieved that so many things intervene.[12]

The 'chorus' in question is the swaying, triple-time waltz music to which the Flowermaidens attempt to seduce Parsifal with their sweet-smelling scents and floral charms (see illustration).[13] Two things are notable about this passage: the tonality of A flat major, to which we will return, and the static harmonies, rotating around tonic and dominant chords. Such tonal stasis, reminiscent of the pastoral style of earlier composers, is remote from the chromatic anguish or harmonic ambivalence of any of Wagner's previous music. We should note in passing, too, that the day before he sketched this section, Wagner heard Mendelssohn's *Reformation* Symphony performed at an amateur concert.[14] Mendelssohn there makes use of the Dresden Amen – a traditional cadence composed by Johann Gottlieb Naumann, Wagner's 18th-century predecessor at the court of Dresden – as would Wagner in *Parsifal*. The cadence, strongly redolent of incense rather than floral aroma, consists of a steady ascent of five notes (the last repeated; see illustration). And, astonishingly, there is

Sketch of 9 February 1876 for the music of the Flowermaidens, Act II of *Parsifal*. Cosima's annotation 'Wanting to be American' (right) refers to the commission for a march to celebrate the American centennial.

The Dresden Amen (top) and the Grail motif from *Parsifal* (bottom), which incorporates it.

a stepwise ascent of five notes in that first sketch for the Flowermaidens (the line, slightly modified, was to be given in the final version to the two top Flowermaidens of the solo group). Already Wagner's creative instinct has shown him the possibility of transforming the sacred into the secular: spirituality and sensuality are to be the twin poles of the new work.

The spiritual pole would come into focus in the August of 1876, with a series of jottings that included the so-called Communion or Last Supper Theme that was to open the work, and the dotted motif associated with Parsifal himself. The Communion Theme is of particular interest because it is quite clearly derived from Liszt's 'Excelsior!' motif as heard in his cantata *The Bells of Strasbourg Cathedral*.[15] Wagner certainly knew the work: not only did Liszt send him a copy of the score in January 1875,[16] but it was performed in Budapest on 10 March that year in a concert jointly conducted by Liszt and Wagner. The 'Excelsior!' motif, heard prominently in the prelude to Liszt's work, rises up through a major triad, striving to achieve – in accordance with the aspirational programme of Longfellow's more famous, earlier poem *Excelsior* ('ever upward!') – the note a tone higher too. Wagner's slightly modified version of the motif retains that rising triad plus extension, and of course aspiration is also a key notion in his Grail-inspired work. Wagner was well aware of his borrowing,[17] and even checked the score of *The Bells of Strasbourg Cathedral* on one occasion to make sure he was not guilty of plagiarism.[18]

As with the Bülow borrowing for *Tristan und Isolde*, it is what Wagner makes of the original that is particularly worthy of comment. In this case a boldly stated, affirmative motif is transformed by a subtle metrical adjustment into something mystical and floating. It is also worth noting that Wagner immediately transposed it into A flat major, always a tonality of special significance for him.[19] On the one hand, it is often associated simply with love (as in the Act II duets of *Tannhäuser* and *Tristan*, and the two scenes between Eva and Sachs of *Die Meistersinger*). But in

Liszt's 'Excelsior!' motif (top) and the opening motif of *Parsifal* (bottom).

Parsifal it inhabits predominantly a sacred, numinous sphere. The two are not mutually contradictory, of course: they are fused in the auratic opening bars of the Liebestod in *Tristan*. And those two early sketches for *Parsifal* – the music of the Flowermaidens and the Communion – demonstrate just how closely the two spheres were intertwined in Wagner's conception from the start.

21 The Silent Sufferer: Cosima Wagner

She worships the Master to distraction.
Ludwig Strecker on Cosima

Photographs of the time are carefully staged to obscure the fact, but Wagner's second wife, Cosima, stood a good few inches taller than the man to whom she looked up in every other respect. For all that she adored him, however – and her self-effacing idolatry was the epitome of anti-emancipation – a close reading of the documents reveals that the dynamics of their relationship were rather more subtle and interesting.

Wagner and Cosima
in front of the Palazzo
Vendramin-Calergi
(land side) in the
winter of 1882–83.

Cosima's mother, Marie d'Agoult, in a portrait by Henri Lehmann, 1839.

To understand Cosima, one needs to be aware of her family background and upbringing. Her father, Franz Liszt, was at the height of his fame as an itinerant pianist, dazzling the audiences of Europe, when she was born on 24 December 1837. Her mother, Marie d'Agoult, descended from the banking family of the Bethmanns, was unhappily married to Count Charles d'Agoult, who, perhaps sensing their incompatibility, had promised before their marriage that he would release her from her vow should she come to regret it. Cosima, like her elder sister Blandine, was weaned by a wet nurse and then placed with a foster mother. Unsuited to, and uninspired by, the prospect of motherhood, Marie, who was prone to bouts of depression and various psychosomatic illnesses, was more or less content to traipse around Italy with her lover, Liszt, though even this lifestyle began to lose its allure. Their relationship, already in decline by the 1840s, was definitively at an end by May 1844.

While acknowledging the paternity of his three illegitimate children (a boy, Daniel, had been born in May 1839), Liszt was an equally clueless father. To Cosima and her siblings he was a 'fantastically legendary phenomenon', but a stern, distant, indeed usually absent father. At the end of 1839 Cosima and Blandine were placed in the care of Liszt's mother, Anna, now resident in Paris. From their surrogate mother they received a basic education (Anna spoke neither French nor German fluently) and a good deal of love. But in 1846 Cosima was sent off to join her sister at a select boarding school in the Rue Montparnasse, run by Louise Bernard and her daughter. They were not unhappy there, but when their estranged mother, Marie d'Agoult, decided to make contact with them at the school, Liszt in fury withdrew them and again placed them temporarily in the care of his own mother.

By this time Liszt was involved with another woman, the fearsomely loquacious, cigar-smoking, fanatically Catholic aristocrat Princess Carolyne von Sayn-Wittgenstein. And it was undoubtedly she who was responsible for the appointment of the children's new governess: a 72-year-old stickler for propriety named Madame Louise Adélaïde Patersi de Fossombroni. Sentimentally attached to the Ancien Régime, Madame Patersi inculcated in the children a contempt for the post-revolutionary bourgeois world and its Enlightenment values. Her own pedagogical regime amounted to a Reign of Terror all of its own. Unquestioning subordination was demanded, and 'entertainment' of any kind abhorred; the children were taught that a woman's life should be regarded as a 'sacrifice', its purpose being to please God and their future husbands. A particular favourite of Madame Patersi was the medieval mystic Thomas à Kempis (c. 1380–1471), whose tome *De Imitatione Christi* became a second Bible to Cosima. Here are a few lines selected at random:

If thou canst be silent and suffer, without doubt thou shalt see that the Lord will help thee. (II.ii)

When a man trusteth in himself, he easily slideth unto human comforts. But a true lover of Christ, and a diligent follower of virtue, does not fall back on comforts, nor seek such sensible sweetnesses; but rather prefers hard exercises, and to sustain severe labours for Christ. (III.ix)

For all worldly delights are either vain or unclean; but spiritual delights are only pleasant and honest, sprung from virtue, and infused by God into pure minds. (III.x)

Thou art deceived, thou art deceived if thou seek any other thing than to suffer tribulations; for this whole mortal life is full of miseries, and signed on every side with crosses. (III.xii)[1]

Indoctrinated with such ideas, Cosima grew up to believe that only suffering offered the key to peace and happiness in this life. A masochistic pleasure in suffering and self-sacrifice came to be the determining features in her personality.

In 1855 the elderly Madame Patersi's health began to deteriorate, and Cosima and Blandine, now seventeen and nineteen respectively, were impelled from one disastrous situation to another. It was decided that they would be farmed out to Franziska von Bülow, the mother of Liszt's most precocious pupil. A tyrannical, demanding woman, she had seen off two husbands and closely monitored the activities of her elder son, Hans, in an attempt to keep him loyal. The boy developed a carapace of cynicism to protect himself, but was prone to severe headaches and psychosomatic illnesses throughout his life. Prodigiously talented but emotionally stunted, a walking disaster in the matrimonial stakes, Hans von Bülow might have been conjured by central casting for the role of husband to the woman raised to believe that suffering was the greatest good.

Cosima (standing) with brother Daniel, sister Blandine, grandmother Anna Liszt and governess Madame de Saint-Mars (right).

A *vanitas* still life by the 17th-century painter Simon Renard de Saint-André. At its centre is the ascetic, masochistic *De Imitatione Christi* by the medieval mystic Thomas à Kempis.

Hans von Bülow at
the age of twenty-five,
painted by Wilhelm
Streckfuss (1855).

Their relationship began, appropriately enough, with Cosima comforting Bülow, her piano teacher, after an ill-fated concert in Berlin that was booed vitriolically, causing him to break down in the green room, briefly losing consciousness. Cosima sat up on her own awaiting the return of Bülow from the theatre and spent the night in the living room trying her best to console him. Their engagement followed immediately. But Bülow was far from convinced that he was worthy of this well-bred daughter of his idol, Liszt. In an uncanny echo of the words of Count Charles d'Agoult, the husband of Cosima's mother, Bülow gave Liszt an assurance that he would 'release [Cosima] were she ever to feel that she had made a mistake with regard to me'.[2] Cosima, for her part, was under no illusions, telling her stepsister Claire de Charnacé: 'I am well aware that it is a bad match.'

Following their wedding at St Hedwig's Cathedral, Berlin, on 18 August 1857, Bülow and Cosima embarked on the honeymoon that was to be the first staging-post in their ill-fated marriage. The itinerary was extended to include a visit to Wagner, at that time living in exile in the Asyl, just outside Zurich. As luck would have it, the other guests included Mathilde Wesendonck, with whom Wagner was infatuated (though the affair was almost certainly platonic), and her husband, Otto. Wagner's wife, Minna, was also there, completing an extraordinary constellation of the composer's past, present and future loves under the one roof.

To Cosima and her sisters, Franz Liszt was a 'fantastically legendary phenomenon', but also a distant father.

Wagner's attention was firmly focused on Mathilde, however, while Cosima for her part seems to have been as repelled by his boorish behaviour as she was attracted by his charisma. There was a further encounter between the two the following year, but they did not see each other again until 1861, and then once more in 1862. It was in the autumn of 1863 that their feelings for each other finally blossomed. By this time Cosima had reportedly attempted to end her life on several occasions, so unhappy was her marital situation, while Wagner's romantic attachments were at their most volatile. At the end of November Wagner found himself in Berlin, and on the afternoon of Saturday 28 November, while Bülow was rehearsing, he and Cosima took a ride through the Tiergarten in a fine carriage. It was during that ride, according to Wagner's subsequent account in his autobiography, that something dramatic happened:

This time we fell silent and all joking ceased. We gazed mutely into each other's eyes and an intense longing for the fullest avowal of the truth forced us to a confession, requiring no words whatever, of the incommensurable misfortune that weighed upon us. With tears and sobs we sealed a vow to belong to each other alone. It lifted a great weight from our hearts.[3]

With Wagner, Cosima finally found happiness, though she continued to be tormented by guilt. This photograph by Fritz Luckhardt was taken shortly after their marriage.

Doubt has occasionally been cast on the genuineness of this 'confession', on the grounds that to outward appearances it marked no particular watershed in Wagner's romantic affections. It is true that the autobiographical account, dictated by Wagner to Cosima herself, may have an element of rosy-hued retrospection about it. On the other hand, it might not be insignificant that the sentence about the sealing of the vow was deleted by Cosima in the first public edition of *Mein Leben* in 1911 – to be restored only in the complete edition of 1963. And it is evident from several entries in her Diaries that 28 November 1863 was a red-letter day for Cosima and her second husband. 'Six years ago R. came through Berlin,' wrote Cosima on 28 November 1869, for example, 'and then it happened that we fell in love; at that time I thought I should never see him again, we wanted to die together. R. remembers it, and we drink to this day.'[4]

By her mid-twenties (she was twenty-five at the time of the carriage ride in the Tiergarten) Cosima had matured into a poised, if somewhat aloof, young lady more confident of her position in society. Though not conventionally beautiful, 'her slim, elegant figure', according to one contemporary witness, 'with its characteristic facial features and abundance of blonde hair, created an emphatically attractive impression in spite of her rather large nose.' The same witness commented on her 'great art of holding an engrossing conversation. She was a highly attractive combination of grande dame and a personality entirely animated by artistic and literary interests.'[5]

Cosima's upbringing drove her to observe matters of etiquette to the point of affectation. Wagner, who was somewhat proud of his humble origins, did not take kindly to being told how to use his knife at the table. But that upbringing had also branded Cosima with an indelible sense of guilt and inferiority. As her Diaries give testimony, on page after page, she was tormented with guilt for her treatment of Bülow: 'thinking with concern and sorrow of Hans. My heart, I know, will never be free of this burden' (16 April 1869); 'I feel guilty ever since Hans told me that he could not do without me' (30 June 1869); 'Willingly and lightly will I bear the world's loathing – Hans's suffering, however, robs me of all joy' (21 May 1869). As Cosima's most recent biographer, Oliver Hilmes, observes, 'Cosima's self-reproaches were fuelled by a powerful sense of inferiority.' Her lack of self-esteem and capacity for suffering can doubtless be traced back to her loveless childhood and to Madame Patersi's religious indoctrination. That much is clear from phrases such as the 'strange ecstasy of suffering' to which Cosima refers,[6] a concept straight out of the Catholic treatises that were her bedtime reading. Furthermore, there is – as Hilmes also notes – a strong element of masochism in Cosima's suffering. Not only does she revel morbidly in her torment, but she even puts barriers in the way of the enjoyment of pleasure.[7]

In the August of 1865 Wagner spent the best part of a fortnight (from the 9th to the 21st) in King Ludwig's hunting lodge on the Hochkopf above the Walchensee, alone apart from his servant Franz Mrazeck. Unable to communicate directly with Cosima, he poured out his feelings

The leatherbound Brown Book, given to Wagner by Cosima, which he used for autobiographical notes, diary jottings and sketches.

for her in a series of entries in his Brown Book (a leatherbound volume Cosima had given him):

Where does delight come from, where does faith? From love? Yes, my soul, from love of <u>you</u>, my wife! Certainly that will work: I know. You still entice my work from my soul. But oh! Give me the peace for it! Stay with me, don't go again. Tell poor Hans openly that without you I cannot manage any longer. Oh heavens, if only you could be my wife to the world! ... I'm going to bed! Good night! <u>You are my wife!</u>[8]

It is perhaps not surprising that Wagner was already fantasizing about Cosima as his wife, for on 10 April of that year a child, Isolde, was born to Cosima who was almost certainly his. Nine months before the birth Cosima had travelled to Starnberg, at his invitation, accompanied only by her two young daughters and a nurserymaid. Bülow had been detained in Berlin. That Wagner and Cosima slept together on that occasion is not in doubt; what remains tantalizingly uncertain is whether Bülow (who arrived at Starnberg on 7 July 1864, Cosima having been installed since 29 June) and Cosima also had sexual relations during this period. It seems unlikely, given the terminal state of their marriage. And yet Bülow, who was capable of striking his wife – as he did repeatedly, even in the presence of the shocked Wagner – may possibly have decided to assert his matrimonial rights. What we do know is contained in the testimony of Wagner's housekeeper, Anna Mrazek, who, when the question of Isolde's paternity came to court in 1914, sketched the scenario of a pitiful bedroom farce in all its sensational and sordid detail. Her testimony was transcribed into the official court records as follows:

The Bülows occupied a common bedroom on the first floor .... Hans von Bülow quite often visited Munich during the day, but regularly spent the nights in the bedroom of his wife ... . Several weeks after the arrival of the Bülows, the husband of the witness (Herr Franz Mrazék) noticed the following: Frau Cosima von Bülow had gone to Wagner in his bedroom. After some time, Hans von Bülow likewise wanted to go into the bedroom, but he found the door blocked. He obviously knew that his wife was in the bedroom with Wagner. Bülow returned quietly back to his bedroom. Once there he lost his self-control. He threw himself to the floor and lashed out with his hands and feet. Herr Mrazék immediately informed his wife, who was busying herself downstairs, about what he had just observed. The Mrazéks believed that a stormy scene was about to develop. But the participants showed the greatest restraint, so that it appeared as if nothing had taken place. The Bülows also retained their shared bedroom. Accordingly, it was certain that when the conception took place, the Bülows were living together for a great part of that time.[9]

At that same trial, Cosima testified that between June and October 1864 she had had sexual relations only with Wagner. This may or may not be true: Wagner (and Cosima) certainly regarded Isolde as his child, though Bülow also, for his own reasons, laid claim to her.

A rare photograph from 1865 of Cosima and Bülow (far right) together, with the violinist Heinrich Wilhelm Ernst and her father, Franz Liszt, at the piano.

Cartoon from the time of the *Tristan* premiere depicting Wagner as Paris abducting Helen (Cosima) to the fury of Menelaus (Bülow).

Ironically, it was not long before Cosima was withdrawing her sexual favours from Wagner too.[10] Yet, despite their ill-matched biological make-ups, Cosima was in many ways the ideal partner for Wagner. Intelligent and well educated, she was able to share his cultural interests: as well as German literature, together they read (usually in translation) Greek, English, French, Russian and Spanish literature, medieval romances, Icelandic sagas, works about history, religion, music, poetry and much

more. Cosima's administrative skills helped to keep the Wagner household out of permanent debt, and of course came into their own when she took over the running of the Bayreuth Festival after Wagner's death. And the love she had for him was never in doubt, providing him with the emotional security he had lacked all his life. It is true, however, that Cosima's willingness to prostrate herself before her idol enabled him to get away with monstrously egotistic behaviour that a wiser wife might have quashed. And when it came to anti-Semitism, Wagner was almost a moderate by comparison with Cosima, who felt a visceral loathing for Jews.

But for all her idolatry, Cosima knew that she was indispensable to Wagner, and she used that knowledge to exert a subtle power over him. For the sake of a quiet life he denied the truth of his affection for others, notably Ludwig and a host of women (all his affairs were 'pure fiction', he once told her). Without her business acumen and moral support, he could scarcely have achieved his life's ambition – the *Ring* tetralogy and its performance at a purpose-built festival. There is more to Cosima than meets the eye.

A more flattering photograph of Cosima, *c.* 1857.

22 Tribschen Idyll: The Lucerne Years

I know of no more beautiful place on earth.
  Wagner's description of Tribschen to Ludwig II

By the end of 1865, the perception of Wagner as a baleful influence on Ludwig and an unacceptable drain on the royal exchequer had created such virulent hostility towards the composer, both in court circles and among the people of Munich as a whole, that Ludwig was finally compelled to give him the order to leave the city. At first Wagner sought a congenial place to live in the south of France, but while travelling in Switzerland with Cosima von Bülow – her husband was away on tour – Wagner discovered the house called Tribschen on a promontory overlooking Lake Lucerne. 'Unimaginably beautiful and holy' is how Wagner described the place to a friend shortly after moving in, and, indeed, it was to provide the setting for some of the happiest and most fruitful years of his life. From April 1866 to April 1872 he lived there with Cosima and their family, free at last from pecuniary worries thanks to his royal patron, and able to devote himself to his musical and literary endeavours in a tranquil and truly idyllic location.

To begin with, Cosima was only a visitor. She first arrived at Tribschen on 12 May 1866 with her three daughters, Daniela, Blandine and Isolde. The first two were from her marriage with Bülow; Isolde was almost certainly Wagner's child (see the previous chapter). In February 1867 Wagner's second child, Eva, was born. Over the following months Cosima spent increasing amounts of time at Tribschen but did not actually move in until November 1868, making the first entry in the diary she was to keep until the day of Wagner's death on 1 January 1869. Only then was Ludwig apprised of the real situation: previously he had been led to believe that Cosima's role was merely that of helpmeet and amanuensis.

Peaceful it may have been at Tribschen, but Wagner hardly led the life of an anchorite. His entourage consisted of more than a dozen people: in addition to Cosima and their five children (a son, Siegfried, was born in June 1869), there were a governess, a nurserymaid, a housekeeper and her niece, a cook and two or three servants. To those must be added two dogs (Russ and Koss, so called to discourage people from abbreviating Cosima's name to Cos), the horse, Fritz, sheep, hens and cats, not forgetting a pair of golden pheasants and the pair of peacocks, Wotan and Fricka,[1] brought from Munich.

Modern photograph of Tribschen, the house in Lucerne where Wagner and his family lived from 1866 to 1872.

View across Lake Lucerne to Tribschen (centre).

The young Hans Richter, employed as a musical secretary with responsibility for organizing house concerts, was also much in evidence, as were regular visitors such as Friedrich Nietzsche, Franz Liszt, Peter Cornelius, the pianist Joseph Rubinstein, the writer and musical historian Edouard Schuré, and the architect Gottfried Semper. Nietzsche in fact made some two dozen visits to Tribschen, described by him in *Ecce Homo* in rapturous terms:

I would not have the days I spent at Tribschen – those days of confidence, or cheerfulness, of sublime flashes, and of profound moments – blotted from my life at any price. I know not what Wagner may have been for others; but no cloud ever darkened *our* sky.[2]

Sadly, those cloudless skies were to become somewhat overcast, if not thunderous, in later years after Wagner's final rift with Nietzsche. Other distinguished visitors included the French writer Judith Gautier and her husband, Catulle Mendès, along with their friend the poet Auguste Villiers de l'Isle-Adam. Their arrival in July 1869 caused something of a stir in the town. When Wagner delivered them to the Hotel du Lac, where rooms had been reserved for them, they were treated with exceptional deference by the staff, the townspeople looking on with great curiosity.

Friedrich Nietzsche, a frequent and welcome visitor at Tribschen, painted in 1869.

It transpired that the men had been mistaken for Ludwig II and his aide Prince Paul von Thurn und Taxis, while Judith was thought, for some reason, to be the singer Adelina Patti.

Judith, the beautiful daughter of the poet Théophile Gautier and almost certainly Victor Hugo's mistress, was herself a writer, one capable of conjuring the mysteries of the Orient without needing to experience them at first hand. Her account of the visit to Tribschen (and of another the following year), published in English translation in 1910 – appropriately enough by Mills & Boon – weaves together fact and fantasy, novelistic observation and star-struck idolatry in highly readable prose.

Having reached the Hotel du Lac, the group was warmly invited to Tribschen, with the suggestion that they should arrive by water. Here is Judith's breathless account of the approach once they had disembarked:

With what deep emotion we set foot upon this sacred soil!

There is no door, no hedge, no limit to this garden; the lake, the hills, the forests, the Alps, the whole world seems a part of it, and even as this thought appeals to our young enthusiasm, so also is it true and prophetic, since the world shall, in truth, become the domain of the great one who dwells here … . We advance slowly, full of emotion and thoughtful, as at the threshold of a temple. Some one has seen us, undoubtedly, as the Master appears at the door of the drawing-room and descends the steps, a big black Newfoundland bounding by his side.

With an air at once ceremonious and cordial, Wagner bids us enter.

A tall and slender young woman, with a noble and distinguished air, a sweet smile and very blue eyes under her beautiful blond hair, stands in the centre of the drawing-room, surrounded by four little girls, one of them an infant.

'Frau von Bülow, who has kindly come with her children to see me', said the Master, in presenting her.[3]

The visitors, no strangers to extramarital liaisons themselves, were neither taken in nor shocked by the subterfuge. Cosima, schooled from infancy in self-restraint, at first found Judith's emotional impetuosity hard to countenance – 'so lacking in manners that I find it downright embarrassing, yet at the same time good-natured and terribly full of enthusiasm' was her initial verdict[4] – but soon came to confide in her.

The visit lasted nine days, during which the French trio became almost part of the family. Judith presented a valuable Chinese fan to Cosima, who felt obliged to let her take a page of Wagner's manuscript in return. 'I found it hard to part with it,' she commented, 'though I do not begrudge it to this remarkable woman.' Wagner had come to regard Judith and Catulle as 'a real enrichment of our lives, and they are certainly an extraordinary, noble couple'.[5] Cosima doubtless revised her opinion as to Judith's 'nobility' a few years later when she could no longer turn a blind eye to the undue intimacy that had developed between her husband and Judith; but for those nine days at least the anti-French sentiments that reigned at Tribschen were suspended.

The return the following year of their three French friends, in the company of the composers Saint-Saëns and Duparc, unfortunately coincided to the day with the declaration of war between Germany and France – presented skilfully by Bismarck as a battle to preserve German liberties in the face of French aggression. Simmering nationalistic tensions came to the boil on the last day of the 1870 visit, when Villiers de l'Isle-Adam offended Wagner with what he criticized as a bombastic reading. Wagner responded to Villiers by deploring the objectionable nature of French rhetorical poetry, an insult on which he was to expand even more offensively later that year in a play entitled *Eine Kapitulation* (A Capitulation). This was a heavy-handed farce that mocked the suffering of the Parisians during the siege of their city. Tasteless as it was, the play was at bottom an attempt to show just how German culture had been swamped by the crowd-pulling frivolity of French or French-inspired works.

Also from this period comes the essay 'Beethoven', which addressed once again the fundamental question of the relationship of poetry to music in the music drama, an issue that had obsessed Wagner since his early Zurich days. Another obsession had been revisited the previous year when Wagner supervised a reprint of his notorious essay 'Jewishness in Music', for which he added a new preface protesting about Jewish persecution – of himself, that is. It was not a gesture designed to win him popularity, despite the incipient anti-Semitism of swathes of the German people, and there were public protests at a performance of *Die Meistersinger* in Mannheim. The opera's Munich premiere was an unequivocal success (with the public, if not the critics), and Wagner was invited to share the royal box, from where he took applause after the second and third acts, in a much criticized breach of protocol. In a letter to Ludwig a few months later, Wagner declared that

the evening of the first performance of the 'Mastersingers' was the high point of my career as man and artist. Just as it will be found, in time, that this work of mine is the most perfect of all that I have written so far, so must I declare that this performance of it – which I owe to your goodness alone – was the best that has ever been given of any of my works: the inestimable honour which you showed me that evening at your side I declare to be the most deeply-felt reward ever bestowed upon a leading artist.[6]

In the same paragraph, however, he goes on to say how the occasion was 'also the very pinnacle of joylessness' for him. Underlying this dissatisfaction was his sense of despair with the state of the German theatre, which was constitutionally incapable of delivering the conditions in which the Wagnerian music drama could thrive. That conviction made him wary of the plan to stage a production of *Das Rheingold* in Munich, even though it was Ludwig himself who was instrumental in bringing it about. Despite the composer's objections, *Das Rheingold* was staged on 22 September 1869, with *Die Walküre* following the next year.

More congenial to Wagner was his ability to work on *Siegfried*, although for a time he deliberately left part of it unscored to prevent premature performance. The full score was finally completed on 5 February 1871. A happy spin-off of that work was the *Siegfried Idyll*, composed as

Turning the tables:
Wagner, with notably
Jewish physiognomy,
is depicted receiving
applause from the royal
box at the Munich
premiere of *Die
Meistersinger* in 1868.

„Habt Dank der Güte
aus tiefstem Gemüthe!
Und darf ich denn hoffen,
steht heut mir noch offen
zu werben um den Preis,
dass ich Meistersänger heiss?"
„Oho! Fein sacht! etc.etc.
(Siehe Textbuch der Meistersinger 2.ᵗᵉ Ausgabe Seite 2i.)

RICHARD WAGNER

LIEBIG'S
FLEISCH-EXTRAKT.

Die Insel der Seligen - Triebschen.
5. Wagner dirigiert das Siegfried-Idyll an der
Haustreppe 1870.

An imaginary recreation of the scene at Tribschen when Wagner conducted the *Siegfried Idyll* outside the bedroom of the waking Cosima, seen here fully dressed with the infant Siegfried.

a birthday present for Cosima and first performed on Christmas Day 1870 (Cosima's birthday was actually the 24th, but she celebrated it on the 25th). The circumstances of the premiere were remarkable, to say the least. This is how they were recorded by Cosima herself:

When I woke up I heard a sound, it grew ever louder, I could no longer imagine myself in a dream, music was sounding, and what music! After it had died away, R. came in to me with the five children and put into my hands the score of his 'Symphonic Birthday Greeting.' I was in tears, but so, too, was the whole household; R. had set up his orchestra on the stairs and thus consecrated our Tribschen forever! *The Tribschen Idyll* – thus the work is called.[7]

The *Siegfried Idyll* was also a celebration of their son, Siegfried, whose birth the previous year had brought such joy to the couple. With the formal dissolution of Cosima's marriage to Bülow, there was now no barrier to their own matrimonial union, which took place in the Protestant church in Lucerne on 25 August 1870. On visiting Bayreuth the following year, they established that the sumptuous Baroque theatre of the Markgräfliches Opernhaus was too small to accommodate the *Ring*. There was nothing for it but to build a new theatre that would do justice to the mighty tetralogy.

23   A Home for the Gods: The Bayreuth Project

Hallowed by the German spirit that shouts to us across the centuries
   Wagner on the Bayreuth Festspielhaus

The story of how Wagner created not only a four-day musico-dramatic work of art, demolishing all established conventions, but also a new kind of theatrical space in which to perform it is one that perfectly embodies the triumph of idealism. Over a period of nearly three decades Wagner conceived his project, persuaded, inspired and cajoled countless others to support him, and finally realized it at Bayreuth, establishing in the process an institution that has held its place at the forefront of international music festivals to the present day.

   Two years after setting down his first outline of what was to become the *Ring* cycle (see Chapter 10: The Rise and Fall of Valhalla), Wagner – in a state of some excitement – began to tell his friends how he planned to present his great 'artwork of the future' to the world. A letter postmarked 14 September 1850 to an old friend from the Paris days, Ernst Benedikt Kietz, adumbrates the scheme:

According to this plan of mine, I would have a theatre erected here on the spot, made of planks, and have the most suitable singers join me here, and arrange everything necessary for this one special occasion, so that I could be certain of an outstanding performance of the opera. I would then send out invitations far and wide to all who were interested in my works, ensure that the auditorium was decently filled, and give three performances – free, of course – one after the other in the space of a week, after which the theatre would then be demolished and the whole affair would be over and done with.[1]

At this point Wagner and his more progressive friends were still hoping that the revolution might come and sweep away all the privileged corruption and superannuated conventions of the existing order. The utopian aspect of his project is even more evident in another letter a week later, to Theodor Uhlig:

After the third [performance] the theatre will be demolished and my score burned. To the people who enjoyed it I shall then say: 'Now go away and do it yourself!'[2]

   As time went on, the somewhat drastic symbolism of adding the score of the *Ring* to Brünnhilde's funeral pyre was quietly forgotten, though

Interior of the Bayreuth Festspielhaus today, with its semi-upholstered seats, the pillars at the ends of rows that form a series of false proscenia, and the functional boxes (right).

the idealistic nature of the project remained. The following November, by which time the work had begun to take further shape, Wagner was still proposing to 'run up a theatre', now on the Rhine, 'and send out invitations to a great dramatic festival'.[3] The element of provisionality is still evident, and the project is still essentially part of his revolutionary programme, but Wagner was obliged to abandon the notion that the world had to change before the work could be performed ('A *performance* is something I can conceive of only *after the Revolution*'[4]) in the light of that revolution's failure.

Just a few months later, Wagner was entertaining the possibility of establishing the festival in Zurich, where he was resident. Liszt supported him wholeheartedly, but the Swiss themselves were slow to open their wallets. Yet it was a setback that allowed him to return to his primary objective of producing a German work for the German people in his native land.

The collapse of the revolutionary ideal inevitably undermined the utopian thrust of the *Ring* project. Yet Wagner made progress with the cycle in the 1850s before setting it aside, temporarily, in 1857, when he paused to carry out the projects of *Tristan und Isolde* and, afterwards, *Die Meistersinger*. Though sustained work on it was not to be resumed until 1869, Wagner published the poem of the *Ring* in 1863, prefacing it with an exposition of the project. In this preface he posits three performances of the cycle in a provisional theatre constructed in 'one of the smaller towns of Germany',[5] suitably appointed, where there would be no conflict with existing institutions. The theatre was to be made, possibly, out of wood and was to feature an amphitheatre-like auditorium and an invisible orchestra. Wagner's preface goes on to foreshadow one of the aspects of the Bayreuth experience that has retained its appeal to pilgrims:

This visit at the height of summer might rightly be regarded by each individual as a refreshing excursion in which his first duty would be to shake off the cares of his daily round. Instead of having, in the usual way after a heavy and worrying day at the counter, in the office or laboratory or wherever his work may be, to seek relaxation and distraction in the evening – a state of mind for which mere superficial entertainment according to taste must seem the best remedy – he will now relax during the daytime and, with the onset of dusk, gather his wits together as the signal sounds for the start of the festival performance. Thus, his faculties refreshed and ready to be stirred, the first mysterious note from the hidden orchestra will arouse in him that contemplative mood without which no true artistic impression is ever possible.[6]

The Festspielhaus on 2 August 1873, the day of the roof-raising ceremony.

Central to Wagner's concerns was his desire to see the work presented as a special occasion: this was not to be the kind of shallow entertainment

offered by conventional theatres, but a life-changing event. The features mentioned earlier in his preface – a wooden structure, an amphitheatre-like auditorium and an invisible orchestra – were incorporated into plans for a festival theatre in Munich, discussed with the architect Gottfried Semper shortly after the accession of Ludwig II in 1864 and marking the first stage of Ludwig's enthusiastic patronage of the composer. That scheme proved abortive, but the 'Festspielhaus', or festival house, that was eventually built in Bayreuth (the roof-raising ceremony took place on 2 August 1873) incorporated all the elements fundamental to Wagner's conception: the wooden construction (the outer walls are lath and plaster); the amphitheatre-like auditorium (both more Greek and more democratic than the traditional horseshoe design with balcony and side boxes); the sunken (and covered) orchestra pit; and a double proscenium (with six pairs of parallel proscenium pillars receding to a final pair at the rear of the stalls). The purpose of these tricks of perspective, and of concealing the orchestral musicians in the pit, was to create a unique theatrical space that would revolutionize the relationship between the spectator and what was onstage:

Between [the spectator] and the scenic picture nothing is clearly visible, only a sense of distance in suspension, achieved by the architectural arrangement of the two proscenia, a phenomenon which presents the removed picture with the unapproachability of a dreamlike vision, while the spectral-sounding music rising up from the 'mystic abyss', like the vapours wafting up from the sacred primeval womb of Gaia beneath the tripod of the Pythia, transports him into that inspired state of clairvoyance in which the scenic picture becomes the truest simulacrum of life itself.[7]

Siegfried Wagner and members of the orchestra in the crowded Festspielhaus pit.

Pouring rain on 22 May 1872 – the day the foundation stone of the Festspielhaus was laid – necessitated the relocation of the performance of Beethoven's Ninth Symphony, under Wagner's baton, to the Markgräfliches Opernhaus.

Having decided that a purpose-built theatre was required in Bayreuth, Wagner and Cosima turned their attention to the raising of capital. A budget of 300,000 thalers was drawn up (the thaler being worth approximately 3 marks in the 1870s; Wagner's annual salary in Dresden had been 1,500 thalers) and a scheme hatched whereby 1,000 'patrons' certificates' would be issued at 300 thalers each. One acquaintance of Wagner, Heinrich Esser, totting up the various production expenses likely to be incurred, queried at an early stage whether 300,000 thalers would be anything like enough ('Now I'm not very good at arithmetic, but Wagner is no good at it at all,' he wrote to Wagner's publisher, Franz Schott, in December 1871). But even that amount proved formidably difficult to raise. At the instigation of Emil Heckel, a music dealer from Mannheim, a network of Wagner Societies was set up that would allow people of more modest means to contribute to the cause. While such a move was broadly in line with Wagner's idealistic intention to make his work available to the masses, there is, as Nicholas Vazsonyi points out in his timely study of the marketing of the Wagner 'brand', an inherent contradiction between Wagner's goal of 'a non-commercial venture where art was enjoyed for art's sake' and the 'relentless effort to attract attention and raise operating capital', which made the venture appear not so different from those of the commercial world he so despised.[8] The popularity of these Wagner Societies was, and remains, unparalleled in the world of classical music, but it was not enough to secure the financial success of the enterprise. The generous subsidies Wagner had been receiving from Ludwig were no longer forthcoming, and in desperation he turned to the Reich, but his appeal was rejected before it even reached the Kaiser. But then Ludwig, in his self-appointed role as Parsifal, once again rode to the rescue:

No, no and again no! It must not end like this; help must be given! Our plans must not founder! Parcival knows his mission and will do everything that lies in his power.[9]

Ludwig chipped in with a loan of 100,000 thalers, enough to make the festival a reality, though of course the repayment of such a loan – as was the case with the patrons' certificates – necessitated the selling of admission tickets. It was a sad but unavoidable betrayal of the revolutionary idealism of the 1850s. This was not a time for ingratitude, however, especially since Ludwig made a further sum available for the completion of the villa next to the gardens of the 18th-century palace. The Wagners moved in on 28 April 1874 and christened their new home 'Wahnfried': 'peace from illusion'.

The first festival, announced for 1873, had to be deferred to 1875, then for a further year. In the meantime Wagner and Cosima set about recruiting the cast. 'Actors who were also singers' was his original desideratum, placing more emphasis on the drama than on the purely musical element of his work. Ultimately, however, he settled for the best voices he could get, developing their potential as singer-actors over the course of extended rehearsals.

Wahnfried today. Note the bust of Ludwig II, by Kaspar von Zumbusch, and the sgraffito by Robert Krausse representing aspects of the Wagnerian music drama.

Josef Hoffmann, the set designer for the *Ring*, depicted satirically with palette and paintbrush as his shield and spear. Caricature from *Der Floh*, 18 March 1877.

Determined not to leave the creation of the stage scenery to 'routine theatrical scene painters', Wagner approached the artist Josef Hoffmann, a painter of historical subjects, who had only limited experience of theatrical work but had already made something of a reputation for himself. Hoffmann's sets for a *Zauberflöte* at the Vienna State Opera were acclaimed for their impeccably researched representation of ancient Egypt, while his horripilant Wolf Glen's Scene for *Der Freischütz* was the talk of Vienna. He undertook the commission for the *Ring* and produced a set of sketches that were widely admired. There were two problems, however. The first was that Hoffmann's precise, architectural treatment of interiors such as those of Hunding's hut or the Gibichung Hall was regarded by Wagner and Cosima as too 'historical'. The mythic world of the *Ring* did not require the historical accuracy that was Hoffmann's forte. The second problem was that, on account of his inexperience in stage matters, Hoffmann was obliged to work with other collaborators appointed by Wagner: the Brückner brothers (Gotthold and Max) for the construction and painting of the sets, Carl Brandt for the design and construction of the stage machinery, and Professor Carl Doepler for the design of the costumes. Hoffmann's inflexibility in dealing with these experienced stage professionals left Wagner with no alternative but to dispense with his services, entrusting the realization of the designs to the Brückners and to Brandt.

It is very difficult for us, more than a century later, to imagine the visual effect of those designs at the first performances. Until quite recently

Gotthold Brückner, who with his brother Max constructed the sets for the first *Ring* in 1876 – a *mise-en-scène* that was to influence productions of the work for decades to come.

all we had to go on was a series of fourteen monochrome photographs taken by Victor Angerer at the artist's request and published in a portfolio as a memento. But two exciting discoveries were to bring us closer than ever to imagining what those sets might have looked like. In the early 1990s a set of five large paintings by Hoffmann came to light, appropriately enough in a castle on the Rhine at Worms, where King Gunther in the *Nibelungenlied* had his residence. These paintings, of scenes from the *Ring*, were made by Hoffmann after he had been dropped by Wagner and essentially represent his impression of what the sets would, and should, have looked like had he been permitted to realize them himself.

But that was not all. In 2005 a further set of fourteen of Hoffmann's oil sketches for the *Ring* was discovered by Max Oppel, a Munich dealer. These sketches, along with the five large canvases, were all acquired, after protracted negotiations, by the Richard Wagner Museum in Bayreuth and exhibited there, after restoration, in 2006. Yet more Hoffmanns surfaced in 2007 in the archive of the Gesellschaft der Musikfreunde in Vienna. These were two of an original set of three paintings, and proved to be impressionistic versions of the *Rheingold* finale and the opening of the third act of *Siegfried*.[10]

Granted that Hoffmann's sketches were not realized entirely in accordance with his intentions, these colour renderings of scenes from the *Ring* evoke unmistakably the world of naturalistic representation within which Wagner and his creative team were operating. Three cycles of the *Ring* were mounted, beginning on 13 August 1876, and musicians, critics, admirers and luminaries descended on Bayreuth from all over the world. What they saw was a staging rooted in naturalism and struggling with inadequate means to create an illusionistic spectacle. But the sheer scale of Wagner's ambition, and the fact that against all the odds he had managed to pull it off, was acknowledged by friends and foes alike.

We get an amusing glimpse of the feverish atmosphere on the Green Hill (as the elevated site of the Festspielhaus came to be known) in August 1876 in a report by the young Edvard Grieg, masquerading as a journalist:

> In the flat next to me there lives a composer of operas, across the corridor a famous singer, below me a celebrated music director and above me a well-known critic. Sitting here I can hear all around me Wagnerian themes being hummed, sung, yodelled and shouted up from the garden. Going to the window I can see Valkyries, Rhinemaidens, giants and dwarfs, gods and mortals, all disporting themselves under the shade of the trees. To get a bit of peace I shut the windows and draw the curtains but Erda's mighty contralto voice pierces the thick walls.[11]

One of the recently discovered oil sketches by Josef Hoffmann, depicting his conception of the cataclysmic final scene of *Götterdämmerung*.

For Tchaikovsky, also visiting the 1876 festival, the main concern was getting enough to eat and drink:

The tables d'hôte prepared in the inns are not sufficient to satisfy all the hungry people; one can only obtain a piece of bread, or a glass of beer, with immense difficulty, by dire struggle, or cunning stratagem, or iron endurance. Even when a modest place at a table has been stormed, it is necessary to wait an eternity before the long-desired meal is served. Anarchy reigns at these meals; everyone is calling and shrieking, and the exhausted waiters pay no heed to the rightful claims of an individual. Only by the merest chance does one get a taste of any of the dishes … . As a matter of fact, throughout the whole duration of the festival, food forms the chief interest of the public; the artistic representations take a secondary place. Cutlets, baked potatoes, omelettes – all are discussed much more eagerly than Wagner's music.[12]

Tchaikovsky would be glad to hear that the professionally organized catering operation at Bayreuth in the 21st century implicitly recognizes that

Scenes from Bayreuth
(1876), drawn by
Ludwig Bechstein.

the pilgrim needs bodily as well as spiritual refreshment. But the culinary privation seems to have addled his brain, for his initial judgment was of a 'truly marvellous staging of the work', even if 'musically, it is inconceivable nonsense'. It is true that relatively few attendees realized just how poorly the staging, for all that it was masterminded by Wagner himself, served his intentions. The more perceptive observers did notice, however; and even those unsympathetic to the 'artwork of the future' had to acknowledge that the artistic achievement was quite out of the ordinary. To be fair to Tchaikovsky, he did, hunger finally satisfied, end his report with an observation that more generously catches the mood of the moment: the *Ring* was, he reported, 'an event of the greatest importance to the world, an epoch-making work of art'.[13]

Wagner on the stage of the Festspielhaus during preliminary rehearsals. Drawing by Adolph von Menzel, 1875.

24 Wagner's Last Card: *Parsifal*

*One of the finest monuments in sound ever to have been raised
to the everlasting glory of music*
Claude Debussy

The sorcerer Klingsor makes a dramatic appearance in 1930s cabaret costume during the narration of Gurnemanz (right) in Stefan Herheim's spectacular Bayreuth production of 2008.

At once Wagner's most sublime and his most problematic work, *Parsifal* ventures into territory remarkable even by Wagner's standards. A pair of monumental acts, each set in a location designated as sacred, frames a third act that features a magic garden peopled by flowermaidens who inescapably evoke the luxuriant decadence of Baudelaire's *Fleurs du mal*. And it is this intertwining of the sacred and the sinful – elements not juxtaposed so sharply since *Tannhäuser* – that makes *Parsifal* the intoxicating brew it is. Described by Wagner himself as his 'last card', *Parsifal* seems to offer the composer's final thoughts on sex and religious faith, alienating many who misunderstand the content and purpose of the imagery. For those willing to investigate its ideological complexity and ambivalence, the opera provides profound insights into the human condition, expressed through transcendental music of unearthly beauty.

The magic garden for Act II of *Parsifal*: a painting by Max Brückner based on Paul von Joukowsky's design.

Wagner first encountered the legendary material for his *Parsifal* during that productive summer holiday he spent in Marienbad in 1845 (see Chapter 4: Under the Yoke), but it was not until 1857 that he made his first prose sketch for the work. In a charming flight of fantasy he describes in his autobiography how the inspiration occurred to him. He and his wife, Minna, had just moved into the little cottage (the 'Asyl') provided by Otto Wesendonck:

On Good Friday I woke for the first time in this house to find the sunshine streaming in. The little garden was in bloom, the birds were singing and I was at last able to sit on the parapet of the little house and enjoy the tranquillity that I had so longed for and which promised so much. Filled with this sentiment, I suddenly said to myself that today was Good Friday and recalled how significant this had once seemed to me in Wolfram's *Parzivâl*. Since the stay in Marienbad, where I had conceived *Die Meistersinger* and *Lohengrin*, I hadn't subsequently concerned myself with the poem. But now its ideal content occurred to me in overwhelming form, and beginning with the Good Friday idea I quickly conceived a complete drama in three acts, sketching it out in a few hasty strokes.[1]

We now know that it was not in fact Good Friday at all – as Wagner admitted much later in life – and in any case that sketchy outline of the work has not survived. Wagner made a more elaborate draft in 1865, but it was not until March and April 1877 that he finally set down the poem. The music was sketched between August 1877 and April 1879, the orchestration occupying him between August of that year and January 1882.

Wagner's chief source for his story of the quest for the Grail was the epic poem *Parzivâl* by Wolfram von Eschenbach, written during the early years of the 13th century. For Wolfram, the Grail was a stone with miraculous powers of sustenance and rejuvenation. Firm associations with the chalice used by Christ at the Last Supper, or the vessel in which Joseph of Arimathea caught the blood of Jesus as he hung on the cross, appeared with the Burgundian poet Robert de Boron (Wolfram's contemporary) and with the first anonymous poets to continue Chrétien de Troyes's *Li Contes del Graal*. Wagner was later scathing about Wolfram's treatment of the legend, and his own certainly effects a skilful compression of the medieval sources. The spear with which Klingsor wounds Amfortas becomes the spear of Longinus, who pierced the side of Christ on the cross. Kundry, the wild woman-cum-seductress, is a convincing, if schizophrenic, conflation of several of Wolfram's characters. And Amfortas recalls the pagan mythical figure of the Fisher King, who rules over a barren wasteland, the condition of which mirrors his own chronic sickness.

A 13th-century illumination showing scenes from Wolfram von Eschenbach's epic *Parzivâl*. From top to bottom: Parzivâl with Arthur and his knights; Parzivâl in a duel with Feirefiz; and Parzivâl recognizing Feirefiz as his half-brother.

Titurel (Ante Jerkunica) prepares to drink the blood of Amfortas (Alan Held) in Act I of Claus Guth's *Parsifal* (2011) at the Gran Teatre del Liceu.

Wagner's portrayal of the ceremony of the Eucharist in the first and third acts of *Parsifal* – the Knights of the Grail gather to partake of Christ's body and blood – has led many to the rash conclusion that it is a Christian work. But what Wagner found of most value in Christianity was its fund of myths and symbols. What he set out to do in *Parsifal* was not to provide a sort of Teutonic church parable or Passion play, but to draw on religious imagery to illuminate universal spiritual truths. Nor is it only Christianity that is so favoured: Wagner's fascination with the ideas of Buddhism, which also dates from the 1850s, is evident too in *Parsifal*, as are the philosophical tenets of Schopenhauer. Central to both is the concept of *Mitleid*, usually translated as 'compassion' or 'pity', but in Wagner bearing also the sense of 'suffering together with'.

In a letter to Mathilde Wesendonck, written shortly after he made that first sketch of *Parsifal*, Wagner captures the essence of the matter with a striking image:

Recently, while I was in the street, my eye was caught by a poulterer's shop; I stared unthinkingly at his piled-up wares, neatly and appetizingly laid out, when I became aware of a man at the side busily plucking a hen, while another man was just putting his hand in a cage, where he seized a live hen and tore its head off. The hideous scream of the animal, and the pitiful, weaker sounds of complaint that it made while being overpowered transfixed my soul with horror.[2]

If this kind of suffering can have any purpose at all, Wagner goes on to say in the letter, it is simply to awaken a sense of fellow-suffering in man, who thereby absorbs the animal's defective existence, and becomes the redeemer of the world by recognizing the error of all existence. (This meaning will one day become clearer to you from the Good Friday morning scene in the third act of Parzival.)[3]

Thus Wagner spells out the central theme of the opera: compassion or fellow suffering as the route to understanding the errors of human existence – a process of enlightenment to which Wagner gives the term 'redemption' or, in more religious mode, 'salvation'. It is this enlightened knowledge to which Wagner refers in a letter to Ludwig, addressing a question that goes to the heart of the work:

'What is the significance of Kundry's kiss?' – That, my beloved, is a terrible secret! ... Adam and Eve became 'knowing'. They became 'conscious of sin'. The human race had to atone for that consciousness by suffering shame and misery until redeemed by Christ who took upon himself the sin of mankind ... . Adam – Eve: Christ. – How would it be if we were now to add to them: – 'Anfortas – Kundry: Parzival?'[4] But with considerable caution! – The kiss which causes Anfortas to fall into sin awakens in Parzival a full awareness of that sin, not as his own sin but as that of the grievously afflicted Anfortas whose lamentations he had previously heard only dully, but the cause of which now dawns upon him in all its brightness, through his sharing the feeling of sin: with the speed of lightning he said to himself, as it were: 'ah! that is the poison that causes him to sicken whose grief I did not understand till now!' – Thus he knows more than all the others.[5]

That 'mother's kiss', in other words, that Kundry plants upon the mouth of the innocent boy in Act II – an osculation that throbs with Freudian tensions – is patently a pivotal moment in the drama. And it is so not least because of the sexual charge it carries. But its function is to awaken Parsifal to the reality of suffering and to its potential as the path to a

Kundry (Jane Dutton) with avian plumage in Nikolaus Lehnhoff's production for the English National Opera (1999, revived 2011).

painful but necessary process of self-enlightenment. Only through fellow suffering can Parsifal achieve wisdom – the wisdom to put aside egoistic desires and impulses in favour of self-denial or the acceptance of moral responsibility.

Such ideas – renunciation, learning through fellow suffering, the desirability of seeking release from the wheel of life in extinction or nirvana – of course chime with those of Schopenhauer (see Chapter 10: The Rise and Fall of Valhalla), but they are also part of a more insidious conceptual nexus that needs to be confronted if we are to penetrate to the essence of *Parsifal*. These are the concepts of racial purity and regeneration formulated by Wagner in the series of late essays (1878–81) dating from the time of *Parsifal* – notably 'Religion and Art', 'Know Thyself' and 'Heroism and Christianity'. The central ideas contained in these essays can be summarized as follows. Humanity has become debased and corrupted primarily through its departure from its natural vegetable diet. The consumption of slaughtered animals has led to a degeneration of the human species because of the assimilation of their blood. A process of regeneration is essential: it must be based on a return to a vegetable diet and rooted in the soil of a true religion. By partaking in the Eucharist and consuming the untainted blood of Christ, even the most degenerate races may be purified.

The concept of racial purity is of course an elaboration of Wagner's lifelong anti-Semitism. Finding it difficult to reconcile the idea of a redeeming saviour with the Jewish God of the Old Testament, in one essay Wagner even floated the concept of the Aryan Jesus. Moreover, the interbreeding of the Jews with the pure Aryan race is partly responsible, he argues, for the degeneration of the species.

The relevance of all this to the heady concoction of ideas in *Parsifal* can scarcely be denied (despite the best attempts of some who ought to know better). Only by expunging Jewishness, Wagner is saying, can humanity regenerate itself and achieve its full spiritual potential. For most of his adult life Wagner had harboured a fantasy: the liberation of the world from impure racial elements, and in particular from Jews. That is part of the message he intended to convey in *Parsifal*, though it by no means defines the whole. Where are the Jewish characters in the opera, Wagner's more naïve apologists ask? It would be easy to point to Kundry, the Middle Eastern, heathen social outcast, condemned like the Wandering Jew to peregrinate through eternity for taunting Christ on the way to his crucifixion, and whose baptism in Act III is of such symbolic significance. But in fact 'real' Jews never inhabit Wagner's operas, which deal in universalized expressions of idealism rather than explicit ideologies. The characterization of Kundry is, in any case, far richer and more positive than that: she is certainly not merely a focus for anti-Semitic sentiment.

How, then, are we to make sense of this witches' brew of Christian compassion, Buddhist/Schopenhauerian renunciation and racial prejudice? The key is the apprehension that the brew's ingredients are not

Parsifal
Kgl. Hofoper Dresden.

Eva Plaschke v.d. Osten.
„Kundry"

M.HERZFELD
DRESDEN 1914

Kundry as exotic temptress. Eva Plaschke von der Osten (mother of the tenor Wolfgang Windgassen) sang the role in Dresden and elsewhere in the early years of the 20th century.

as heterogeneous as they might appear: each infuses the others. Just as the notions of compassion and fellow suffering are common to both Christianity and Buddhism, so hatred – in this case of other races – may be seen as the obverse of love. Two sides of the same coin, love and hate add up to a world view formulated on the concepts of racial purity and regeneration of the species. Wagner's own compassionate conduct in his daily life receives far less attention than his egregious outbursts against particular individuals, especially Jews. It is well documented none the less. More important than whether Wagner himself was a charitable man is the plethora of compassionate utterances in both the so-called 'regeneration writings' mentioned earlier and in the text of *Parsifal* itself. In the opera, for example, Gurnemanz chides the Esquires for their uncompassionate treatment of Kundry, and then Parsifal for the thoughtless act of shooting down the swan. The final act begins with the welcome accorded the weary traveller and the washing of his feet, moving to the healing of Amfortas.

And then of course there is the music. Was there ever a more poignant expression of compassionate suffering than the Good Friday Music in Act III? If this passage, like the shimmering harmonies of the prelude (returning at the end of the opera) and the evocation, in Gurnemanz's Narration, of the 'sacred solemn night' when the Grail was brought down from heaven, touches the sublime, it does so as a sonic instantiation of a moral virtue. For all the pernicious aspects of Wagner's race-inspired

The Grail Hall, modelled on the interior of Siena Cathedral. Painting by Max Brückner based on a design by Paul von Joukowsky.

ideology – and this has its place in the work too – there is no denying that the light of compassion burns brightly throughout this work. Compassion and an obsession with racial purity are its twin poles.

It is all too easy to be diverted from the work's ideological orientation, or to wish to suppress it, on account of the transcendentally rapturous quality of the music. Certainly it has an aura unique even to Wagner's oeuvre. Debussy famously described the score as 'lit from behind',[6] while Wagner himself said that his instrumentation would be 'like cloud layers that disperse and reform'.[7] Nietzsche, too, for all his ambivalent relationship with the work ('I don't like hysterical women' was one of his first reactions to it[8]), had to admit that the music was 'incomparable and bewildering': just a few bars were enough to transport him to realms otherwise inaccessible. But what makes *Parsifal* truly remarkable is the fusion of the transcendental and the morally virtuous with an insidious ideology that was questionable even in Wagner's day, and that in the light of history most civilized people would come to regard with contempt.

That is the Faustian bargain on offer, however, if we are to understand *Parsifal* as its creator intended. Of course there are ways of recalibrating, even subverting, the message – and these have been fully and rightly explored by stage directors seeking to interpret the opera for modern-day audiences – but *Parsifal* remains a work whose glory will always be shrouded in its dark ambiguities.

In Stefan Herheim's Bayreuth production of *Parsifal* (2008), the rear window of Wahnfried looked out onto a bed and, beyond it, Wagner's grave, thus binding the history of modern Germany into a searching interpretation.

Amfortas (Detlof Roth) painfully holds aloft the Grail in Act I of Herheim's *Parsifal*.

25 Death in Venice: The Events of Wagner's Last Days

Triste – triste – triste. Wagner è morto.
  Giuseppe Verdi

The deaths of luminaries are seldom reported with forensic accuracy. Too often the testimony of the eyewitness is compromised by either the momentousness of the occasion or the desire to accord the narrator a higher place in the affections of the departed than is their due. That is certainly the case here, but – as always with Wagner – the process of mythification at the same time tells us a good deal about the subject and the way he was perceived by the world.

Wagner's 1882–83 visit to Venice was the last of several he made to La Serenissima. The family arrived there on 16 September 1882, moving two days later into one of the great Renaissance palaces on the Grand Canal, the Palazzo Vendramin-Calergi at San Marcuola. In poor health and suffering occasional heart spasms, Wagner was under the supervision of Dr Friedrich Keppler, a local physician and surgeon. The electrical storms and heavy rain on Tuesday 13 February 1883 might almost, for the

Venice as Wagner might have seen it: a view of the Grand Canal by Guglielmo Ciardi, 1889.

superstitiously minded, have portended an event of major significance. 'Today I must take care of myself,' said Wagner to his valet, Georg Lang, that morning. That much is documented, as is the fact that Wagner spent most of the morning working on what he had said would be his final essay, 'On the Feminine in the Human'. This is a fascinating fragment expatiating on the degeneration of the human species, marriage, polygamy, the Buddha and the emancipation of woman. Essentially his argument is that humankind has degenerated because the pure love of which it is capable has been corrupted by abuse of the institution of marriage. Only when the love between a man and a woman is liberated from considerations of goods and property will humanity achieve its higher state: polygamy is not the answer. The Buddha once felt obliged to exclude woman from the possibility of sainthood, but

> It is a beautiful feature of the legend that shows the Victoriously Perfect one [the Buddha] determined to admit woman. However, the process of the emancipation of woman proceeds only in ecstatic convulsions. Love – tragedy.[1]

What is less clear is whether or not Wagner and Cosima also had a blazing row that morning – as was attested by their daughter Isolde – supposedly over the announced visit of one of the Flowermaidens from the previous year's *Parsifal*: Carrie Pringle, an English soprano with whom, it is alleged, the composer was having an affair. The evidence for such an affair is slender, and while it cannot be proved decisively one way or the other, there are good grounds for concluding that the whole episode is merely the final flourish in a lifetime devoted to the propagation of myths.[2]

Carrie Pringle, the English flowermaiden. Lack of evidence for an affair between her and Wagner has not prevented extravagant speculation on the subject.

Early in the afternoon, at about 1.45 pm, Cosima sat down at the piano. Totally absorbed in her task, she played Schubert's song *Lob der Tränen* (In Praise of Tears). Although she had been a fine executant in her youth, Cosima rarely played the piano; Siegfried later said that he had never heard her play before that day. Paul von Joukowsky, the designer of *Parsifal* and now a family friend, arrived for lunch, and at 2 o'clock Wagner sent word that they should not wait for him as he was feeling unwell. Cosima went to check on her husband and reported that he had had further heart spasms. She stationed the maid Betty Bürkel outside Wagner's door in case of emergencies, and the company proceeded to lunch. When Wagner suffered his final, fatal heart attack, Betty was the only one to hear his cry for help. The most comprehensive account of what happened next comes from a novelist, Henriette Perl, who supplemented evidence from the household servants and from the report by Dr Keppler with colourful details from her own imagination. 'Frightened to death,' Perl reports,

the servant plunged immediately into the room, which ... was divided by a curtain into two sections. – Behind this curtain, however, she saw the Master laid out on his sofa, half-covered by his furs and his feet propped on an adjacent armchair.

As the girl later reported, the Master's facial lines were frightfully distorted, while weakly and painfully the words escaped from his lips: 'Call my wife and the doctor.'

These were his last words![3]

Those may indeed have been Wagner's last words, or they may have been simply the last words heard by Betty Bürkel. According to another

The sofa on which Wagner breathed his last, now in the Richard Wagner Museum in Bayreuth.

account, for which Wagner's valet, Georg, was probably responsible, his last words were actually 'Meine Uhr'. (In theory, this could suggest something along the lines of 'My hour has come', but more likely reflects the possibility that his pocket watch, a gift from Cosima, had slipped from its place as he struggled for breath.) A third tradition, apparently started by Hans Richter, has it that Wagner's last words were 'My son should ...'. However, if this was indeed Wagner's final utterance, his intentions for Siegfried remained tantalizingly unarticulated.[4] Betty Bürkel, finding Wagner in distress, ran to Cosima, who in turn hurtled into her husband's room, colliding, according to the later testimony of Siegfried, so violently with the half-open door that it almost splintered. The doctor was called, but it was at least an hour before he arrived to find Wagner with his head resting on his wife's breast. Realizing that he was not sleeping but dead, Keppler lifted him onto the heavily decorated lounging bed. On being told the truth, the distraught Cosima flung herself on her husband's body, and all efforts to prise her from it were in vain: throughout the night and into the afternoon of the following day she remained inseparable from the corpse. Keppler's report located the primary disorders in Wagner's stomach and intestines, but he notes that the consequent strain on his heart was exacerbated by his vigorous participation in a wide range of social and artistic issues. Keppler went on to make an intriguing and much-quoted observation:

The actual attack which precipitated the abrupt end of the Master's life *must* have had a similar cause, but I cannot engage in speculation on the subject.[5]

Did Keppler either know or surmise what had so agitated Wagner on that last day? Was his discretion inspired by a suspicion that Wagner's final heart attack was provoked by the reported argument with Cosima that morning – and that that row might have been instigated by the composer's undue affection for a Flowermaiden? This can only remain speculation, as can the allegations of unprofessionalism levelled at Keppler after his patient's death.

But if the doctor's report can be read to some extent as an exculpation, and if Henriette Perl's account attempts to claim more inside information than she in reality possessed, the subsequent rewriting of history by Wagner's 'faithful gondolier', Luigi Trevisan, takes the prize. Trevisan was indeed in and around the Palazzo Vendramin-Calergi on 13 February 1883: he was one of three messengers dispatched to find Dr Keppler. He seems to have realized at an early stage the potential for an embroidered account of Wagner's last hours, one that promoted the gondolier himself to the role of chief confidant to his distinguished fare. A quarter of a century after the event, an article, for which we must assume Trevisan was the chief source, appeared in an Italian newspaper according him a more central role than ever. According to this highly tendentious account, the gondolier himself saw Wagner fall to a couch clutching his heart, he himself gathered the composer in his arms and heard his last words ('Frau! ... Doctor! ... Frau! ... Doctor!') and placed him on the bed 'enveloped in his scarlet silks'.[6]

A sculptor called Benvenuti made a death mask and the body was embalmed. Notices appeared in the local newspapers, and it was estimated that the family received more than 300 telegrams of condolence from all parts of the world. On Friday 16 February the coffin, brought from Vienna, was carried from the Palazzo Vendramin-Calergi and placed on a draped gondola. The family followed in a second gondola, as described in Henriette Perl's purple prose:

> Silently they entered into the black-bedecked gondola, silently in the lifeless vessel they glided through the long watery planes of the Grand Canal, their eyes directed steadily toward the little boat that floated before them and that carried the sarcophagus, richly decorated with laurels and palms, in which rested the dear departed.
>
> The sun shone brilliantly in the day of February 16, it sparkled wantonly in the green-and-blue flow of water, thoroughly warmed by the sun; sadly the trees, agitated by the wind in the garden of the Palazzo Vendramin, bent their branches, as if to offer their farewell salute to the great dead man. – From the distance sounded the bells of one of the towers of this city so rich in campanili, it was the only music that the widow's ear, become so sensitive and intolerant, was unable to exclude. – A fearfully sad tolling, with which her tears began anew to flow uncontrollably and her heart almost stopped in its anguish.[7]

The local newspaper described the transfer, at the railway station, to a train, omitting to mention only that the 'funeral car' was a decorated goods wagon:

The exterior casket (since there were three other internal ones) was in metal bronzed in three shades, with a crucifix, cherubs, foliage, lions' heads, in Renaissance style. The funeral car on the inside was decorated in black and silver. With the catafalque placed in the mortuary car, some 20 *corone* [imitation floral wreaths] were set in it, and then it was closed, and the municipal physician, dottor Gallina, affixed there the lead seals.[8]

The body was conveyed with due ceremony by rail to Bayreuth, where the town was in mourning. Black flags fluttered from the buildings and the bells of all the churches tolled as the funeral procession wound its way from the station to the gates of Wahnfried. The burial took place in private, in the grounds of Wahnfried. The apotheosis and death cult, which were of suitably heroic proportions, are another story.

Cosima Wagner alights from the funeral car at Bayreuth (right) after journeying from Venice. The following day a solemn funeral procession wound through the streets of Bayreuth (below), as black flags fluttered from buildings and the town's bells tolled.

26 Perfect and Imperfect Wagnerites: The Spread of the Wagner Cult

Em'ly, this excitement is breaking me up fast!
    anonymous American lady to companion during performance
    of *Parsifal* in 1894, reported by Walter Crane

Caricatures from *Charivari* depicting the reception in Paris of Wagner's 'music of the future', 1860.

The sharply polarized opinions on Wagner and his work that are such a notable feature of his posthumous reception have been in evidence since the man and his art were first before the public. The colourful abuse indulged in by the London critics on the occasion of his visit to the English capital in 1855 constitute a breathtaking indictment of their profession. Allowed column after column (articles of many thousand words were commonplace), they paraded their fears and prejudices about the 'music of the future', which they knew only from Wagner's theoretical writings or from reports of them. They then proceeded to demolish the series of concerts in which Wagner conducted standard repertoire alongside excerpts from a handful of his recent works (*Tannhäuser* and *Lohengrin*, it should be noted, rather than *Das Rheingold* or *Die Walküre*, the latter not even yet complete). Of the overture to *Tannhäuser*, the critic of *The Times*, J. W. Davison, for example, wrote as follows:

A more inflated display of extravagance and noise has rarely been submitted to an audience; and it was a pity to hear so magnificent an orchestra engaged in almost fruitless attempts at accomplishing things which, even if readily practicable, would lead to nothing.[1]

Elsewhere he lambasted Wagner for what he regarded as his erratic conducting, his supposedly communist world view and his inability to spin a simple melody *à la* Auber or Rossini. Other writers, including Henry Smart of the *Sunday Times* and H. F. Chorley of the *Athenaeum*, displayed comparable critical acumen in their reports.

It is true that these critics were to some extent avenging themselves for a perceived slight (see also Chapter 9: The Zurich Years) – but it is also the case that their antipathy to Wagner's aesthetic theories was shared by many of their compatriots. Davison himself managed to come to terms, to some extent, with the Wagnerian *Gesamtkunstwerk* when the *Ring* was first staged in 1876, while his German-born colleague Francis Hueffer, who joined *The Times* in 1878, was an enthusiastic and well-informed proselytizer for the Wagnerian cause. The German critic Eduard Hanslick, though generally regarded as Wagner's chief nemesis, was actually more measured in many of his criticisms, which were motivated primarily by

An early parody of the *Ring* (1876–77) by Paul Gisbert (Paul Pniower), in which Wotan attempts to shore up the ailing financial system through a bank raid on two Jewish capitalists called Alberich and Mime.

a diametrically opposed aesthetic outlook, one that championed Brahms and other proponents of absolute music over those who advocated such notions as music drama and programme music.

Among composers of Wagner's era who rallied to his flag were Liszt (see Chapter 11: 'Most Excellent Friend'), Wolf and Bruckner. Berlioz expressed more guarded approval, while Grieg reported enthusiastically from the first *Ring* performances for a Norwegian newspaper. The *grand maître* of French music, César Franck, studied Wagner's scores closely and was clearly influenced by them, but maintained a certain distance from the Wagner cult, deciding, for example, not to make the pilgrimage to Bayreuth. The Master's disciples were less strong-willed, however. Guillaume Lekeu fainted during the prelude to *Tristan* at the Bayreuth Festival and had to be carried out. Chabrier resigned his government post and became a composer on hearing *Tristan* in Munich; his opera *Gwendoline* is plastered with leitmotifs and other Wagnerian fingerprints. Chausson and Duparc are among other notable French composers heavily influenced by Wagner.

The tone of this devotional posture was set early by Charles Baudelaire, who attempted to express in a letter to Wagner what he found potent about the music:

You immediately feel carried away, under a spell. One of the strangest pieces and one which gave me a new musical sensation is the one which is intended to portray a feeling of religious ecstasy. The effect produced by the Entry of the Guests [*Tannhäuser*] and the Bridal Procession [*Lohengrin*] is immense. I felt all the majesty of horizons far wider than ours. And another thing: I often experienced quite a strange feeling, the pride and enjoyment of understanding, of being engulfed, overcome, a really voluptuous sensual pleasure, like rising into the air or being rocked on the sea.[2]

The erotic strain in Wagner's work was to appeal to other French men of letters too, notably Mallarmé, Catulle Mendès and Villiers de l'Isle-Adam, while Joris-Karl Huysmans's novel *A rebours* (Against the Grain), first published in 1884, helped to establish the reputation of Wagner as a sensualist and decadent. The *Revue Wagnérienne*, which appeared in 1885, did much to popularize the Wagnerian aesthetic by publishing translations of his writings and analyses of the music dramas.

The *Revue Wagnérienne* was also the house journal of the Symbolists, who in both literature and the visual arts took much of their inspiration from Wagner. From the use of symbolism and leitmotif to stream-of-consciousness techniques it was but a short step, and if James Joyce and Virginia Woolf perfected the latter, then no one deployed leitmotif with more subtlety and ingenuity than Proust in *A la recherche du temps perdu*. Wagnerian symbolism and mythology permeate the novels of D. H. Lawrence and Thomas Mann, and a host of other writers, from Joseph

Anton Bruckner, a fervent admirer of Wagner, sought and obtained permission to dedicate his Third Symphony to him. After a tense examination of two of Bruckner's scores, the two composers drank beer together.

Conrad to Anthony Burgess in the modern era, also paid their dues. In Burgess's case the debt has often been expressed through parody, as for example in *The Worm and the Ring*, with its portrayal of 'Albert Rich' in pursuit of three giggling schoolgirls through the rain. The Wagnerian resonances of E. M. Forster's *Howards End* have long been acknowledged, but an important recent study by Alexander H. Shapiro has demonstrated how the novel is actually a reconfiguring of the fundamental crisis of *Die Walküre* – Brünnhilde's challenge to Wotan – as a bourgeois drama.[3] Shapiro shows in the same article how the plot of *Tristan und Isolde* is similarly reconfigured by Ian McEwan in his novel *Atonement*, making clear in the process how central Wagner's art is to McEwan's preoccupations.

In the visual arts, countless minor practitioners of the 19th and 20th centuries paid allegiance to Wagner in canvases that echoed the themes, symbols and *mises-en-scène* of his operas. Among major artists, it was again the Parisian avant garde that set the pace. The terms 'Symbolist' and 'Wagnerian' were almost interchangeable when applied to such artists as Gustave Moreau and Odilon Redon, while Henri Fantin-Latour's lithographs and paintings of Wagnerian scenes dated back to the Impressionist

Aubrey Beardsley identified Wagner's music (not unsympathetically) with the Decadent movement, as evidenced by the sour faces and décolletage of the affluent, predominantly female audience in *The Wagnerites* (1894).

The Third Tableau of 'Das Rheingold' by Aubrey Beardsley (1896), in which an effeminate Loge (centre), with 'rapid, flaming, tongue-like movements', provokes Alberich to transform himself into a dragon while Wotan looks on.

era of the 1860s; Renoir, too, painted a pair of overdoor panels illustrating scenes from *Tannhäuser*. German and Austrian artists, such as Max Klinger and Gustav Klimt, received their inspiration from Wagner via the Parisians; and Aubrey Beardsley, Van Gogh, Gauguin and Cézanne all came under the Wagnerian spell. Kandinsky's experiments with synaesthesia were influenced in part by the work of Scriabin, but his desire to combine several arts in a *Bühnengesamtkunstwerk* unmistakably reflects the expansionist ambitions of Wagner.

Russia also proved to be fertile Wagnerian territory, in spite of the composer's tenuous association with the country in his lifetime. The spiritual dimension of his art struck a chord with practitioners of the mystical,

Symbolist-inspired movement that swept the country at the turn of the 20th century. Wagner's theories and aesthetic ideas were actually discussed more than the works themselves were performed, and after the Revolution it was the anti-capitalist tendency of such essays as 'Art and Revolution' that appealed to Bolsheviks and intellectuals alike. Mass festivals were organized, often involving thousands of people, in a grand synthesis of music, dance, rhythmic declamation and decorative arts that demonstrably, though tacitly – art of the past not being officially approved – invoked the spirit of the Wagnerian *Gesamtkunstwerk*.

In Britain, Wagner's music was much better known: the *Ring* was performed in London as early as 1882, and only with World War I did German music temporarily disappear from the repertoire. His influence on the harmonic language of composers such as Parry, Stanford and Elgar is self-evident. Other late Romantics influenced by Wagner include Granville Bantock, Arnold Bax (born in the year Wagner died, 1883) and, most notoriously, Rutland Boughton. In the case of Boughton, only his early music sounds at all Wagnerian, but his keen espousal of the principles of the *Gesamtkunstwerk* inspired the conception of a commune of artists, living and working together, composing an English equivalent (the 'choral drama') based on Arthurian legend. No less important a role in the spread of the Wagnerian gospel was played by two key non-practitioners: the indefatigable translator and editor William Ashton-Ellis, and the critic George Bernard Shaw, who in addition to regular and trenchant reviews of Wagner performances, both at home and at Bayreuth, produced in 1898 a commentary on the *Ring* with a socialist perspective that irrefutably reflected Wagner's preoccupations at the time of writing the tetralogy.

Neither in Britain nor in France did the Great War result in the wholesale rejection of Wagner and his music that one might have expected. For a time in France the cloud of nationalism did indeed cast its shadow. As one commentator put it:

Siegfried, Brünnhilde, the Valkyries, Wotan, Valhalla, and the Rhine were emblems of German provocation and glory, offensive and hateful in a moment when we were fighting for our land and our lives. These broad identifications and the pressures exerted by public instinct, which had a certain logic and justice, gave rise to no opposition.[4]

But there certainly was opposition to the taboo on Wagner and, as Paul du Quenoy shows in a recent study,[5] the enthusiasm for his music engendered in the last decades of the 19th century continued unabated in certain influential quarters. Vincent d'Indy, for example, argued that Wagner's technical innovations – not least his emancipation of dissonance – had had an entirely salutary effect on French music. And in general the perception was that Wagner's importance transcended both ideology and national boundaries.

For Americans of the Gilded Age, Wagner struck a chord as much with his ideas as with his music. His critique of rampant capitalism, atrophied aristocracy and debased human values appealed strongly to those who yearned for the restoration of moral and spiritual truths. But the music gave them something else too. Around the conductor Anton Seidl developed a Wagner cult whose members were ripe for its intoxicating vapours. Respectable middle-aged women stood and screamed when Seidl conducted. For middle-class women of this period, Wagner's music offered a magic potion enabling them to forget their tedious, unfulfilling lives as housewives. As Joseph Horowitz noted in his ground-breaking study of the phenomenon, Lilli Lehmann's hypnotic delivery of Isolde's Liebestod at the Metropolitan Opera House delivered an out-of-body experience for many members of the audience too: 'The bad effects of husband and bedroom were silenced by a musical–dramatic orgasm as explicit and complete as any mortal intercourse.'[6]

The intensity of such experiences was evoked by the novelist Willa Cather in her short story of 1904, *A Wagner Matinee*, in which Aunt Georgiana, a former music teacher at the Boston Conservatory, now sallow of complexion and possessed of sagging shoulders and badly fitting false teeth, is taken to a Wagner concert by her nephew, Clark. As Clark relates:

The second half of the programme consisted of four numbers from the Ring, and closed with Siegfried's funeral march. My aunt wept quietly, but almost continuously, as a shallow vessel overflows in a rain-storm … .

Anton Seidl, whose Wagner evenings gave American ladies of the Gilded Age a sensual thrill they did not always experience in real life.

The deluge of sound poured on and on; I never knew what she found in the shining current of it; I never knew how far it bore her, or past what happy islands. From the trembling of her face I could well believe that before the last numbers she had been carried out where the myriad graves are, into the gray, nameless burying grounds of the sea ... .

The concert was over ... . I spoke to my aunt. She burst into tears and sobbed pleadingly, 'I don't want to go, Clark, I don't want to go!'[7]

Adulation of Wagner in Germany itself inevitably became entwined with the upsurge of Wilhelminian nationalism. Kaiser Wilhelm II visited and subsidized Bayreuth, and had his car horn tuned to a Wagnerian leitmotif. The spirit of 'Bayreuth Idealism' was enshrined in its most unadulterated form in the *Bayreuther Blätter*, the periodical established by Wagner and Hans von Wolzogen in 1878. Wolzogen's six-decade occupation of its editorial chair ensured a platform for Germany's leading racists and anti-Semites, who interpreted the canon, and especially *Parsifal*, as harbingers of a true Aryan culture. A regular contributor to the *Bayreuther Blätter* was Houston Stewart Chamberlain, whose *Grundlagen des 19. Jahrhunderts* (Foundations of the 19th Century) was a formidably influential proto-Nazi tract. The association of Wagner's works with Hitler and the Third Reich was to cast a long shadow that had still not been completely dissipated by the second decade of the 21st century (see Chapter 28: Swastikas Over Bayreuth).

Opening page of the inaugural issue of the *Bayreuther Blätter* (January 1878), edited by Hans von Wolzogen but a mouthpiece for the views of Wagner, author of the introductory exhortation.

A trio of solid supporters of the Wagner project: (left to right) Heinrich von Stein (tutor to Siegfried), Carl Friedrich Glasenapp (author of a somewhat protectionist biography of Wagner) and Hans von Wolzogen, editor of the *Bayreuther Blätter*.

Houston Stewart Chamberlain, Wagner's son-in-law, reading to Cosima in Bordighera, 1913. An influential proto-Nazi figure, he was regarded as a spiritual godfather by Hitler.

*If my grandfather were alive today, he would undoubtedly
be working in Hollywood.*
        Wolfgang Wagner

With its implicit suggestion that the Wagnerian *Gesamtkunstwerk* aspires
to the medium of cinema, or perhaps that the music dramas could most
effectively be realized through the use of cinematic techniques, Wolfgang
Wagner's comment quoted above belongs to a tradition of such observa-
tions almost as old as film itself. Making ironic reference to Nietzsche's
Wagnerian formulation 'the birth of tragedy out of the spirit of music',
Theodor W. Adorno in a famous essay suggested that in Wagner's works
'we witness the birth of film out of the spirit of music'.[1] For the Marxist
Adorno, deeply critical of the burgeoning culture industry of the early
20th century, such a parturition served only to confirm the decadent
features of the Wagnerian music drama he had previously identified:
film, in this sense, was 'derisively fulfilling the Wagnerian dream of the
Gesamtkunstwerk – the fusion of all the arts into one work'.[2]

The twin ideas that on the one hand Wagner's music is characterized by a proto-cinematic element, and on the other that soundtracks of
Hollywood films typically deploy Wagnerian harmonies, sonorities and
other features have long been commonplace. But it is only in recent years
that scholars, toiling at the interface of musicology and film studies, have
begun to anatomize the affinity of Wagner and cinema with anything
approaching systematic rigour.

The starting point for this brief conspectus of the subject is the
proto-cinematic nature of Wagner's works in terms of both the music
and the *mise-en-scène*. Wagner's own programme note for the prelude to
Lohengrin, describing the descent of a host of angels bearing the Holy
Grail, reads like a cinematic scenario:

At the beginning of the piece, the clearest blue of ethereal heaven seems, to
the rapturous gaze of those whose hearts are fired by the greatest yearning for
otherworldly love, to condense to a wondrous vision, a vision scarcely visible yet
one that holds our attention in thrall as though by magic force; in infinitely delicate outline the host of wonder-bringing angels emerges with ever-increasing
certainty, bearing the sacred vessel in their midst as imperceptibly they descend
from empyrean heights. The vision becomes yet more distinct as it wings its way
downwards, ever more visible, to this earthly vale of ours, till perfumes of ravishing sweetness well forth from its womb: entrancing fragrance wafts from within

it like clouds of gold, usurping the onlooker's startled senses and filling the innermost depths of his quivering heart with wondrously hallowed emotion.[5]

A visual picture of this scene, akin to that painted by Fantin-Latour in 1902, was evidently in Wagner's mind as he composed the prelude, and he was no less eager for members of his audience to conjure that picture in their own imaginations. For the Transformation Scenes in Act I and III of *Parsifal*, which effect the progression from the forest to the Grail Temple, Wagner and his production team devised a *panorama mobile* in which the landscape, painted on three huge canvas scrolls stretched between vertical rollers on either side of the stage, moved behind Parsifal and Gurnemanz as they pretended to walk. During the orchestral interlude linking Scenes 1 and 2 of *Das Rheingold*, the *mise-en-scène* moves

Prelude to Lohengrin (1902), Henri Fantin-Latour's depiction of the descent of a host of angels bearing the Grail.

Josef Hoffmann's depiction of the final tableau of *Das Rheingold* captures the proto-cinematic nature of Wagner's conception. The colour versions of Hoffmann's paintings and sketches came to light only recently.

in what has been felicitously described by Peter Franklin as 'an elaborate upward panning shot',[4] from the depths of the Rhine to an open space on a mountain summit. As Franklin points out, the music 'plays a continuity role here in smoothing over a disjuncture in the narrative' – as it often does in film.[5] But the changing scene and the music are also intended to be closely synchronized. The stage directions, from which the following are an extract, are distributed carefully over the relevant bars of the score – a cue-sheet of the future, as it were:

The whole stage is filled from top to bottom with black billowing water, which for a time seems to keep on sinking. Gradually the waves turn into clouds, which resolve into a fine mist as an increasingly bright light emerges behind them. When the mist has completely disappeared from the top of the stage in the form of delicate little clouds, an open space on a mountain summit becomes visible in the dawning light.[6]

Wagner's works are replete with proto-cinematic associations of this kind. Indeed, the orchestral preludes and interludes have often been staged by directors – Stefan Herheim's 2008 *Parsifal* and Hans Neuenfels's 2010 *Lohengrin*, both at Bayreuth, are just two notable examples. But another feature of Wagner's scores is a precursor of a specific cinematic technique: the mimicking by musical means of movements and gestures assigned to characters in the drama, known in film technique as 'Mickey-Mousing' after its ubiquitous use in Walt Disney cartoons. One example of this is the Dutchman's Monologue, 'Die Frist ist um', in Act I of *Der fliegende Holländer*. In his 'Remarks on Performing the Opera *Der fliegende Holländer*', Wagner stipulates the following:

The first notes of the ritornello in the aria (the deep E-sharp of the basses) accompany the Dutchman's first step on shore; his rolling gait, which is peculiar to sailors who have spent a long time away at sea, is accompanied by a wave-like figure for the cellos and violas; with the first crotchet of the third bar he takes his second step, – still with folded arms and bowed head; the third and fourth steps coincide with the notes of the eighth and tenth bars.[7]

Hopelessly over-prescriptive as these directions are for the modern theatre, they do serve to exemplify Wagner's preoccupation with obtaining a precise correspondence between actions on the stage and gestures in the music. Another example of Mickey-Mousing occurs in Act I Scene 1 of *Die Walküre*, where Sieglinde's movements are replicated directly in the music. The stage direction for her to approach the sleeping Siegmund on the hearth corresponds to three lightly syncopated gestures suggesting three forward steps. Then, as she bends over him and listens, we hear an arching motif at once eloquent of her tender concern and suggestive of her bodily motion. We need to remind ourselves, of course, that such 'mimomania' is not exactly unprecedented: it was a feature of 19th-century opera and melodrama generally,[8] while the *panorama mobile* can be traced back to the Baroque theatre.

The prelude to *Lohengrin*, as staged by Hans Neuenfels in his Bayreuth production of 2010. The titular hero creates a laboratory in which concepts such as truth and deceit, fidelity and treachery are to be tested.

Music and movement mimic each other as Sieglinde (portrayed here by the Belgian soprano Jeanne Paquot d'Assy) encounters the sleeping Siegmund (Georges Imbart de La Tour); Covent Garden, 1909.

Given the prolific nature of proto-cinematic elements in Wagner's music, it is hardly surprising that those scores should in turn have been plundered by the cinema. An early link was forged via a piece called the 'Nibelungen-Marsch', composed by a bandmaster named Gottfried Sonntag (1846–1921) working in Bayreuth. Sonntag's march, based on the fanfares used at the Festspielhaus to announce the start and resumption of performances, makes liberal use of the basic leitmotifs associated with the sword, Siegfried's horn call, Valhalla, and so on. With its title anglicized as the 'Nibelungen March', Sonntag's Wagnerian medley proved a vital resource to those compiling accompaniments for silent films. The march appears on cue sheets throughout the silent era, though, as Scott D. Paulin points out, its somewhat dubious pomposity served 'both for *really* bad Germans and for comically bad ones'.[9]

Sonntag's march was also much in demand, however – even, without any sense of irony, in Nazi Germany, where it provided a soundtrack for official Nazi events. The Ride of the Valkyries, too, was used in German newsreels reporting on Nazi air strikes. But the latter piece, along with other Wagnerian motifs, had in the meantime been appropriated by Hollywood in cartoons of the period, such as *Bugs Bunny Nips the Nips* (1944). This film, which unfolds the encounter of the insouciant herbivore with Japanese soldiers on a Pacific island, achieves the implausible by depriving Wagner's music of its German resonance, redeploying it to celebrate US militarism (Bugs's victory over the Japanese is here a metaphor for the superiority of American forces over German).[10]

Other Warner Bros cartoons made similar use of Wagner, and one study has found music from 10 of Wagner's works appearing in 120 cartoons.[11] Wagner's music, then, was at this point frequently, if inconsistently, inscribed with Nazi associations in films emanating from Hollywood studios. And, as we shall shortly see, the association was so powerfully engrained that it could still be drawn on at the turn of the 21st century.

In the post-war period, however, Wagnerian motifs were being deployed equally stereotypically in a different genre. Scores by Dimitri Tiomkin and Bernard Herrmann for respectively *The Thing from Another World* and *The Day the Earth Stood Still* (both 1951) draw on a stock of menacing neo-Wagnerian tropes, including tritones rasped by brass low in their register, recalling the Dragon motif in *Das Rheingold* (Scene 3) and *Siegfried* (Act I Scene 1). To some extent 'alien invasion' movies of this sort reflect characteristics of earlier horror and monster movies such as *King Kong* (1933) or the Frankenstein films.

Of the many films of this era freighted with Wagnerian allusions of one kind or another, both musical and otherwise, one may serve for many: *Pandora and the Flying Dutchman* (1951). The story and screenplay were written by the film's director, Albert Lewin, and based on the legend of the Flying Dutchman. In this mesmerizing and lushly Technicolor work, re-released in a meticulously restored version in 2010, a glamorous Ava Gardner stars as Pandora who, like Senta, gives up everything, including her life, for a 17th-century Dutch sea captain condemned to sail the oceans for eternity on account of a blasphemous oath. The charismatic James Mason plays Hendrik, the sea captain. The score, by Alan Rawsthorne, may not be Wagnerian, but the emotional intensity certainly is.

In subsequent decades, George Lucas's *Star Wars* movies (1977–2008) deployed pseudo-Wagnerian music – grandiloquent and

Pandora and the Flying Dutchman: Ava Gardner and James Mason in a Technicolor reworking of the legend, directed by Albert Lewin (1951).

Avenging furies: helicopter gunships attack a Vietnamese village to the amplified strains of the Ride of the Valkyries in Coppola's film *Apocalypse Now*.

aspirational – to underscore good-versus-evil confrontations on an intergalactic scale, outstripping even Wagnerian ambitions. In Francis Ford Coppola's *Apocalypse Now* (1979) there is an infamous scene in which the Ride of the Valkyries is blasted over loudspeakers by Lt. Col. Kilgore, as his helicopter gunships attack a Vietnamese village. The overtones of militarism and heroism in this stirring music were clearly major factors in its choice by Coppola, as they were for the commander who used the same piece to psych up his troops for an aerial attack on Iraq, early in the war that started in 2003.[12]

But there are deeper cultural associations at work here too. This is by no means an isolated example of Wagner's music being identified in the popular imagination with nationalistic triumphalism. It has been convincingly argued that the Wagnerian resonances of Hans Zimmer's score for Ridley Scott's epic blockbuster *Gladiator* (2000) draw on a repertoire of associations linking Wagner and Nazi Germany.[13] The nostalgic heroism of Siegfried's Funeral March is just one point of musical reference, and it is consistently reinforced by visual iconography (the eagle, and the legions and spectators geometrically ranged in the manner of Leni Riefenstahl's *Triumph of the Will*). In the process of creating an identifiable modern image for the imperial power of Classical antiquity, Scott and Zimmer have, then, dragooned Wagner into service. Much as one may deplore the facile linkage of Wagner and Nazism by means of the images they have in common, those associations are evidently so deeply engrained in the Western cultural imagination that even modern cinema-goers, many endowed with a less than profound sense of history, can be relied upon to decode them.

It remains to mention some of the many films that have concerned themselves primarily with Wagner, the man and his music. A very early example is the silent *Parsifal* (1904), directed by Edwin S. Porter, in which the action and music are compressed into eight scenes lasting less than half an hour in total. Not the least ambitious aspect of this film, which was released and screened in New York barely ten months after

Scene from a landmark early film of *Parsifal* by Edwin S. Porter (1904), in which Kundry washes Parsifal's feet. The tableau reappears in an advertisement from the *New York Clipper*, 13 November 1904 (below).

the controversial stage premiere of the original at the Metropolitan Opera House, was the attempt (not entirely successful) to synchronize the action with special phonograph cylinder recordings using the Edison Kinetophone system. Other early silents include versions of *Lohengrin* (1907), *Tristan* (1909 and 1911), *Siegfried* (1912) and another *Parsifal* (1921), wittily described by its maker, Max Reinhardt, as a 'Kinoweihfestfilm' ('a festival film for the consecration of a screen').

Another early landmark was Carl Froelich's feature-length (it lasted about 90 minutes) silent biographical film *The Life and Works of Richard Wagner* (1913). Not only was this one of the very first biographical films

Giuseppe Becce both wrote the score for the early silent *The Life and Works of Richard Wagner* (1913) and starred as the composer himself – a role for which his remarkable resemblance to Wagner ideally equipped him.

ever made, but it was also one of the earliest to feature a specially written score. Although successful in securing the rights from the Wagner estate to use the music, Froelich was not able to afford the astronomical fee it demanded (close to half a million marks) and instead commissioned a new score from a young Italian composer called Giuseppe Becce. The challenge for Becce was to conjure a Wagnerian mood without actually quoting a bar of his music. In fact, Becce's score draws on music by Haydn, Mozart, Beethoven and Rossini, with interpolations of his own.[14] But Becce made an even more crucial contribution: when the actor originally contracted to play the part of Wagner unexpectedly withdrew from the project, the producer, Oskar Messter, suggested that Becce take his place. With his ability to act the part of a conductor or pianist, Becce more than adequately fulfilled the demands then made of film actors; moreover, he even bore an uncanny resemblance to Wagner.

Among the other representations of Wagner on film deserving of mention are William Dieterle's *Magic Fire* (1955), starring Alan Badel as the composer, and with music arranged and conducted by Korngold; Ken Russell's *Lisztomania* (1975), in which the blood of Liszt drunk by a vampiric Wagner symbolizes the music supposedly stolen from him; and Tony Palmer's epic *Wagner* (1983) – shown abridged as a mini-series on American television – featuring Richard Burton in the title role and meticulous reconstructions of the events of Wagner's life. This film was reissued in 2011 in a remastered, wide-screen version ('as the director intended') lasting a mere 7 hours 46 minutes.

Joachim Herz's *Der fliegende Holländer* (1964) was not a biopic but a nearly full-length production of the opera – indeed, the first of any of Wagner's operas to be filmed. With its debts to F. W. Murnau, G. W. Pabst and Ingmar Bergman, it is notable both for its sophisticated cinematography and for the insights Herz's socialist-realist production brought to the work.[15]

Wagner (played by Alan Badel) surrounded by female admirers in the poster for William Dieterle's film *Magic Fire* (1955).

Stellar casting in Tony Palmer's epic *Wagner* (1983): the composer and his second wife, Cosima – here played by Richard Burton and Vanessa Redgrave – share an intimate moment.

Senta (Anna Prucnal) is pursued by the film team and director in Joachim Herz's remarkable cinematic version of *Der fliegende Holländer* (1964), which presented the action as Senta's dream.

In the early 1970s there appeared a pair of notable films about Ludwig II that inevitably contained a strong focus on Wagner. Luchino Visconti's *Ludwig* (1973), starring Trevor Howard as the self-absorbed composer, nostalgically re-creates the world of high culture of the 19th century, drawing on Wagner's music with none of the guilt-by-association it was later to acquire. Hans Jürgen Syberberg's *Ludwig – Requiem for a Virgin King* (1972), by contrast, suggests that the king's kitsch adoration of Wagner represented a harmless irrationalism in the German psyche that would be replaced by a far more pernicious version. Syberberg's subsequent *Parsifal* (1982) was an even more ambitious attempt to exorcise the ghosts of the Nazi appropriation of Wagner. Deploring the critical, socio-political interpretations of contemporary stage directors, which he believed had criminalized the German cultural heritage by associating it with Nazism, Syberberg wished to salvage the irrational, Romantic essence of Wagner, while nevertheless subjecting it to his own socio-political interrogation. The result was a cinematic staging of Wagner's last opera, located not in the forest or the Grail Hall but on and inside a hugely enlarged death mask of the composer.[16]

Since the turn of the new century, film and video have been incorporated, to a greater or lesser extent, into numerous stage productions of Wagner operas. The *Ring* cycles in Stockholm (Staffan Valdemar

The central role in Hans Jürgen Syberberg's filmed version of *Parsifal* (1982) is taken by two characters: a shock-headed youth (below left) and a virginal young woman (below right), representing animus and anima. Their final embrace signifies the healing of the psyche.

Cutting-edge digital video projection and 3D animation were deployed to remarkable effect in the production of the *Ring* by La Fura dels Baus for Valencia (2009).

Holm, 2008), Valencia (La Fura dels Baus and Carlus Padrissa, 2009) and New York (Robert Lepage, 2012), together with the stagings of *Parsifal* and *Lohengrin* by Stefan Herheim and Hans Neuenfels, respectively, at Bayreuth, are just some of the more notable examples. Syberberg, dismissing many decades of innovative work in the theatre, may have believed that film was now in a position to supersede theatre in the realization of the Wagnerian *Gesamtkunstwerk*; a more objective view would be that, while advances in film technology have enabled directors to capture the cinematic potential of Wagner's dramaturgy in ever more vivid ways, the theatre is in little danger of becoming extinct.

28 Swastikas Over Bayreuth: Wagner and the Third Reich

I was captivated at once.

> Adolf Hitler, recalling a performance of *Lohengrin* he attended at the age of twelve

As operagoers and the international press arrived in Bayreuth for the festival in 1933, they were greeted by swastikas fluttering from every building, by images and souvenirs of Adolf Hitler in every shop window and by Nazi propaganda wherever they turned. Ernest Newman, writing for the *Sunday Times*, described with mordant irony how, on settling into their hotel rooms, visitors found them well stocked with the texts of Hitler's

The Festspielhaus decorated and illuminated on the occasion of Hitler's 50th birthday, 20 April 1939.

The Führer greeting crowds from King Ludwig's annex.

Der Führer in Bayreuth-Festspiele 1940.

speeches and other material, together with 'a big book from which we learned, in three languages, that, far from the Jews being ill-treated in Germany, they were really having the time of their lives in that tolerant country'.[1] During the intervals in performances at the Festspielhaus, Hitler would appear at the window of King Ludwig's annex to acknowledge the stretched-arm salutes and ecstatic acclamation of the crowds.

Shocking as such images are to us today, the identification of Hitler with Bayreuth was no coincidence: this was not a case of a demagogue subverting an innocent institution. On the contrary, there were deep historical connections between Hitlerism and the Bayreuth ideal, and the ground had been well prepared. To go back no further than the turn of the 20th century, one can see the ideological battlelines between the traditionalists and the modernists being drawn. While the latter were entertaining such dangerous notions as parliamentary democracy, universal suffrage and secular liberalism, the former were consolidating their forces behind fortifications buttressed by concepts of nationhood and religious faith. Terms such as 'spiritual renewal', 'regeneration', 'redemption' and 'Germanness' were much bandied around. And as anybody with even a superficial knowledge of his writings can testify, such concepts go to the heart of Wagner's *Weltanschauung*, or philosophy of life. Convinced that modern Germany was in the throes of moral decline,

Wagner promulgated, both in his prose works and in his operas, an ethic of spiritual regeneration rooted in an atavistic notion of Germanness that celebrated the pure Aryan blood of the *Volk*. By the 1920s such ideas had become so endemic in the Wahnfried circle that its members could routinely unburden themselves of such sanctimonious nonsense as this:

Bayreuth is not only a sanctuary, a refuge, but also a power station of the spirit of that inner world that we might in a word term idealism. And so we who gladly call ourselves idealists should be as it were the conduits through which the spiritual power of idealism flows forth to other distant souls, as many as are responsive to it, in the world outside, which cannot satisfy truly living souls … . So we silently, constantly stand in guard over the treasure of art that may one day with God's grace transform itself again into a Holy Grail.[2]

To the Bayreuthians, parliamentary democracy and the supposedly decadent, liberal values of the Weimar Republic were anathema. Thus they were ripe for the emergence of the burgeoning nationalist movement of the 1920s.

Convergences between Hitler's world view and Wagner's are not difficult to find: the ideals of the heroic, the Teutonic and the 'myth of blood', or racial purity; notions of *Heimat* and anti-Semitism; even the predisposition towards anti-vivisectionism and vegetarianism. And yet there is little

Franz Stassen's design for a war monument at Bayreuth (1916) features an Aryan Siegfried, his sword, Nothung, and an inscription – 'Nothung, Nothung, New and Rejuvenated' – that echoes Siegfried's triumphant cry in Act I of the opera.

Hitler in the royal
box at the Munich
National Theatre
for a performance of
Lohengrin, 1938.

solid evidence that it was from Wagner's works or writings that Hitler
drew his inspiration. All we know for sure is that he was a passionate
and well-informed opera-goer with a particular predilection for Wagner,
whose works he knew intimately from his student years in Vienna.

To add to this aesthetic affinity, there also developed a close personal
association between Hitler and Wahnfried: not so much with Siegfried
Wagner as with his young English-born wife, Winifred. Fearful that
the homosexual Siegfried would produce no heirs, the Wahnfried circle
groomed the eighteen-year-old Winifred to bear his progeny and continue the Wagnerian line. The couple were married in Wahnfried on
22 September 1915. Winifred's first meeting with Hitler was eight years
later at a social event in Bayreuth, in September 1923. Swept off her
feet by him – less by his anti-Semitism (which she did not share) than
by his sheer charisma and those hypnotic blue eyes – Winifred invited
the charming, if socially gauche, demagogue to Wahnfried the following
morning. Before encountering Winifred at that hotel reception on the
night of 30 September 1923, Hitler had already paid his respects to the
great guru of Bayreuth, Houston Stewart Chamberlain – the English-
born propagandist who was married to Wagner's daughter Eva, and the
author of the best-selling racist tract *Die Grundlagen des 19. Jahrhunderts*
(Foundations of the 19th Century). Such was Chamberlain's reputation
that the ambitious young politician could not resist the opportunity to
seek his endorsement. Chamberlain was by this time too ill to communicate properly with anyone except Eva, but a week later he wrote a letter
to Hitler:

You are actually not at all a fanatic such as has been described to me; I would
rather prefer to characterize you as the complete opposite of a fanatic. The
fanatic inflames people's minds; you warm their hearts ... .

Houston Stewart
Chamberlain,
influential racial
propagandist and
Wagner's son-in-law.

Siegfried and Winifred Wagner with their children, Wolfgang, Verena, Wieland and Friedelind, in 1922.

Hitler enjoying the company of Winifred Wagner and sons at Wahnfried, 1938. From left: Artur Kannenberg (Hitler's household steward), Wolfgang Wagner, Winifred, an adjutant, Hitler, Julius Schaub (an adjutant) and Wieland Wagner.

The ideal of politics would be to have *none*. But these non-politics should frankly be stood up for and forced with all one's might on the public. Nothing will succeed as long as the parliamentary system holds sway; for this the Germans have, God knows, not a spark of talent! I hold its domination to be the greatest misfortune; it can only lead again and again into the quagmire and bring all plans for the recovery and uplifting of the fatherland to ruin ... .

That Germany in the hour of its greatest need brings forth a Hitler bears witness to its vitality.[3]

For Hitler, Chamberlain's benediction was significant not only as the first major endorsement of his rabble-rousing party, but also as a conferment of spiritual authority. The next day he was conducted around Wahnfried by Siegfried and Winifred. Standing in respectful silence for a long time beside Wagner's grave, he saluted him as the greatest German of all time. For Siegfried, allegiances were more complicated. On the one hand, he inherited the nationalist, conservative views of his mother. On the other, he was a more tolerant, less bigoted man than many of his contemporaries. Thus it was in 1924, when the Festival opened for the first time since the war, that the old imperial flag flew over the Festspielhaus, in unabashed repudiation of the Weimar Republic; the official Festival guide dripped with proto-Nazi propaganda. At the end of the *Meistersinger* that opened the season, the audience spontaneously rose to its feet and launched into three verses of *Deutschland über Alles*. Siegfried was alarmed. For all that such patriotic fervour chimed with his own ideological inclinations, he was astute enough to see that outbursts of this sort would play badly with large sections of the German audience, not to mention international supporters. Siegfried acted firmly, banning any overt association of the Festival with the National Socialists. A notice was displayed reading as follows: 'The public is strongly urged not to sing at the conclusion of *Die Meistersinger*. What matters here is art!' That quotation, from *Die Meistersinger* itself, where it is uttered in apparent naivety by Eva, was to be shamelessly exploited by successive generations of Wagnerites, not least at Bayreuth, to cover up dubious ideological connections.

Winifred more than made up for such aloofness, however, with the hospitality she offered Hitler. He visited her frequently at Wahnfried, often after dark, helping to put the children to bed and reading them stories. He called her 'Winnie', and she and the children were among the select few able to use Hitler's nickname 'Wolf'. Whether or not the relationship between Winnie and Wolf was carried into the bedroom is not a question that can be answered decisively. On balance, it seems not: Hitler put his mission of saving the fatherland above all personal and emotional considerations. But there is no doubt that they were very close indeed. Not only did Hitler make generous funding available for the Festival, but Winifred was also able to appeal successfully to him when she wished to hire Jews or homosexuals: Max Lorenz, Franz von Hoesslin, Alexander Kipnis and Emanuel List all benefited from her advocacy. Hitler absented himself from the Festival, however, from 1926 until 1933, when he came to power, on the grounds that he did not wish to cause an embarrassment.

Hitler leaving the
Siegfried Wagner
House, next to
Wahnfried, where he
stayed on his visits
Bayreuth. The whole
house was put at his
disposal, though he
always liked to be
joined for a meal
by Winifred (also
pictured) or another
member of the
Wagner family.

The productions seen at Bayreuth in the years between the post-war reopening (1924) and Siegfried's death (1930) did not stray far from the orthodoxy established by Cosima. Venerable stagings of the *Ring*, *Parsifal* and *Die Meistersinger* were dusted off, and there were two new productions: *Tristan* in 1927 and *Tannhäuser* in 1930. With regard to the former, Siegfried wrote to his stage assistant, Kurt Söhnlein: 'I do not wish to alter the staging arrangements etc. that have been traditional since Munich in 1865.'[4] It was hardly the resounding mission statement of a radical. And yet the staging did in fact incorporate a modest degree of innovation, in that a good deal of the stage detail was either removed or simplified. For *Tannhäuser* Siegfried engaged the avant-garde choreographer Rudolf von Laban to stage the Bacchanal, and his own handling of the chorus contrasted markedly with the stylization that had characterized Cosima's. The notion of Cosima's and Siegfried's productions as unremittingly dark is something of a myth: Siegfried's correspondence with the designer Max Brückner suggests that he was interested in exploring colour.[5] Otherwise, apart from some imaginative lighting, there was little to offend the Old Norns, to borrow Hans Mayer's felicitous description of the old guard (Siegfried's sisters Eva and Isolde and half-sister Daniela led the rear offensive).

In April 1930, Cosima, long since a reclusive shadowy presence at Wahnfried, finally succumbed to fate at the ripe age of ninety-two. Devastated by her death, and exhausted by personal and political tensions on the Green Hill, Siegfried suffered a heart attack, from which he never recovered. His *Tannhäuser* had already hit the boards, but Siegfried never saw it.

Given Cosima's long reign as Wagner's successor, it should not have come as a surprise that Winifred felt able to take over from her own husband at the helm of the Festival. There was huge resistance, however,

For his new production of *Tannhäuser* in 1930, Siegfried Wagner commissioned choreography from the pioneer of avant-garde 'expressive' dance, Rudolf von Laban.

Siegfried and Cosima in 1911, by which time Wagner's widow had passed the mantle to her son.

from the Old Norns and their associates, who questioned her legitimacy, especially as a foreigner. Winifred moved swiftly to establish her credentials, appointing as her general manager Heinz Tietjen, who as head of the Prussian state theatre system was already in charge of the Berlin State Opera, the Kroll Opera, and the operas of Wiesbaden, Kassel and Hanover, making him the most powerful intendant in Germany.

For the post of music director, the main contenders were Toscanini and Furtwängler, who jointly presented an interesting paradox. Toscanini was a renowned anti-fascist, a radical, but he regarded the musical text as holy writ, under no circumstances to be diverged from. Furtwängler, by contrast, was far more conservative, but his readings were notable for considerably more subjectivity and interpretative latitude. Winifred decided on Furtwängler, who as a German offered perhaps the line of least resistance, but hedged her bets by inviting Toscanini to conduct a *Parsifal* and a *Tannhäuser*. As the singer Rudolf Bockelmann shrewdly observed at the time: 'Two popes in one house; that will lead to schism.'[6] His words were all too prophetic, and much of Winifred's energy over the succeeding years was spent in pacifying one or other pontiff.

Many years later, Toscanini admitted to Winifred's daughter Friedelind that he had been 'madly in love' with Winifred at this time and 'regretted not having had the courage to have an affair with her'.[7] But Winifred's affections were bestowed elsewhere: not so much on Hitler as with Tietjen. For all that her children referred to him as 'the orangutan', Winifred was besotted enough with her intendant to be planning a permanent relationship and cohabitation with him.

A fortnight after Hitler's accession to power (30 January 1933) came, fortuitously, the 50th anniversary of Wagner's death. To celebrate, Hitler

Winifred and 'the orangutan', Heinz Tietjen (centre), with whom she fell in love, in the garden at Wahnfried. Winifred's children, from left to right, are Wieland, Verena, Wolfgang and Friedelind.

staged a grandiose memorial ceremony in Leipzig. It was this event that saw the first major apotheosis of Wagner as 'the fullest embodiment of the national ideal' and 'the herald of National Socialism', as Hitler's propagandist, Josef Goebbels, put it. Though not known for his passion for Wagner's music, Goebbels claimed that he had always been stirred by the great choral acclamation 'Awake! Soon will dawn the day' at the climax of the third act of *Die Meistersinger*. Now it should act as the clarion call to the German people, he declared, continuing:

Of all his music dramas the *Meistersinger* stands out as the most German. It is simply the incarnation of our national identity. In it is contained everything that conditions and inspires the German cultural soul. It is a brilliant compendium of German melancholy and romanticism, of German pride and German energy, of that German humour which, as they say, smiles with one eye and cries with the other.[8]

And so the work was appropriated by the Nazi regime, coming to be performed on all important party and state occasions. Not that *Die Meistersinger* is quite the uncomplicated work of light, love and laughter that its more innocent admirers like to believe; and yet the Nazis' exploitation of it was cultural abuse on a criminal scale.

The Festival Meadow scene of *Die Meistersinger* staged in 1933 by Heinz Tietjen and Emil Preetorius. Its massive forces were made possible through Hitler's financial assistance.

Hitler returned to Bayreuth each year from 1933 to 1939, but the Festival was never under party control, and the Nazis did not interfere consistently with artistic policy as they did elsewhere. It is true that Winifred consulted Hitler on major policy decisions, but she also succeeded in holding the line against both him and his associates on many

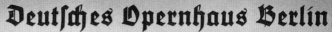

Deutsches Opernhaus Berlin

Zur Wiedereröffnung am Sonntag, dem 17. November 1935, 18 Uhr

Öffentliche Festaufführung

die Meistersinger von Nürnberg

in neuer Einstudierung und Inszenierung.

Oper in 3 Aufzügen von Richard Wagner · Musikal. Leitung: Artur Rother.
Inszenierung: Wilhelm Rode · Bühnenbilder und Kostüme: Benno von Arent.

Hans Sachs, Schuster	Wilhelm Rode
Veit Pogner, Goldschmied	Wilhelm Schirp
Kunz Vogelsang, Kürschner	Rudolf Schramm
Konrad Nachtigall, Spengler	Hans Heinz Nissen
Sixtus Beckmesser, Schreiber	Eduard Kandl
Fritz Kothner, Bäcker	Hans Reinmar
Balthasar Zorn, Zinngießer	Hans Florian
Ullrich Eißlinger, Würzkrämer	Harry Steier
Augustin Moser, Schneider	Georg Rathjen
Hermann Ortel, Seifensieder	Edwin Heyer
Hans Schwarz, Strumpfwirker	Hans Gillmann
Hans Foltz, Kupferschmied	Wilhelm Spering
Walther von Stolzing, ein junger Ritter aus Franken	Eyvind Laholm
David, Sachsens Lehrbube	Valentin Haller
Eva, Pogners Tochter	Constanze Nettesheim
Magdalene, Evas Amme	Marie-Luise Schilp
Ein Nachtwächter	Ludwig Windisch

Nürnberg, um die Mitte des 16. Jahrhunderts.

Chöre: Hermann Lüddecke. Der Bruno Kittelsche Chor. Technische Leitung: Kurt Hemmerling.
Nach dem ersten Aufzug folgt eine kürzere, nach dem zweiten Aufzug eine längere Pause.

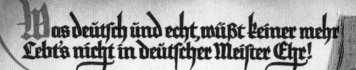

Was deutsch und echt, wüßt keiner mehr
Lebt's nicht in deutscher Meister Ehr!

Poster for a new production of *Die Meistersinger* at the Deutsche Oper, Berlin, in 1935. The designer, Benno von Arent, was beloved by Hitler for his grandiose, monumental effects.

occasions. Though regarded with suspicion, even hatred, by the party functionaries, Tietjen and his chief stage designer, Emil Preetorius, were broadly allowed to get on with their jobs unimpeded. Production style at Bayreuth was never subjected to the grotesque Nazification that was visited on most cultural organizations; nor were the Festspielhaus interior or specific props ever adorned with swastikas.

Hitler was in any case not always on the side of the reactionaries. When in 1933 a new production of *Parsifal* was mooted, the old guard deplored the idea in characteristically sanctimonious terms:

The sets, *upon which the Master's eyes had once rested*, still convey today the special, inimitable language which is insolubly linked to the consecration of the entire work … . Therefore, the undersigned old and young friends of Bayreuth urgently request that the Festival management not produce the Festival music drama Parsifal in any other form than in its original set design of 1882, and in this way it will erect a living monument to the Master of Bayreuth which pays worthy tribute to the completely unique and unforgettable essence of his art.[9]

The signatories to this so-called '*Parsifal* Petition', who included Richard Strauss, appear to have been ignorant of the fact that Siegfried had already designed a new magic garden for his 1911 revival (the idea that no changes had been made since 1882 is another tenacious myth). Hitler, however, was not only in favour of a new production: he even suggested

More or less willing 'guests of the Führer' on their way to the Festspielhaus in summer 1940.

Alfred Roller's cautiously secularized designs for Heinz Tietjen's 1934 *Parsifal* found favour neither with the traditionalists nor with those who wished for innovation.

Alfred Roller – responsible for the iconoclastic *Tristan* with Mahler in 1903 – as the director.[10] Roller's staging, as it turned out, was not the radical break with tradition many had feared: the Grail Temple may have been secularized somewhat, but the outlines of its revered predecessor were still present. The production was a disappointment to many, including Hitler; so, too, was the stylistically retrogressive one designed by the twenty-year-old Wieland Wagner to replace it.

Far more successful was the *Lohengrin* of 1936, not least because it was conducted by Furtwängler and featured a starry cast including Franz Völker and Max Lorenz alternating as the Swan Knight. However this, like the 1933 *Meistersinger*, was also a deeply political production, in that it was set up to celebrate the thousandth anniversary of the death of King Heinrich (Henry the Fowler), the first German monarch (876–936). But more than that, Hitler wished the new production to run in tandem with the Olympic Games being held in Berlin that year. As a result, the production became one of the most lavish ever seen, the stage filled with extravagantly decked out supernumeraries. Tietjen had a predilection for massive choral forces, which played into the party's desire for a monumental demonstration of strength, and so pleased was Hitler with the outcome that he offered the entire production and performers to Covent Garden in honour of Edward VIII's coronation. The offer was diplomatically declined. This overt politicization of Bayreuth was, it should be stressed, the exception rather than the rule.

On the outbreak of war in 1939, Hitler was insistent that the Festspielhaus should remain open for business and the following year he instituted the so-called War Festivals, mounted for military personnel and workers in the war industries. Winifred and Tietjen remained in artistic control, but the administration was coordinated by an organization called Kraft Durch Freude (Strength Through Joy). While Hitler wished his genuine passion for Wagner's music to be shared by the common people,

Monumentalism and triumphalism were once again the keynotes of Tietjen's *Lohengrin* in 1936. In the pit was Wilhelm Furtwängler.

the party propagandists saw it more as an opportunity for disseminating German culture. Wagner's idealistic vision of an audience attending free of charge was much invoked; the reality for these press-ganged attendees was rather different. Arriving *en masse* in special trains, they were fed, watered and quartered overnight before receiving a booklet and lecture on Wagner and his works the following day. Each of the five War Festivals was attended by some 20,000–30,000 'guests'. History does not record how many returned to the Festspielhaus in peacetime.

29 Regime Change:
The Grandsons Usher In the Era of New Bayreuth

Every generation needs a new revolution.
Thomas Jefferson

In the immediate aftermath of World War II, as Germans came to terms with the devastation of their country, and with the trauma and shame of the holocaust unleashed in their name, a new generation in Bayreuth had to decide how best to salvage the Festival from the taint of its wartime association with Hitler and the Nazis. Winifred was initially categorized by the denazification process as a 'major offender', the punishment for which included a five-year term in a labour camp. Perhaps to her credit, Winifred never denied her friendship with Hitler – nor did she until the end of her days – but she was able to argue extenuation in terms of the many persecuted individuals she had personally helped. Some fifty-four credible witnesses testified to that effect, and Winifred was transferred to a 'lesser incriminated' category.

A picture that symbolizes the necessary reconstruction process undertaken by Wieland and Wolfgang Wagner at Bayreuth.

Winifred Wagner with lawyer Fritz Meyer at her denazification trial in 1947. Her extenuating plea that she assisted numerous victims of Nazi oppression was accepted.

Wieland (left) and Wolfgang Wagner with 'Uncle Wolf'.

There could be no question of her retaining direction of the Festival, however, and of her children it was Wieland and Wolfgang who eventually emerged as the likely successors. But were they completely free of guilt? All the Wagner children had worshipped Uncle Wolf, and both sons had benefited from his protection during the war. Wieland, moreover, had maintained contact with Hitler right until the end, even visiting him in his bunker in Berlin. The innovations espoused by Wieland in particular over the following two decades largely obscured two facts, which have become widely acknowledged only in recent years. First, Wieland was not merely a member of the party, but an enthusiastic camp-follower well into the 1940s. And, as was finally revealed only in the early years of the present century, the so-called Institute for Physical Research, at which he held a post (possibly even as deputy to the director, his brother-in-law Bodo Lafferentz) from September 1944 to April 1945, was actually a satellite of the Flossenbürg concentration camp where the inmates were scientists working on a secret weapon.[1] Second, the designs and productions for which Wieland was responsible up to that time show little sign of his later iconoclasm – in fact they were deeply traditional.

But in 1945 Wieland took himself off to his mother's summer house at Nussdorf on Lake Constance, where he remained until 1948. It was a period he later referred to as his 'creative black years': a confrontation with the demons of the past, but also a fundamental reappraisal of his whole aesthetic outlook. Wieland read voraciously and immersed himself in a wide range of modernist culture, previously regarded with suspicion on the Green Hill. The writings of Freud and Jung, Brecht and Sartre were plundered, the art of Klee and Picasso absorbed, and the parallels between Greek and Nordic drama explored. New research by Ingrid Kapsamer reveals the particular interest Wieland showed in Freud under the influence of Victor Rosenfeld, an Austrian refugee who had emigrated to London in 1938.[2] All this bore fruit when the Festival finally reopened in 1951 under the joint direction of the two brothers, Wieland taking chief responsibility for staging, Wolfgang for the management and finance. Surrounding himself with intellectuals of the left, often Jewish – Theodor W. Adorno and Ernst Bloch among them – Wieland got to grips with the task of sweeping out the Augean stables of Nazified Wagnerism.

Given the economic devastation of post-war Germany, funding was inevitably a problem. One quarter from which finance was more readily available was unfortunately that inhabited by conservative nationalists and ex-Nazis, and the Society of the Friends of Bayreuth they founded in 1949 provided them with a boot in the door. The new productions decided on for the reopening were *Parsifal* and *Die Meistersinger*, to which the *Ring*, no less, was subsequently added. Wolfgang nevertheless very nearly succeeded in making the books balance, while Wieland set about forging the austere production style that defined New Bayreuth. (The *Meistersinger*, however, was a conventional production by Rudolf Hartmann.) Harnessing the anonymity and sparseness of Greek drama to the mythic universality of Jungian symbolism, Wieland stripped his stage to a bare minimum of props, deployed lighting to create 'musical spaces' and replaced the flesh-and-blood characters of the realist tradition with shadowy but resonant archetypes. The conductor Hans Knappertsbusch spoke for many when he affected to believe during rehearsal for *Parsifal* that the sets were still to arrive. Audiences and critics were divided as to whether this sacrilege was a dereliction of theatrical responsibilities or an inspired, richly allegorical reinvention of timeless masterpieces.

The thinking behind Wieland's bold aesthetic was expounded in an essay translated as 'Tradition and Innovation':

> Wagner's stage directions reflect the taste of his age ... . He himself was tragically disappointed with the realisation of his own instructions ... . Should one keep on blaming these defects exclusively on the insufficient technical facilities of the period? Certainly the argument would not hold true in regard to the costumes. The shortcomings suggest that Wagner's stage directions represent inner visions rather than practical demands, and that these, through the dictates of current taste and the practical limitations of realisation, changed of their own accord from imagined perfection to the best that was possible in the circumstances – the price any lofty vision must pay when it insists on assuming visible form.[3]

The iconic image of New Bayreuth. Siegfried (Bernd Aldenhoff) and Brünnhilde (Astrid Varnay) on the mountain top (1952). Wieland Wagner's radical staging swept away representational scenery in favour of classical, archetypal forms and stark visual economy.

New productions of *Tristan* and *Tannhäuser* were added in 1952 and 1954 respectively, and then in 1956 came another scandal: Wieland's notorious '*Mastersingers* without Nuremberg', in which the cobbled streets of the second act were replaced by a virtually empty stage overhung by a vast ball of leaves and flowers, and the colourfully attired guildsmen of the third

No trace remained of Teutonic supremacy in Wieland Wagner's 1956 *Meistersinger*. Instead, a handful of props suffused in violet-blue light evoked the midsummer Nuremberg night.

Wieland Wagner's 'blue and silver' *Lohengrin* of 1958 rejected supernaturalism in favour of medieval mystery. The swan was a projected image, while the immobile Greek-style chorus directly faced the audience.

act gave way to uniformly dressed spectators of the festivities. *Lohengrin* (1958) and *Der fliegende Holländer* (1961) completed the canon, and then Wieland began to revise his productions, starting with a new *Tannhäuser* in 1961.

Many of the leading conductors of the day available to Wieland were tainted by their associations with the Third Reich. Furtwängler, Böhm, Knappertsbusch, Karajan and Krauss had all to a greater or lesser extent collaborated with the regime or profited from the exile of those less fortunate or more principled than they. They were all nevertheless invited to

Furtwängler appeared at Bayreuth on its post-war reopening in 1951, but only to conduct Beethoven's Ninth Symphony. On his return there in 1954, he conducted the same work just three months before his death.

Martha Mödl (left) and Astrid Varnay take part in an impromptu three-wheeled Ride of the Valkyries in the Marktplatz, Bayreuth, during the 1953 festival.

the reopened Festival, though it was Knappertsbusch and Karajan alone who presided over the first year. Furtwängler was originally invited to be chief conductor, but on account of the involvement of Karajan, whom he loathed, he agreed to conduct only the inaugural performance of Beethoven's Ninth Symphony. The minutes of the Society of Friends of Bayreuth amusingly record his indecision:

Wieland has again been negotiating with Furtwängler, who, after saying 'yes' three times and 'no' five times, has finally said 'yes' on condition that 1951 turns into a Richard Wagner's Bayreuth, not a Herr von Karajan's Bayreuth.[4]

As for singers, Wieland first asked Kirsten Flagstad to be his Brünnhilde. She declined but recommended Astrid Varnay, who was accepted without audition. The wisdom of that choice became evident in recent years when Varnay's peerless Brünnhilde – regal yet deeply sympathetic – was heard again on the recording of the 1955 *Ring* under Keilberth.[5] Generally speaking, for financial reasons it was lesser-known, young singers who were cultivated in these years, though such names as Martha Mödl, Wolfgang Windgassen, Hermann Uhde and Ludwig Weber ring down through the ages. So, too, do those of singers subsequently added to the roster: Birgit Nilsson, Anja Silja, Hans Hotter, Theo Adam, George London, Gustav Neidlinger, Leonie Rysanek and many more.

Wieland's untimely death from lung cancer in 1966 left at the helm his brother Wolfgang, who was already resenting the adulation that Wieland by this time commanded. Wolfgang destroyed models of Wieland's productions on his death, and removed most of his brother's staff. He also began to cast aspersions on Wieland's ideological convictions (repeatedly drawing attention to his Nazi connections), on his revolutionary achievements and on the extent of his role in re-establishing the Festival.

Wolfgang's own productions (*Lohengrin* 1953, *Hollander* 1955, *Tristan* 1957) were simple and stylized but lacked Wieland's genius. The set for the *Ring* consisted of a huge disc whose many planes were

Theo Adam as Wotan and Ursula Boese as Fricka in Wieland Wagner's 1965 *Ring*.

The skeletal infrastructure of the disc that formed the centrepiece of Wolfgang Wagner's *Ring*, revived in 1970.

broken up and reassembled. Props such as swords, spears and drinking horns, banished by Wieland, reappeared, but the stagecraft was inept. Dissenting voices began to be heard, from within the Bayreuth circle as well as the press, expressing dissatisfaction with Wolfgang's abilities as a director. Wolfgang remained unperturbed, turning out a *Meistersinger* in 1968 that was unashamedly reactionary in its restoration of romantic, realistic detail.

Wolfgang's revived *Ring* of 1970 was more subtle dramaturgically than before, while his romantic, colourful *Parsifal* of 1975 courted controversy by allowing Kundry to survive at the end, thus establishing the female principle in the process of redemption. There were further criticisms at this time, which concerned a perceived decline in quality of conductors, the faltering standard of the orchestra and the fact that high-calibre singers were not responding to the call. Partly in response to the criticism and partly to obviate testamentary problems that might arise on the death of Winifred, now in her seventies, the Wagner family concluded an agreement in 1973 for the Festival to be turned into a national foundation: the Richard-Wagner-Stiftung Bayreuth. By the terms of this agreement, ownership of the Festspielhaus, Wahnfried and the Wagner archive was transferred to the Foundation, the executive board of which comprised representatives of the federal government, the *Land* of Bavaria, the four branches of the Wagner family, the Society of Friends of Bayreuth, and various other local governments and foundations. The Foundation assumed responsibility for the choice of Festival director and did what was expected of it by selecting Wolfgang.

Underpinned both financially and morally by support from all levels of political society, Wolfgang could have been forgiven for hunkering down behind a barricade of safe, ideologically neutral productions of the kind he himself favoured. Astonishingly, he did the exact opposite. Beginning with Götz Friedrich's *Tannhäuser* of 1972, he inaugurated an era of trailblazing productions as challenging in their dramaturgical innovation as they were radical in their ideological orientation. Friedrich's *Tannhäuser*, which related the work's spiritual battle to Wagner's own struggle against oppressive social conditions, was all the more piquantly provocative in that Friedrich was a Marxist practitioner of the Felsenstein school from East Berlin's Komische Oper. In his secularized view of the work, the pilgrims became ordinary people in everyday working clothes responsible for finding their own salvation. If this was not controversial enough, the provocation was unintentionally compounded, as Wolfgang amusingly relates in his autobiography. For reasons connected with the set and the acoustics a group of twenty-four chorus members, previously invisible, was required to appear on stage. Costumes had to be made for them at short notice, and some excess supplies of imitation leather were used for the purpose.

The first-nighters were very disturbed by the sudden appearance on stage of such a preponderance of leather-coated figures because they evidently associated them with members of the Gestapo and Security Service – a possibility that had never entered our heads. But that was not the end of our unintentional provocations ... . Many of the audience thought they glimpsed undergarments of infamous communist red beneath the chorus's stylized cowls of grey-blue net. Some claimed that the pilgrims had sung the East German anthem, not 'Hail to the miracle of grace!', others that they had heard the strains of the *Internationale*, and still others that they had seen fists raised in the communist salute – a blasphemous accompaniment to the pilgrims' hallelujahs.[6]

There was another reason why Friedrich's production irritated the traditionalists. The latter, forgetting that Wieland himself had once been the innovator, now regarded his work as normative. Friedrich, however, was not convinced by

the permanent half-darkness, the displacement of concrete human action into the far distance. I thought it must be possible to achieve a concretization of the human action which Wieland never found.[7]

His solution was to attempt to combine Wieland's shadowy mythic symbolism with 'intensive human action'. That mode of narrative realism, imported from the Komische Oper, was to have a huge impact on production style at Bayreuth and far beyond.

Yet the *Tannhäuser* scandal was but a premonitory rumble of thunder to the storm that erupted over the centenary *Ring* of 1976. The French team in charge of the cycle – Patrice Chéreau (director), Richard Peduzzi (designer) and Pierre Boulez (conductor) – essayed an audacious interplay of the mythical and contemporary planes on which the work is constructed, setting the action against the socio-political backdrop of the *Ring*'s first century, roughly 1876 to 1976. Equally radical was the degree of realism Chéreau brought to the acting style – theatricality as

Siegmund (Peter Hofmann) pulls the sword Nothung from the tree to the joy of Sieglinde (Jeannine Altmeyer) in Patrice Chéreau's landmark *Ring* production of 1976.

immediate and thrilling as it was rare on the operatic stage in the 1970s. For Chéreau, the performance of Wagner's works implies the rejection of the norms that preceded them and of the conventions with which the opera is encumbered.[8]

Responding to criticisms that he dressed Siegfried in a dinner jacket, Chéreau said:

People have come to realise in the course of the years that these are merely details that one must see in connexion with a greater idea.[9]

And, for Chéreau, that 'greater idea' involved a searching analysis of the extent to which Siegfried was truly free.

Two years later another East German director, Harry Kupfer, delivered a landmark production of *Der fliegende Holländer* that provided both an incisive psychological reassessment of Senta's predicament, in terms of socially induced alienation and neurosis, and an electrifying theatrical experience. Kupfer's *Ring* (1988), like that of Chéreau, emphasized the relevance of the work to the world of the late 20th century. In particular, the ecological aspect was forcefully engaged, the entire action taking place in a world already ravaged by a catastrophe, presumably nuclear. Kupfer's reading highlighted the message of the *Ring* that the abandonment of love and humanity's finer sensibilities in favour of territorial aggrandizement and enhanced material possessions leads to the despoliation of nature and ultimately to global extinction.

Other radical productions from these decades could be mentioned, including the *Tristan*s of Jean-Pierre Ponnelle (1981) and Heiner Müller (1993). Wolfgang's own stagings in the final quarter of the last century – the *Ring* (1970–75), *Parsifal* (1975–81), *Die Meistersinger* (1981–88), *Tannhäuser* (1985–93) and *Parsifal* again (1989–93) – increasingly came to seem like survivors from a prehistoric age of operatic production; and Peter Hall's *Ring* (1983) was one of a handful of productions that similarly flew the flag for a traditional, non-interventionist approach. The two strands, progressive and conservative, existed side by side, occasionally intertwining.

The cynic might opine that a series of scandals was orchestrated purely to keep the Festival in the headlines. A more charitable view would be that Wolfgang grasped the imperative for constant renewal, even when he was unable to generate it himself.

Harry Kupfer used the full depth of the Bayreuth stage (50 metres) and laser lighting to create a 'Weltstrasse', or street of world history, for his 1988 *Ring*. Here, Alberich (Günter von Kannen) and a Rhinemaiden appear in Scene 1 of *Das Rheingold*.

30 Renewing the Legacy: Bayreuth Today and in the Future

Open the shrine!
    Parsifal, Act III

With Wolfgang Wagner very nearly eighty years of age and the Wagner family as bitterly divided as ever over the past, present and future of Bayreuth, the turn of the 21st century seemed set to bring the question of the succession to a crisis. If the directorship were to stay in the family – the general assumption had always been that it should – then the most likely contenders were Gudrun (Wolfgang's second wife, an experienced but controversial administrator who had been with the Festival since the mid-1960s, latterly as Wolfgang's personal assistant), Gottfried and Eva (Wolfgang's son and daughter), and Wolf Siegfried and Nike (Wieland's children). None of the next generation, however, was deemed

Brass fanfares from the balcony of the King Ludwig's annex summon festival-goers to the performance.

Wolfgang Wagner
with his second wife,
Gudrun, and their
daughter Katharina.

up to the task by Wolfgang, who wanted Gudrun to take charge, eventually handing over to their daughter Katharina. Then, in March 1999, five months before his eightieth birthday, Wolfgang dropped a bombshell, announcing that the time had come to begin the search for a new director. That was the signal for a revving up of the hostilities that already existed between the various sides of the family; needless to say, the ensuing slanging match was lapped up by the media. Gottfried and Wolf Siegfried made it clear that, for different reasons, they would not be standing. That left Eva, Nike and Wolfgang's favourite, Gudrun.

In order to counter the objection that they were insufficiently experienced, Eva and Nike both selected running mates with impressive credentials. Eva's lieutenant was Wieland Lafferentz, the son of Verena (Wolfgang's sister), who after a stint in orchestral administration in Dresden was now running the Salzburg Mozarteum. He, in due course, was to jump ship and mount his own challenge for the Bayreuth

Wieland Wagner's son Wolf-Siegfried demonstrates the Siegfried horn to his sisters Daphne and Nike.

job. Nike's choice fell on Elmar Weingarten, the general manager of the Berlin Philharmonic.

Nike, formidably intellectual but bitter at her exclusion from the inner circle (of Gudrun she opined: 'We all know that she owes her position to her place in the marital bed, rather than any understanding of art and culture'), staked her claim in a series of statements that set out an alternative agenda for Bayreuth. Her proposals were as follows: that Wagner's earlier works – *Die Feen*, *Das Liebesverbot* and *Rienzi* – should be added to the Festival repertoire, as should operas by such precursors of Wagner as Weber, and a handful of Wagner's non-operatic works; the operas should be presented in imaginative, thematically grouped ways; the relationship between stage and pit should be coordinated with greater sensitivity, so that 'a steely, futuristic staging should not be entrusted to a romantically minded and over-reverential conductor';[1] and Bayreuth's connection to musical history should also be explored through the performance of works by Bruckner, Berg, Henze and others.

Eva – or Eva Wagner-Pasquier, as she is now known – for her part already had valuable experience, having held administrative posts at Covent Garden, Opéra Bastille, Houston Opera, the Festival d'Aix-en-Provence and the Metropolitan, New York. And it was indeed Eva who was chosen by the Richard Wagner Foundation (which has had ultimate control of the Festival since 1973) as the new director, with the stipulation that Wolfgang should step down after the 2002 season. This was not what Wolfgang had in mind at all, and he had no intention of going quietly. His series of contracts (twenty-six in all) with the Foundation, drawn up in and after 1973, made him secure as long as he was in a position to do the job. He also held a right of veto over the appointment of his successor. Once Wolfgang had made it clear that he felt he was perfectly capable of continuing, Eva eventually retired from the fray. But this left the question of what would happen if and when Wolfgang were to die. Realizing that the Foundation would be unlikely to hand the crown to either Gudrun,

Eva and Gottfried, the children of Wolfgang Wagner's first marriage.

rejected by them previously, or Katharina, who was still relatively inexperienced, Wolfgang moved to appoint a figure acceptable to all parties who could work with him for the time being and take over, at least temporarily, in the event of his demise. That figure was Klaus Schultz, former head of the opera houses of Aachen and Mannheim, and now of the Gärtnerplatz Theatre in Munich. Schultz was appointed as 'freelance associate to the Bayreuth Festival management', whereupon there was a temporary lull in the succession feud. Eva returned to her jobs in Paris and Aix, while Nike took over the summer festival in Weimar, renaming it 'Pèlerinages' to underline the association with her great-great-grandfather Franz Liszt.

Katharina, meanwhile, began to earn her spurs as a director in her own right, mounting controversial productions of *Der fliegende Holländer* in Würzburg and *Lohengrin* in Budapest, as well as works by such composers as Lortzing and Puccini elsewhere. Whatever the merits or otherwise of those productions – and they demonstrated a strongly interventionist approach – she proved herself triumphantly with her first assignment at Bayreuth: a new production of *Die Meistersinger* in 2007. Grappling with the troubling ideology that underpins the work, as well as its consequent appropriation by the Nazis, she presented a remarkably original take on the issue of progressive versus conservative values in a production of breathtaking stagecraft. It is fair to say that it polarized opinion, but

nobody could deny that, compared with the work of her father, it was a breath of fresh air.

Four months after that production opened, Gudrun's death was announced, a development that once again threw the question of the succession wide open. A period of manoeuvring and negotiation ensued, ending with the surprising but somewhat elegant solution of a partnership between Katharina and Eva. The half-sisters had discovered, the world was told, that they actually got on rather well. Relieved that some hatchets had at last been buried – though Gottfried and Nike kept up their sniping from the sidelines – the Foundation rubber-stamped the new joint directorship in September 2008. Wolfgang, now on the verge of ninety and physically and mentally incapable of running the Festival, had at last stood down. He died in March 2010, having held the reins since 1951.

Despite negative predictions from commentators who would have liked to see the marriage of convenience founder, the progress made in the years since the inauguration of the joint directorship has been impressive. While Katharina has demonstrated her commitment to a radical vision for the staging of Wagner's works, Eva has supplied the managerial and administrative expertise that any such enterprise demands.

The new regime wasted no time in opening up the Bayreuth experience to a wider public. The first 'public viewing' of a Bayreuth production, in 2008, drew an audience of up to 38,000 people who watched Katharina's *Meistersinger* on a big screen in the town's so-called Volksfestplatz. In the same year a new reduced-price category of supporters, called the Young Friends of Bayreuth, provided the chance to attend dress rehearsals; and a further programme of Wagner for children has been developed. Further opportunities for the recording, transmission and/or streaming of productions have been grasped, and the utilization of new technologies in other spheres, with the aim of broadening the appeal of Bayreuth and

A public viewing of
Die Meistersinger in
the Volksfestplatz,
27 July 2008.

Wagner's works, is equally encouraging. It was further announced in 2010 that Wagner's three early operas would be performed at Bayreuth in the bicentenary year, though not in the Festspielhaus.

Nor is the roster of guest directors and conductors likely to be anything less than adventurous, judging by what has been announced in the way of forward planning. Katharina intends to mount productions of her own, as well as inviting radical directors to re-energize the canon without necessarily expanding it. This seems eminently sensible. The Bayreuth Festival is as successful as it is because it is single-minded in its approach and provides the resources for executants to give of their best. Given that every ticket for the Festival as currently mounted could be sold many times over, it seems perverse to change the brand. There might be a case for an Easter or Whitsun festival, which would allow access to the Festspielhaus for greater numbers and could be used for a wider range of repertoire spread over various locations in the town. But a compelling case has yet to be made for changing an institution that gets so much right.

Criticism has been levelled at Bayreuth in recent years for the quality of its casting. This is indeed a problem, but the solution does not lie in the dream-casting in which some critics like to indulge. In the first place, Bayreuth has far from unlimited means and is not willing or able to pay the exorbitant fees demanded by many top singers (and their agents). A ceiling is rightly imposed and, if singers do not find the experience and honour of appearing at Bayreuth a sufficient incentive, then they are not retained. In the second place, the exacting rehearsal schedule necessitated by the demands of Wagner's peculiarly taxing works makes it difficult for top singers to devote the required time in the midst of a host of rival summer engagements. There are signs that Bayreuth, post-Wolfgang, might be relaxing its demand for exclusivity, but any advantage in the possibility of securing otherwise unavailable top-flight singers has to be balanced against the dangers of 'drive-thru rehearsal syndrome'.

Neither is the wider question of Bayreuth's baleful legacy easily resolved. Plans for the comprehensive refurbishment of Wahnfried by 2013 include a standing exhibition on Wagner and the Third Reich. Moreover, the new regime announced in 2009 that it was to open the Wagner archives to independent historians in order to lay bare, once and for all, the truth of the connections of family and Festival to the Third Reich. This is all very commendable as far as it goes, for historians of the Bayreuth Festival have been wilfully and obdurately impeded in their research for more than half a century. But the truth is that the really inflammatory material is not in the Festival archives. One day in the summer of 1976 Winifred Wagner and her daughter Verena cleared out all Winifred's private papers, as well as documents and correspondence left by her husband, Siegfried. Everything was loaded into a car and driven, on Winifred's instructions, to the Munich flat belonging to Verena's own daughter, Amélie. There they have resided to the present day, shielded from public scrutiny. Among this cache of documents is believed to be correspondence between Siegfried and Hitler, Winifred and Hitler, and Winifred and Wolfgang. It is these, and any similar papers, that need to be urgently handed over to historians in order that the full story can be told. There will still be plenty of room for subjective interpretation, but this will then be based on the facts rather than on briefings and leaks from disgruntled family members. Short of some kind of Truth and Reconciliation Commission, it is difficult to see the generation of great-grandchildren ever being mollified. The next generation, however – and in that one may include Katharina, as a younger great-grandchild – has less of a personal investment in the decades-long struggle of the Wagner dynasty. With Wolfgang's veto no longer in place, it is even conceivable that, when the time comes for Katharina to move on, her place could be occupied by a non-family member. As Wolfgang himself once observed, the succession should be decided by 'personal accomplishments, not by the inherited shape of chins or noses'. In the meantime, the world will be watching events on the Green Hill with no less fascination than in the past, as bemused by the still-unfolding saga of the Wagner dynasty as it is impressed by the calibre of its unique achievements.

Chronology of Wagner's Life and Works

1813
22 MAY Birth in Leipzig, in house known as the Red and White Lion in the Brühl. His putative father, Carl Friedrich Wagner, is a municipal official.

JUL.–AUG. His mother, Johanna, embarks on trip through war-torn territory from Leipzig to Teplitz, where she stays with family friend Ludwig Geyer, an actor and painter.

16 AUG. Baptised in the Thomaskirche, Leipzig.

23 NOV. Carl Friedrich dies.

1814
28 AUG. Johanna and Geyer marry.

1820
Looked after by Pastor Christian Wetzel at Possendorf, near Dresden, where he has piano lessons.

1821
30 SEP. Geyer dies.

1822
2 DEC. Enters Dresden Kreuzschule as Richard Geyer.

1826
DEC. Stays in Dresden with the family of schoolfriends when his own family relocates to Prague.

1827
Visits inspirational Uncle Adolf in Leipzig, then rejoins own family now back in that city.

1828
21 JAN. Enters Nicolaischule in Leipzig as Richard Wagner.

SPRING/SUMMER Completes grisly tragedy called *Leubald* and studies J. B. Logier's *Thorough-Bass*.

AUTUMN Harmony lessons with Christian Gottlieb Müller.

1829
First compositions: two piano sonatas and string quartet (all lost).

1830
EASTER Leaves Nicolaischule.

16 JUN. Enrols at Thomasschule, Leipzig.

SUMMER–DEC Studies violin briefly and writes four overtures (all lost).

1831
EARLY 1831 Composes Seven Pieces for Goethe's *Faust* (voice and piano) and Piano Sonata in B flat for Four Hands.

23 FEB. Matriculates at Leipzig University.

AUTUMN Studies with Christian Theodor Weinlig; writes Piano Sonata in B flat (op. 1) and Fantasia, also for piano.

1832
EARLY 1832 Composes Grosse Sonate in A major.

APR.–JUN. Composes Symphony in C major

SEP.–OCT. Brief infatuation with daughter of Count Pachta, on whose estate at Pravonin, near Prague, he stays. Begins to sketch opera, *Die Hochzeit* (later abandoned).

1833
JAN./FEB. Joins brother Albert in Würzburg, taking post as chorus master at theatre. Text for *Die Feen* (music completed 6 Jan. 1834). Brief fling with soprano Therese Ringelmann.

1834
21 JAN. Returns to Leipzig, where he encounters Young Germany.

END JUL. Becomes musical director of Heinrich Bethmann's travelling company based in Magdeburg.

SUMMER Falls in love with actress Minna Planer; conducts *Don Giovanni*.

1835
JAN. Begins *Das Liebesverbot*.

1836
29 MAR. Premiere of *Das Liebesverbot* in Magdeburg.

APR. Bankruptcy of Bethmann company.

24 NOV. Marries Minna in Königsberg-Tragheim.

1837
MAR. Composes *Rule Britannia* Overture.

1 APR. Appointed musical director at Königsberg Theatre.

MAY–JUL. Minna leaves him; he pursues her and they stay at Blasewitz, near Dresden, where he reads Bulwer-Lytton's novel *Rienzi*, on which subject he sketches an opera.

JUN. Appointed musical director at theatre in Riga.

1838
SUMMER Begins Singspiel *Männerlist grösser als Frauenlist*, but abandons after completing only two numbers.

AUG. Completes poem of *Rienzi* and begins music.

1839
JUN.–JUL. Burdened with debts and now unemployed, he leaves Riga clandestinely with Minna. Minna suffers miscarriage. Turbulent crossing to London (arrives 12 Aug.).

AUG.–SEP. Continues to France, eventually arriving in Paris.

24 NOV. Premiere of Berlioz's *Roméo et Juliette* makes deep impression.

DEC. Begins what is to become *Faust* Symphony.

1840
6 MAY Sends prose sketch of *Der fliegende Holländer* to Scribe and (Jun.) to Meyerbeer.

MAY–JUL. Begins music of *Holländer*.

OCT./NOV. Narrowly escapes debtors' gaol.

19 NOV. Completes *Rienzi*.

1841
18–28 MAY Writes poem of *Holländer*.

NOV. Completes score of *Holländer*.

1842
7 APR. Leaves Paris with Minna and heads for Dresden.

JUN.–JUL. Summer holiday in Teplitz, where he makes prose draft of *Tannhäuser*.

20 OCT. Premiere of *Rienzi* in Dresden under Reissiger is resounding success.

1843
2 JAN. Premiere of *Der fliegende Holländer* under Wagner's own baton virtually assures him of job offer of Kapellmeister at king of Saxony's court.

2 FEB. Accepts job, after some hesitation.

APR. Completes poem of *Tannhäuser*.

6 JUL. Conducts gala performance, with some 1,200 singers, of new choral work *Das Liebesmahl der Apostel* in Dresden Frauenkirche.

1 OCT. Moves to more spacious apartment in the Ostra-Allee, where he begins to assemble an impressive library of ancient and contemporary material.

1844
14–15 DEC. His *Trauermusik* played at ceremony for transferral of Weber's remains from London to Dresden, followed by delivery of oration at graveside.

1845
13 APR. Completes score of *Tannhäuser*.

3 JUL. Visits Marienbad with Minna, dog and parrot to take waters; immerses himself simultaneously in Parzivâl and Lohengrin legends.

16 JUL. Prose draft for *Die Meistersinger* completed.

3 AUG. Prose draft for *Lohengrin* completed.

19 OCT. Premiere of *Tannhäuser* in Dresden.

1846
2 MAR. Submits report about reorganization of royal orchestra.

5 APR. Performance of Beethoven's Ninth Symphony at traditional Palm Sunday concert under his baton is a triumph in both musical and public-relations terms.

30 JUL. Finishes first complete draft of *Lohengrin*.

OCT. Prose sketch for five-act work (probably an opera) on legend of Friedrich Barbarossa.

1847

24 FEB. Conducts own version of Gluck's *Iphigénie en Aulide*.

29 AUG. Finishes second complete draft of *Lohengrin*.

(1847) Reads several Greek plays in translation, including *Oresteia* trilogy.

1848

9 JAN. Death of mother in Leipzig.

FEB. Uprising in Paris.

MAR. Uprising in Vienna, greeted enthusiastically by Wagner.

28 APR. Completes score of *Lohengrin*.

MAY Submits radical *Plan for the Organization of a German National Theatre for the Kingdom of Saxony*, which oddly fails to find favour with his superiors.

14 JUN. Delivers address to republican Vaterlandsverein. Around this time meets Russian anarchist Bakunin.

4 OCT. Prose résumé for *Ring*, called *Der Nibelungen-Mythus*.

AUTUMN Above résumé turned into libretto, called *Siegfrieds Tod*.

1849

JAN.–APR. Scenario for five-act drama (probably opera): *Jesus von Nazareth*.

APR.–MAY Active in revolutionary struggle, narrowly escaping arrest; flees to Switzerland and thence Paris.

JUL. Settles down in Zurich; writes 'Art and Revolution'.

4 NOV. Completes 'The Artwork of the Future'.

DEC. Begins prose draft for opera *Wieland der Schmied* (not completed).

1850

JAN. Annual allowance of 3,000 francs proposed by Julie Ritter and Jessie Laussot.

MAR.–MAY Affair with Laussot in Bordeaux, but subsequent elopement to Greece or Asia Minor thwarted by her husband.

3 JUL. Returns to Zurich and Minna.

SUMMER Musical sketches for *Siegfrieds Tod* (later *Götterdämmerung*).

28 AUG. Premiere of *Lohengrin* in Weimar under Liszt.

SEP. Publishes 'Jewishness in Music'.

WINTER Writes 'Opera and Drama' (completed 10 Jan. 1851).

1851

MAY Sketches *Der junge Siegfried* (later *Siegfried*), then writes poem (Jun.).

JUL.–AUG. Writes 'A Communication to my Friends'.

15 SEP. Begins rigorous regimen at the Albisbrunn hydropathic establishment, in the hope of alleviating erysipelas and constipation.

AUTUMN Prose sketches for *Rheingold* and *Walküre*.

DEC. Wagner, still hoping for revolution, expected to start in France, refuses to acknowledge 1852.

1852

FEB. Meets Otto and Mathilde Wesendonck, and subsequently François and Eliza Wille, and Georg Herwegh.

APR.–MAY Conducts *Holländer* in Zurich.

1 JUL. Verse draft of *Walküre* completed.

3 NOV. Verse draft of *Rheingold* completed.

NOV.–DEC Revisions of texts for *Der junge Siegfried* and *Siegfrieds Tod*.

(1852) Suffers depression and contemplates suicide; these moods continue until 1857.

1853

Publishes fifty copies of complete *Ring* poem and reads it to invited audience at Hôtel Baur au Lac in Zurich.

JUL. Liszt visits and impresses Wagner with his *Faust* Symphony and symphonic poems.

AUG.–SEP. Italian holiday, during which inspiration for opening of *Rheingold* supposedly occurs in a dream experience in a La Spezia hotel.

10 OCT. Meets fifteen-year-old Cosima Liszt in Paris.

1 NOV. Begins complete draft of *Rheingold*.

1854

28 JUN. Begins complete draft of *Walküre*.

SEP. Otto Wesendonck settles his debts in part, providing regular allowance in exchange for receipts from future performances.

SEP./OCT. Herwegh introduces him to philosophy of Schopenhauer. Conceives *Tristan*, presumably under pressure of infatuation with Mathilde Wesendonck.

1855

MAR.–JUN. Conducts eight concerts in London for Philharmonic Society.

1856

MAY Prose sketch for projected Buddhist opera *Die Sieger*.

SEP. Begins composition of *Siegfried*.

19 DEC. First dated musical sketches for *Tristan*.

1857

APR. Occupies the Asyl, adjoining the Wesendoncks' villa in the Zurich suburb of Enge. Conceives *Parsifal*.

9 AUG. Breaks off composition of *Siegfried* at end of Act II.

SEP. Hans von Bülow and his bride, Cosima, stay with the Wagners on their honeymoon.

(1857) Passion for Mathilde Wesendonck reciprocated; works on *Tristan* and sets five of Mathilde's poems to music.

1858

17 AUG. Marital tensions on the Green Hill force departure from Asyl.

29 AUG. Arrives in Venice with Karl Ritter and stays in apartment in Palazzo Giustiniani on Grand Canal. Works on Act II of *Tristan* and confides feelings to 'Venice Diary'.

1859

24 MAR. To Lucerne, where he completes Act III of *Tristan*.

6 AUG. Completes full score of *Tristan*.

SEP. Otto Wesendonck buys copyright in four *Ring* scores for 6,000 francs each.

10 SEP. Settles in Paris, where he remains until Jul. 1861.

17 NOV. Minna arrives with dog and parrot; attempt to salvage marriage.

1860

JAN.–FEB. Conducts three concerts of his music in Paris.

12 AUG. Partial amnesty allows him to return to Germany, but not yet to Saxony.

1861

MAR. Fiasco orchestrated by Jockey Club forces *Tannhäuser* to be withdrawn from stage of Paris Opéra after three performances.

NOV. Visits Wesendoncks in Venice. Embarks on *Die Meistersinger*.

1862

28 MAR. Full amnesty enables him to re-enter Saxony.

NOV. Last meeting with Minna in Dresden.

23 NOV. Public reading of *Meistersinger* poem in Vienna, where he is now staying in luxurious style, with the help of the milliner and seamstress Bertha Goldwag.

1863

JAN.–APR. Gives concerts of his music in Prague, St Petersburg and Moscow.

MAY Decks out new apartment in Penzing, near Vienna, in luxurious style.

JUL.–DEC. Further concerts in Budapest, Prague, Karlsruhe, Breslau and Vienna.

NOV. Wagner and Cosima von Bülow commit themselves to each other 'with sobs and tears' (*Mein Leben*).

1864

MAR. Mounting debts force Wagner to leave Vienna to escape arrest; takes refuge with Eliza Wille at Mariafeld.

10 MAR. Solvency crisis solved by accession to power of eighteen-year-old King Ludwig II of Bavaria, who pays off his debts and subsequently authorizes generous annual stipend. Wagner moves into house near royal castle Schloss Berg, overlooking Lake Starnberg, near Munich.

JUN. Cosima arrives at Starnberg with two daughters; union with Wagner consummated.

OCT. Moves into spacious house at 21 Briennerstrasse in Munich.

1865

10 APR. Wagner's first child, Isolde, born to Cosima.

10 JUN. Premiere of *Tristan* in Munich under Bülow. Begins to dictate autobiography *Mein Leben* to Cosima.

10 DEC. Forced to leave Munich following pressure from court officials and press.

1866

25 JAN. Minna dies in Dresden.

8 MAR. Cosima joins him in Geneva; they decide to make the house Tribschen, on Lake Lucerne, their home.

1867

17 FEB. Birth of second daughter, Eva.

APR. Bülow appointed court Kapellmeister to Ludwig and director of proposed music school.

24 OCT. Full score of *Die Meistersinger* finished.

23 DEC. Returns to Munich and stays there until early 1868.

1868

21 JUN. Triumphant premiere of *Die Meistersinger* in Munich under Bülow.

SEP.–OCT. Travels to Italy with Cosima.

8 NOV. Meets Nietzsche in Leipzig.

16 NOV. Cosima finally moves into Tribschen with Isolde and Eva.

1869

1 MAR. Resumes work on the *Ring* with Act III of *Siegfried*.

SPRING 'Jewishness in Music' reprinted.

6 JUN. Birth of son, Siegfried; Nietzsche present at Tribschen and visits frequently thereafter.

JUL. Visited by three French admirers: Judith Gautier, her husband, Catulle Mendès, and the poet Villiers de l'Isle-Adam.

22 SEP. *Rheingold* performed in Munich under Franz Wüllner, despite Wagner's strenuous efforts to prevent it.

DEC Reads *Parsifal* sketch to Nietzsche.

1870

26 JUN. Premiere of *Die Walküre* in Munich.

JUL. Bülows' marriage legally dissolved. Outbreak of Franco-Prussian War coincides with visit by another French entourage.

25 AUG. Marriage of Wagner and Cosima in Protestant church in Lucerne.

7 SEP. Completes 'Beethoven' essay.

25 DEC. *Siegfried Idyll* performed on staircase at Tribschen in honour of Cosima's birthday.

1871

5 FEB. *Siegfried* completed.

APR. Wagners visit Bayreuth and decide to build new theatre.

NOV. Friedrich Feustel, chair of Bayreuth town council, offers any site Wagner chooses for theatre.

1872

FEB. Selects site adjoining palace gardens in Bayreuth for future home, Wahnfried, and the 'Green Hill' of Bürgerreuth for theatre itself. Society of Patrons of the Bayreuth Festival established.

22 MAY Foundation stone of theatre laid.

END SEP. Move into temporary home in Bayreuth at Dammallee 7.

OCT. Liszt makes first visit to Bayreuth. Cosima converts to Protestantism.

NOV.–DEC. Wagner and Cosima undertake tour of Germany's opera houses in search of singers.

1873

JAN.–FEB. (also Apr.) Further tours to scout for artists. Wagner also conducts fundraising concerts.

SEP. Bruckner visits Wagner in Bayreuth and requests permission to dedicate symphony to him.

NOV. In view of threat to Festival through lack of funds, Wagner approaches Ludwig for help.

1874

JAN. Ludwig initially refuses help but subsequently extends loan of 100,000 thalers.

28 APR. Wagners move into new home, Wahnfried.

JUN.–SEP. Rehearsals for *Ring* with conductor Hans Richter and singers.

21 NOV. Finishes score of *Götterdämmerung* and thus entire *Ring*.

1875

FEB.–MAY Concert tours of Vienna, Budapest and Berlin; travels also to Leipzig, Hanover and Brunswick.

JUL.–AUG. Rehearsals for the *Ring* with soloists and orchestra. All energies directed towards realization of Festival the following year.

1876

FEB.–MAR. Composes *Grosser Festmarsch*, a commission to celebrate centennial of American Declaration of Independence. Lacking inspiration, 'he can think of nothing but the 5,000 dollars he has demanded and perhaps will not get', reports Cosima.

3 JUN. Rehearsals for *Ring* begin.

13–30 AUG. First Bayreuth Festival, consisting of three complete *Ring* cycles under Hans Richter, attended by luminaries and musicians from all over Europe. Nietzsche is present but leaves before end of festival in

severe physical pain; he and Wagner meet for last time in Sorrento in Oct. Festival deficit is 148,000 marks. Intimacy with Judith Gautier continues until Feb 1878.

1877

19 APR. *Parsifal* text completed.

7–29 MAY Series of eight concerts given in recently opened Royal Albert Hall in London; profits of £700 do little to reduce Festival deficit.

SEP. Begins composition of *Parsifal*.

1878

JAN. First issue of *Bayreuther Blätter* published under editorship of Hans von Wolzogen.

12 MAR. Finishes 'Modern', first of series of 'regeneration writings'.

31 MAR. Bayreuth deficit settled by agreement with Ludwig II.

1879

OCT. Open letter on subject of vivisectionism.

31 DEC. Advised by doctor to seek milder climate, he leaves Bayreuth with family *en route* for Italy.

1880

4 JAN. Family take up residence in Villa d'Angri, overlooking Bay of Naples. Joined by Paul von Joukowsky, future stage designer for *Parsifal*.

MAY Moorish-style castle and exotic garden of Palazzo Rufolo at Ravello provide model for stage setting of Act II of *Parsifal*: 'Klingsor's magic garden is found!'

21 AUG. Cathedral in Siena provides similar inspiration for Hall of the Grail.

12 NOV. Conducts private performance for Ludwig of *Parsifal* prelude. Last meeting with the king.

17 NOV. Returns to Bayreuth.

1881

5 NOV. Family arrive in Palermo.

DEC. Suffers chest spasms.

1882

13 JAN. Finishes score of *Parsifal*.

15 JAN. Portrait sketched by Renoir.

END MAR. First major heart attack.

APR. Family travel through Messina, Naples and Venice, arriving back in Bayreuth on 1 May.

26 JUL. Premiere of *Parsifal* in Bayreuth. Sixteen performances in Jul and Aug.

14 SEP. Departure for Venice, where family and entourage occupy a wing of the Palazzo Vendramin-Calergi.

1883

13 FEB. Fatal heart attack; dies in Cosima's arms.

18 FEB. Private burial in garden of Wahnfried.

Notes

Abbreviations

CT: *Cosima Wagner: Die Tagebücher 1869–1883*, ed. Martin Gregor-Dellin and Dietrich Mack, 2 vols (Munich, 1976–77); trans. Geoffrey Skelton, 2 vols (London, 1978–80)

ML: *Mein Leben*, ed. Martin Gregor-Dellin (Munich, 1963; 2nd edn 1976); trans. Andrew Gray and ed. Mary Whittall as *My Life* (Cambridge, 1983)

PW: *Richard Wagner's Prose Works*, trans. and ed. William Ashton Ellis, 8 vols (London, 1892–99)

SB: *Richard Wagner: Sämtliche Briefe*: I–IX, ed. Gertrud Strobel, Werner Wolf et al. (Leipzig, 1967–2000); X–XIX, ed. Andreas Mielke, Martin Dürrer and Margret Jestremski (Wiesbaden, 1999–2011)

SLRW: *Selected Letters of Richard Wagner*, trans. and ed. Stewart Spencer and Barry Millington (London, 1987)

SS: *Sämtliche Schriften und Dichtungen*, Volks-Ausgabe, 16 vols (Leipzig, n.d.)

WDS: *Wagner: A Documentary Study*, ed. Herbert Barth, Dietrich Mack and Egon Voss (London, 1975); trans. P. R. J. Ford and Mary Whittall

Translations

Except where otherwise stated, translations are generally the author's own. For convenience of reference the relevant page numbers of standard translations have also been given.

1. Father of the Man: Paternity and Childhood

1. William Ashton Ellis, *Life of Richard Wagner*, I (London, 1900), p. 48. Ellis began his *Life* as a free translation of the six-volume biography by C. F. Glasenapp (Leipzig, 1876–1911), though it developed into an independent study of its own.
2. 'Neue Wagner-Ermittlungen (Das Geheimnis der Mutter)', *Programmhefte der Bayreuther Festspiele* (1985): *Parsifal*, pp. 21–32 (Eng. trans.).
3. By way of comparison, Geyer's salary as an actor was 1,040 thalers.
4. ML, pp. 17–18; Eng. trans. p. 11.
5. Obituary by August Böttiger, *Abend-Zeitung*, Dresden (29/30 Oct. 1821).
6. ML, p. 20; Eng. trans. pp. 13–14.

2. Learning the Craft: Youthful Apprenticeship

1. Autobiographical Sketch, 1843; WDS, p. 11.
2. Letter to Franz Hauser, March 1834; SLRW, p. 18.
3. WDS, pp. 151–52.
4. John N. Burk (ed.), *Letters of Richard Wagner: The Burrell Collection* (London, 1951), p. 15.

5. Letter to Ottilie Wagner, 3 March 1832; SLRW, p. 13.
6. Berthold Litzmann, *Clara Schumann*, I (Leipzig, 1902), p. 55; WDS, pp. 153–54.
7. Autobiographical Sketch, 1843; WDS, p. 13.

3. Earning his Keep: First Professional Appointments

1. *Allgemeine Musik-Zeitung*, Berlin, 14 Oct. 1910.
2. ML, pp. 82–83; Eng. trans. pp. 74–75.
3. Letter to Theodor Apel, 13 Sep. 1834; SLRW, p. 23.
4. ML, p. 98; Eng. trans. p. 89.
5. ML, p. 108; Eng. trans. p. 99.
6. *Neue Zeitschrift für Musik*, Leipzig, 3 May 1836; WDS, p. 158.
7. Letter of 4 Nov. 1835; SLRW, p. 34.
8. The two numbers were performed in the UK for the first time in a realization by James Francis Brown (published by Music Haven, London, 2010) at the Linbury Studio Theatre, Royal Opera House, London, on 13 October 2007. For full details of the project see Barry Millington, 'Happy Families: A Wagner Singspiel Rediscovered', *The Wagner Journal*, I/3 (2007), pp. 3–18.

4. Under the Yoke: Kapellmeister in Dresden

1. Letter to Samuel Lehrs, 7 April 1843; SLRW, p. 107.
2. Letter to Cäcilie Avenarius, 22 Oct. 1843; SLRW, p. 115.
3. Letter to Ferdinand Heine, 6 Aug. 1847; SLRW, p. 137.
4. Karl Gutzkow, *Rückblicke auf mein Leben* (Berlin, 1875); Eng. trans. WDS, p. 168.

5. The Eternal Wanderer: *Der fliegende Holländer*

1. ML, p. 172; Eng. trans. p. 162.
2. SS, p. 323; PW, p. 370 (trans. Mary Whittall).
3. Nila Parly, *Vocal Victories: Wagner's Female Characters from Senta to Kundry* (Copenhagen, 2011), p. 46.
4. WDS, p. 166.
5. See John Warrack, 'Behind "The Flying Dutchman"', ENO Opera Guide to *Der fliegende Holländer*, ed. Nicholas John (London, 1982), p. 11.

6. Desperately Seeking Venus: *Tannhäuser*

1. ML, p. 223; Eng. trans. p. 212.
2. Quoted in Laurence Dreyfus, *Wagner and the Erotic Impulse* (Cambridge, Mass., 2010), p. 81.
3. See chap. 15 of the present book and Dreyfus (above, n. 2) for more on Wagner's erotics.
4. SS IV, p. 279; PW I, pp. 322–23 (trans. Stewart Spencer).
5. Trans. by Rodney Blumer in ENO Opera Guide to *Tannhäuser*, ed. Nicholas John (London, 1988), p. 74.

6. *Ibid.*, p. 79.
7. *Ibid.*, p. 86.
8. Wagner's note on the overture to *Tannhäuser* was written for a concert in Zurich on 16 March 1852; SS V, pp. 178–79; PW III, p. 231 (trans. Stewart Spencer in *Wagner*, XI [1990], p. 32).
9. Nila Parly, *Vocal Victories: Wagner's Female Characters from Senta to Kundry* (Copenhagen, 2011), pp. 49–82, esp. pp. 76, 81.

7. Swansong to Traditional Opera: *Lohengrin*

1. The editions of *Parzivâl* and *Titurel* in question were those of Karl Simrock (1842) and San-Marte (1841). The anonymous version of *Lohengrin* was in the 1813 edition by Ferdinand Gloekle, with its introduction by Joseph von Görres. Wagner also drew on the *Deutsche Sagen* of Jacob and Wilhelm Grimm (1816–18), Jacob Grimm's *Deutsche Rechtsalterthümer* (1828) and Leopold August Warnkönig's three-volume *Flandrische Staats- und Rechtsgeschichte bis zum Jahr 1305* (1835–42). The latter two sources filled out the picture of 10th-century Brabant for the composer.
2. ML, p. 315; Eng. trans. pp. 302–3.
3. ML, p. 316; Eng. trans. p. 303.
4. SS IV, pp. 295–96; PW I, p. 341.
5. SS IV, p. 302; PW I, p. 347.
6. SS IV, p. 300; PW I, p. 346.
7. SS IV, p. 291; PW I, p. 336.
8. SS IV, p. 298; PW I, p. 343.
9. Liszt's essay was written in French and translated into German by two of Wagner's young acolytes, Karl Ritter and Hans von Bülow. It was published in the Leipzig *Illustrirte Zeitung* on 12 April 1851 (XVI/406, pp. 231–35, 238–41). An English translation, probably the work of Charles Ainslie Barry, was published in *The Monthly Musical Record*, VI (1 Feb.–1 May 1876), pp. 19–22, 31–35, 51–54, 70–72. The latter translation was reprinted, with an introduction and annotation by David Trippett, in *The Wagner Journal*, IV/1 (2010), pp. 4–21; IV/2 (2010), pp. 28–40; IV/3 (2010), pp. 43–57.
10. *Ibid.*, IV/3 (2010), p. 56.
11. *Ibid.*, IV/3 (2010), pp. 56–57.

8. Revolutionary Road: Uprising in Dresden

1. Eda Sagarra, *An Introduction to Nineteenth-Century Germany* (Harlow, 1980), p. 93.
2. Golo Mann, *Deutsche Geschichte des 19. und 20. Jahrhunderts* (Frankfurt am Main, 1958); trans. as *The History of Germany Since 1789* (London, 1968), p. 172.
3. SS XII, p. 223; PW IV, p. 139.
4. SS XII, p. 224; PW IV, p. 140.

5. Eduard Devrient, *Aus seinen Tagebüchern: Berlin–Dresden 1836–1852*, ed. Rolf Kabel (Weimar, 1964).

6. Woldemar Lippert, *Wagner in Exile: 1849–62*; trans. Paul England (London, 1930), p. 22.

7. From the diary of Clara Schumann. Berthold Litzmann, *Clara Schumann*, II (Leipzig, 1907), pp. 189–90; Eng. trans. WDS, p. 173.

8. Letter to Minna Wagner, 14 May 1849; SLRW, p. 146.

9. The Zurich Years: Wagner's Exile in Switzerland

1. Chris Walton's *Richard Wagner's Zurich: The Muse of Place* (Rochester, N.Y., 2007) admirably describes the intellectual outlook of Zurich in the extended period leading up to Wagner's stay.

2. Letter to Theodor Uhlig. 11 Nov. 1851; SLRW, p. 231.

3. Letter of 26/27 June 1850; SLRW, p. 203.

4. See Barry Millington, 'After the Revolution: The Ring in the Light of Wagner's Dresden and Zurich Projects', *University of Toronto Quarterly*, LXXIV/2 (2005), pp. 677–92, for full details of the interim projects.

5. Daniel H. Foster's *Wagner's 'Ring' Cycle and the Greeks* (Cambridge, 2010) is the most recent study in English of the influence of Greek drama on Wagner.

6. Minna's daughter Natalie reported the incident to Wagner's friend Gustav Kietz, who retailed it in an article published in the *Richard Wagner-Jahrbuch* of 1907. Quoted by Walton in *Richard Wagner's Zurich* (n. 1), p. 86.

7. See Walton, *Richard Wagner's Zurich* (n. 1).

8. See Joachim Köhler, *Richard Wagner: The Last of the Titans* (New Haven, Conn., and London, 2004), pp. 418–29, for an enlightening perspective on Wagner's reception of Schopenhauer.

9. Quoted 'at portentous length' in William Ashton Ellis, *Life of Richard Wagner*, V (London, 1906), p. 267.

10. Royal Archives, Windsor, quoted in Stewart Spencer, *Wagner Remembered* (London, 2000), p. 93.

11. Letter of 12 June 1855; SLRW, p. 348.

10. The Rise and Fall of Valhalla: *Der Ring des Nibelungen*

1. Timings vary considerably. Hans Richter took fourteen and a half hours at the first performances in 1876. Daniel Barenboim's Teldec recording spans 14 hours 48 minutes.

2. SS IV, p. 312; PW I, pp. 358–59.

3. Letter to Theodor Uhlig, 12 Nov. 1851; SLRW, pp. 232–33.

4. Letter of 31 May 1852; SLRW, pp. 260–61.

5. Simon Goldhill, 'Wagner's Greeks: The Politics of Hellenism', chap. 4 in *Victorian Culture and Classical Antiquity* (Princeton, N.J., and Oxford, 2011), pp. 125–50, esp. pp. 133–34 and 145–48.

6. Daniel H. Foster, *Wagner's 'Ring' Cycle and the Greeks* (Cambridge, 2010), p. 177, also pp. 157–76.

7. SS IV, p. 329; PW I, p. 376.

8. Christian Thorau, *Semantisierte Sinnlichkeit: Studien zu Rezeption und Zeichenstruktur der Leitmotivtechnik Richard Wagners* (Stuttgart, 2003).

9. *Das Wesen des Christentums* (Leipzig, 1841); trans. George Eliot (repr. Amherst, N.Y., 1989), p. 33.

10. Letter of 25/26 Jan. 1854; SLRW, p. 307.

11. Letter of 3 Oct. 1855; SLRW, p. 351.

12. See Bryan Magee, *The Philosophy of Schopenhauer* (Oxford, 1983), pp. 322–25.

13. 'Versuch über das Theater', repr. in *Im Schatten Wagners: Thomas Mann über Richard Wagner: Texts und Zeugnisse 1895–1955*, ed. Hans Rudolf Vaget (Frankfurt am Main, 2005), p. 24. See also *Thomas Mann: Pro and Contra Wagner*, ed. Erich Heller (London, 1985), p. 31.

14. *Versuch über Wagner* (Berlin and Frankfurt am Main, 1952); Eng. trans. *In Search of Wagner* (London, 1981), p. 140.

15. Letter to Röckel, 25–26 Jan. 1854; SLRW, p. 309.

16. 'A Communication to my Friends', SS IV, p. 328; PW I, p. 375.

17. *Thomas Mann: Pro and Contra Wagner* (n. 13), pp. 180–81.

18. *Discours sur l'origine et les fondements de l'inégalité parmi les hommes* (Amsterdam, 1755), trans. G. D. H. Cole in *Jean-Jacques Rousseau: The Social Contract and Discourses* (London, 1913), pp. 207–38.

19. *The Perfect Wagnerite* (London, 1898; 4th edn 1923, repr. 1967), esp. pp. 71–85.

20. The full text of *Siegfrieds Tod*, together with an English translation and commentary, is given in Edward R. Haymes, *Wagner's 'Ring' in 1848* (Rochester, N.Y., 2010).

21. See Udo Bermbach, *Richard Wagner in Deutschland* (Stuttgart and Weimar, 2011), esp. pp. 388–99.

11. 'Most Excellent Friend': Franz Liszt

1. Berthold Kellermann, *Erinnerungen* (Erlenbach and Leipzig, 1932), p. 195.

2. The complete essay appears in English translation in *The Wagner Journal*, iv (2010), nos 1–3.

3. Letter of 20 Nov. 1851; SLRW, pp. 234–35.

4. Letter to Otto Wesendonck, 13 July 1853; SLRW, p. 285.

5. See SLRW, p. 165, and, for a detailed analysis of the creative exchange between Wagner and Liszt, Ian

Beresford Gleaves, 'Liszt and Wagner: An Exploration of a Key Relationship', *Wagner*, VI/3 (1985), 77–99.

6. John Deathridge, Martin Geck and Egon Voss, *Wagner Werk-Verzeichnis (WWV): Verzeichnis der musikalischen Werke Richard Wagners und ihrer Quellen* (Mainz, 1986), p. 366.

7. See Jonathan Kregor, 'Liszt's Wagner', *The Wagner Journal*, v (2011), pp. 17–43, for a judicious treatment of the subject.

8. Letter of 20 July 1856; SLRW, p. 354.

9. Letter to Hans von Bülow, 7 Oct. 1859; SLRW, p. 472.

10. CT, 15 July 1882.

12. Muses, Mistresses and Mother-Figures: Wagner's Women

1. See Chris Walton, 'Voicing Mathilde: Wagner's Controlling Muse', *The Wagner Journal*, 1/2 (2007), pp. 3–18. The essay also appears as chap. 10 in Walton's *Richard Wagner's Zurich: The Muse of Place* (Rochester, N.Y., 2007), pp. 201–42.

2. Letter of 20 Aug. 1858; SLRW, p. 399.

3. Quoted in Alan Walker, *Hans von Bülow* (New York, 2010), p. 106.

4. Letter of 16 April 1850; SLRW, p. 192.

5. The correct birthdate of Jessie Laussot has only recently been ascertained. See David Cormack, 'An Abduction from the Seraglio: Rescuing Jessie Laussot', *The Wagner Journal*, VI/1 (2012), pp. 50–63.

6. Letter of 26/27 June 1850; SLRW, p. 204.

7. *Ibid.*; SLRW, p. 202.

8. See Joanna Richardson, *Judith Gautier: A Biography* (London, 1986), esp. pp. 251–52.

9. See, for example, Joachim Köhler, *Richard Wagner: The Last of the Titans* (New Haven, Conn., and London, 2004), esp. pp. 5–7, 157–59, 581–91; Martin Gregor-Dellin, *Richard Wagner: His Life, His Work, His Century* (London, 1983), trans. J. Maxwell Brownjohn, pp. 21–24; and Chris Walton, *Richard Wagner's Zurich* (n. 1), esp. pp. 193–96.

10. Eva Rieger, *Richard Wagner's Women* (Woodbridge, 2011), esp. pp. 168–83. This book is highly recommended for its many insights into the links between Wagner's sensual instincts and his works.

11. Letter of 3 Aug. 1863; SLRW, p. 570.

13. The Behemoth of Bayreuth: Wagner's Personality

1. Stewart Spencer's *Wagner Remembered* (London, 2000) is a particularly rich source of contemporary reminiscence.

2. Robert von Hornstein, *Memoiren* (Munich, 1908); Spencer (n. 1), p. 97.

3. Friedrich Pecht, *Aus meiner Zeit* (Munich, 1894); Spencer (n. 1), p. 176.

4. Edouard Schuré, *Richard Wagner: Son oeuvre et son idée* (Paris, 1933); Spencer (n. 1), p. 180.

5. Peter Cornelius, *Ausgewählte Briefe*, II (Leipzig, 1905), pp. 25–26; WDS, p. 207.

6. Malwida von Meysenbug, *Memoiren einer Idealistin* (2nd edn Stuttgart, 1877), III, pp. 286–88; WDS, p. 188.

7. Eliza Wille, *Richard Wagner an Eliza Wille: Fünfzehn Briefe des Meisters nebst Erinnerungen und Erläuterungen von Eliza Wille* (Berlin and Leipzig, 1908); Spencer (n. 1), p. 155.

8. Gustav Schönaich, quoted in Spencer (n. 1), pp. 153–54.

9. Barry Emslie, *Richard Wagner and the Centrality of Love* (Woodbridge and Rochester, N.Y., 2010), p. 203.

14. Always Short: Wagner and Money

1. Letter to Robert von Hornstein, 12 Dec. 1861.

2. Letter to Liszt, 31 Dec. 1858; SLRW, p. 435.

3. Letter to Liszt, 15 Jan. 1854; SLRW, p. 297.

4. Letter to Otto Wesendonck, 24 Aug. 1859; SLRW, p. 461.

15. In the Pink: The Role of Silks and Satins in Wagner's Life

1. Ludwig Kusche, *Richard Wagner und die Putzmacherin oder Die Macht der Verleumdung* (Wilhelmshaven, 1967), pp. 29–30; Eng. trans. by Stewart Spencer in Joachim Köhler, *Richard Wagner: The Last of the Titans* (New Haven, Conn., and London, 2004), p. 455.

2. Sebastien Röckl, *Ludwig II und Richard Wagner*, I (Munich, 1913), pp. 245–46; Eng. trans. in Ernest Newman, *The Life of Richard Wagner*, III (New York, 1941), p. 439.

3. Letter to Marie Völkl, 6 Dec. 1863; SLRW, p. 572.

4. Köhler, *Titans* (n. 1), p. 454.

5. From 'Zwei Nietzsche Anekdoten', *Frankfurter Zeitung*, 9 March 1904, quoted in Sander L. Gilman and Ingeborg Reichenbach (eds.), *Begegnungen mit Nietzsche* (Bonn, 1981), p. 163; Eng. trans. Laurence Dreyfus in *Wagner and the Erotic Impulse* (Cambridge, Mass.), 2010, p. 135.

6. Dreyfus (above, n. 5), pp. 135–50.

7. Barbara Eichner and Guy Houghton, 'Rose Oil and Pineapples: Julius Cyriax's Friendship with Wagner and the Early Years of the London Wagner Society', *The Wagner Journal*, I/2 (2007), p. 29.

8. Loc. cit.

9. Stewart Spencer, 'Wagner and Gaetano Ghezzi', *The Wagner Journal*, I/1 (2007), pp. 23, 27.

10. Dreyfus (n. 5), p. 142.

11. See, for example, CT, 20 July 1881, for an amusing word-play of Wagner's, reported by Cosima, on lines from the final chorus of Goethe's *Faust*, Part 2: 'The Indescribable, here it is done: the pleasant and soft things one likes to put on.'

12. *Gazzetta di Venezia*, 15 Feb. 1883, cited in Stewart Spencer, '"Er starb, – ein Mensch wie alle": Wagner and Carrie Pringle', *Wagner*, XXV/2 (2004), p. 66. More detail on the death and various obituaries is given in John W. Barker, *Wagner and Venice* (Rochester, N.Y., 2008).

13. Letter of 23 Oct. 1877; SLRW, p. 873.

14. Laurence Dreyfus, 'Siegfried's Masculinity', *The Wagner Journal*, IV/3 (2010), pp. 4–26. But see also *Wagner and the Erotic Impulse* (n. 5) for a full discussion of Wagner's erotics and incisive analysis of the music in this context.

16. 'My Adored and Angelic Friend': Ludwig II

1. Wendelin Weissheimer, *Erlebnisse mit Richard Wagner, Franz Liszt und vielen anderen Zeitgenossen nebst deren Briefen* (Stuttgart and Leipzig, 1898); Stewart Spencer, *Wagner Remembered* (London, 2000), pp. 161–62.

2. Diary of Julius Fröbel, quoted in Spencer (above, n. 1), pp. 182–83.

3. Letter to Mathilde Maier of 23 Feb. 1865.

4. Reported by Judith Gautier in *Wagner at Home* (London, 1910), p. 36; trans. Effie Dunreith Massie.

5. Letter of 4 May 1864; WDS, p. 204.

6. Joachim Köhler, *Richard Wagner: The Last of the Titans* (New Haven, Conn., and London, 2004), p. 477.

7. Friedrich Pecht, *Aus meiner Zeit* (Munich, 1894), II, pp. 134–35; Eng. trans. WDS, p. 205.

8. Köhler (n. 6), p. 471.

9. Köhler (n. 6), p. 474.

17. Fatal Attraction: *Tristan und Isolde*

1. Letter of 20 Aug. 1858 to Clara Wolfram; SLRW, p. 400.

2. Arthur Schopenhauer, *Die Welt als Wille und Vorstellung* (Dresden, 1818 [though 1819 appears on title page]); Eng. trans. E. F. J. Payne in *The World as Will and Representation* (Indian Hills, Colo., 1958, repr. 1966), p. 319.

3. Letter of 29 Oct. 1859; SLRW, p. 475.

18. 'Art is What Matters Here': *Die Meistersinger von Nürnberg*

1. ML, pp. 315–16; Eng. trans. p. 303 (author's trans.).

2. Frederic Spotts, *Bayreuth: A History of the Wagner Festival* (New Haven, Conn., and London, 1994), p. 143.

3. Notwithstanding the radical neo-Elizabethan production of 1963 by Wieland Wagner, which like the later production by his niece adopted an ironic view of the work.

4. Letter to Franz Schott, 30 Oct. 1861; SLRW, pp. 526–27.

5. Act III Scene 2.

6. Barry Emslie, *Richard Wagner and the Centrality of Love* (Woodbridge and Rochester, N.Y., 2010), esp. pp. 167–222.

19. Grit in the Oyster: The Role of Anti-Semitism in Wagner's Life and Work

1. Translation by Stewart Spencer (of the text as published in the *Neue Zeitschrift für Musik* of 3 and 6 September 1850) in *Wagner*, IX (1988), p. 25.

2. *Ibid.*, p. 24.

3. *Ibid.*, p. 27.

4. This often overlooked aspect is demonstrated by David Conway in *Jewry in Music: Entry to the Profession from the Enlightenment to Richard Wagner* (Cambridge, 2011).

5. Karl Marx, 'On the Jewish Question', Karl Marx and Friedrich Engels, *Collected Works* (London, 1975), III, pp. 146–74.

6. SS V, p. 85. Author's trans. of the ending as it appears in the 1869 version.

7. Letter to Liszt, 18 April 1851; SLRW, pp. 221–22.

8. *Ibid.*, p. 222.

9. Letter to Friedrich Nietzsche, 23 Oct. 1872; SLRW, p. 812.

10. CT, 2 July 1878.

11. CT, 22 Nov. 1881.

12. See Barry Emslie, *Richard Wagner and the Centrality of Love* (Woodbridge and Rochester, N.Y., 2010), esp. chap. 8, for a perceptive treatment of this aspect.

13. See Barry Millington, 'Nuremberg Trial: Is there anti-semitism in *Die Meistersinger*?', *Cambridge Opera Journal*, III (1991), pp. 247–60, for the full thesis.

14. 'Jewishness in Music', SS V, pp. 69–70; trans. Stewart Spencer in *Wagner*, IX/1 (1988), p. 23.

15. On this point see Marc A. Weiner, 'Wagner and the Perils of Reading', *Wagner*, XVIII (1997), pp. 59–82. On the wider question of anti-Semitism in Wagner's works, see Marc A. Weiner's landmark study *Richard Wagner and the Anti-Semitic Imagination* (Lincoln, Nebr., and London, 1995).

16. See Barry Emslie, 'Puppy Love' [review of Michael Tanner's *Faber Pocket Guide to Wagner*], *The Wagner Journal*, IV/3 (2010), pp. 83–86, esp. p. 85.

17. The phrase is Thomas S. Grey's. See the judicious treatment of the whole subject in his *Cambridge Companion to Wagner* (Cambridge, 2008), pp. 203–18.

18. Quoted in *ibid.*, p. 214.

19. For more on the subject, see also the chapters on these works in the present book.

20. Creative Spark: Sources of Inspiration in Wagner's Work

1. ML, p. 512; Eng. trans. p. 499.

2. John Deathridge, 'Wagner's Sketches for the *Ring*', *Musical Times*, CXVIII (1977),

pp. 383–89, esp. p. 387; and 'Cataloguing Wagner' in *The Richard Wagner Centenary in Australia*, ed. Peter Dennison, *Miscellanea Musicologica: Adelaide Studies in Musicology*, XIV (Adelaide, 1985), pp. 185–99, esp. pp. 193–97.

3. I have been among the sceptics with regard to the La Spezia 'vision': see, for example, my *Wagner* (London, 1984), pp. 198–99.

4. Letter of 16(?) Dec. 1854; SLRW, pp. 323–24. The black flag was a motif present in certain versions of the legend but not used in the opera.

5. CT, 30 July 1879.

6. *Das Braune Buch. Tagebuchauf- zeichnungen 1865–1882*, ed. Joachim Bergfeld (Zurich/Freiburg, 1975); trans. George Bird as *The Diary of Richard Wagner 1865–1882: The Brown Book* (London, 1980), p. 105.

7. See his illuminating study of the genesis of the opera in 'Die "schwarze und die weiße Flagge": zur Entstehung von Wagners "Tristan"', *Archiv für Musikwissenschaft*, LIV/3 (1997), pp. 210–27.

8. ML, p. 524; Eng. trans. p. 511.

9. Letter to Bülow of 26 Oct 1854; SLRW, p.321.

10. Letter of 9 Sep. 1864; SLRW, p. 621.

11. Letter of 3 Mar. 1860; SLRW, p. 486.

12. CT, 16 Feb. 1876.

13. The sketch of 9 February 1876 illustrated here was preceded by a not dissimilar sketch, possibly of the same date or slightly earlier – the first surviving sketch used in *Parsifal*.

14. CT, 8 Feb. 1876.

15. William Kinderman discusses this borrowing in his introductory chapter to *A Companion to Wagner's 'Parsifal'*, ed. W. Kinderman and K. Syer (Rochester, N.Y., and Woodbridge, 2005), pp. 20–23. His later chapter ('The Genesis of the Music', pp. 133–75) is a comprehensive and invaluable account of the compositional process of *Parsifal* from the earliest stages.

16. See CT, 28 Jan. 1875, where the arrival of the score is noted, along with the comment: 'a curious work, done with great effect, but so alien to us'.

17. See Arthur W. Margret, 'Liszt and *Parsifal*', *Music Review*, XIV (1953), pp. 107–24.

18. See CT, 28 Dec. 1877.

19. See Robert Gauldin, 'Tracing Mathilde's Ab Major', in *Richard Wagner for the New Millennium: Essays in Music and Culture*, ed. M. Bribitzer-Stull, A. Lubet and G. Wagner (New York, 2007), pp. 27–42, though I prefer a more fundamental association of A flat with love in general.

21. The Silent Sufferer: Cosima Wagner

1. Thomas à Kempis, *Of the Imitation of Christ: Four Books* (Oxford, 1849).

2. Letter of 20 April 1856, cited in Marie von Bülow, *Hans von Bülow in Leben und Wort* (Stuttgart, 1925), p. 68.

3. ML, pp. 745–46; Eng. trans. p. 729.

4. CT, 28 Nov. 1869.

5. Rosalie Braun-Artaria, *Von berühmten Zeitgenossen: Erinnerungen einer Siebzigerin* (Munich, 1918), p. 100; quoted in Oliver Hilmes, *Cosima Wagner: The Lady of Bayreuth* (New Haven, Conn., and London, 2010), p. 87.

6. CT, 27 Feb. 1876.

7. See Hilmes (n. 5), p. 106.

8. *Das Braune Buch. Tagebuchauf- zeichnungen 1865–1882*, ed. Joachim Bergfeld (Zurich/Freiburg, 1975); trans. George Bird as *The Diary of Richard Wagner 1865–1882: The Brown Book* (London, 1980), p. 105.

9. Quoted in Alan Walker, *Hans von Bülow: A Life and Times* (New York, 2010), p. 120.

10. See for example CT, 6 Aug. 1869; 24 Nov. 1869; 16 May 1870; 11 and 12 Nov. 1870; and 14 Feb. 1871.

22. Tribschen Idyll: The Lucerne Years

1. The latter's name was also rendered 'Frigge' in a nod to Nordic nomenclature.

2. *The Complete Works of Friedrich Nietzsche*, ed. Oscar Levy (Edinburgh and London, 1909–13), XVII: *Ecce Homo*, trans. Anthony M. Ludovici, p. 41.

3. Judith Gautier, *Le Troisième Rang du Collier* (Paris, 1909); trans. Effie Dunreith Massie as *Wagner at Home* (London, 1910).

4. CT, 16 July 1869.

5. CT, 18 July 1869.

6. Letter of 14 Oct. 1868; SLRW, p. 731.

7. CT, 25 Dec. 1870.

23. A Home for the Gods: The Bayreuth Project

1. SLRW, pp. 216–17.

2. Letter of 20 Sep. 1850; SB III, p. 426.

3. Letter to Uhlig, 12 Nov. 1851; SLRW, p. 234.

4. *Ibid*.

5. SS VI, p. 273; PW III, p. 274.

6. 'Preface to the Edition of the Poem of the Stage Festival Play *Der Ring des Nibelungen*', SS VI, p. 276; trans. by Geoffrey Skelton in *Wagner in Thought and Practice* (London, 1991), pp. 96–97.

7. 'The Festival Playhouse in Bayreuth', SS IX, p. 338; PW V, p. 335.

8. Nicholas Vazsonyi, *Richard Wagner: Self-Promotion and the Making of a Brand* (Cambridge, 2010), pp. 184–85.

9. Letter of 25 Jan. 1874 from Ludwig II to Wagner.

10. Oswald Georg Bauer, the scholar responsible for bringing these paintings and sketches to light, reproduces them

in *Josef Hoffmann: Der Bühnenbildner der ersten Bayreuther Festspiele* (Munich and Berlin, 2008). A selection is also reproduced in Patrick Carnegy's engrossing account of the mystery surrounding them: 'Designs on the Ring', *The Wagner Journal*, IV/2 (2010), pp. 41–55.

11. *Bergenposten*, 12 Aug. 1876, quoted in Robert Hartford, *Bayreuth: The Early Years* (London, 1980), p. 64.

12. Article submitted to the *Russky Viedomosty*, quoted in Modeste Tchaikovsky, *The Life and Letters of Peter Ilich Tchaikovsky*, trans. Rosa Newmarch (London, 1906,) p. 182.

13. *Ibid.*, p. 185.

24. Wagner's Last Card: *Parsifal*

1. ML, p. 561; Eng. trans. p. 547.

2. Letter to Mathilde Wesendonck of 1 Oct. 1858; SLRW, p. 422.

3. *Ibid.*, p. 424.

4. The forms Anfortas and Amfortas coexist in the manuscript tradition of Wolfram's *Parzivâl*. Not until 1877 did Wagner settle on the second alternative, as well as on the familiar spelling of Parsifal.

5. Letter of 7 Sep. 1865; SLRW, p. 664.

6. Letter to André Caplet of 25 Aug. 1912; E. Lockspeiser (ed.), *Lettres inédites à André Caplet* (Monaco, 1957).

7. CT, 27 Apr. 1879.

8. Letter to Reinhart von Seydlitz of 4 Jan. 1878.

25. Death in Venice: The Events of Wagner's Last Days

1. SS XII, p. 345; PW VI, p. 337, and VIII, p. 398.

2. As Stewart Spencer points out in his impeccably researched '"Er starb, – ein Mensch wie alle": Wagner and Carrie Pringle', *Wagner*, XXV/2 (2004), pp. 55–77, there is no incontrovertible evidence that the couple were engaged in an affair, or that a visit from Ms Pringle provoked a furious row with Cosima that led to Wagner's fatal heart attack. On the other hand, such affairs are generally not conducted in such a way as to leave a trail of evidence for future historians.

3. Henriette Perl, *Richard Wagner in Venedig* (Augsburg, 1883). See John Barker, *Wagner and Venice* (Rochester, N.Y., and Woodbridge, 2008), p. 128, and chap. 7 generally for copious quotations from Perl.

4. See Barker (above, n. 3), pp. 306–7 for more on 'Wagner's last words'.

5. See Barker (n. 3), esp. pp. 298–99, for detailed extracts from Keppler's report.

6. See Barker (n. 3), pp. 308–10; also chap. 15 of the current book, and the furs in Henriette Perl's account, quoted above.

7. Barker (n. 3), p. 135.

8. *La Gazzetta di Venezia*, 16 Feb. 1883; Eng. trans. in Barker (n. 3), p. 95.

26. Perfect and Imperfect Wagnerites:
The Spread of the Wagner Cult

1. *The Times*, 16 May 1855, quoted in
   William Ashton Ellis, *Life of Richard
   Wagner*, v (London, 1906), p. 277.
2. Letter of 17 Feb. 1860; WDS, p. 193.
3. Alexander H. Shapiro, 'McEwan and
   Forster, the Perfect Wagnerites', *The
   Wagner Journal*, v/2 (2011), pp. 20–45.
4. Camille Mauclair, 'Wagner après la
   Guerre', quoted in Paul du Quenoy,
   *Wagner and the French Muse: Music,
   Society, and Nation in Modern France*
   (Palo Alto, Calif., 2011), p. 127.
5. *Wagner and the French Muse* (above,
   n. 4). See also '"Honeymoon to
   Bayreuth": French Appreciations
   of Richard Wagner in the Interwar
   Era', *The Wagner Journal*, v/1 (2011),
   pp. 46–64.
6. *Wagner Nights: An American History*
   (Berkeley, Calif., and Los Angeles,
   1994), p. 216.
7. *Ibid.*, p. 220.

**27. Panning for Gold: Wagner
and Cinema**

1. T. W. Adorno, *Versuch über Wagner*
   (Berlin and Frankfurt am Main, 1952);
   trans. as *In Search of Wagner* (London,
   1981), p. 107.
2. T. W. Adorno and Max Horkheimer,
   Dialektik der Aufklärung; trans. as
   The Dialectic of Enlightenment (London,
   1972), p. 124.
3. Wagner's programme note was
   written for the concerts he conducted
   in Zurich on 18, 20 and 22 May 1853.
   SS v, pp. 179–81; PW III, pp. 231–33.
   This translation by Stewart Spencer in
   Wagner, XI (1990), pp. 110–11.
4. 'Underscoring Drama – Picturing Music'
   in *Wagner & Cinema*, ed. Jeongwon Joe
   and Sander L. Gilman (Bloomington,
   Ind., 2010), p. 55.
5. *Ibid.*
6. Stage direction for transition linking
   Scenes 1 and 2 of *Das Rheingold*.
   Translation from Stewart Spencer and
   Barry Millington (eds), *Wagner's Ring
   of the Nibelung: A Companion* (London,
   1993), p. 69.
7. Translation by Melanie Karpinski from
   the ENO Opera Guide to *Der fliegende
   Holländer*, ed. Nicholas John (London,
   1982), p. 37.
8. See Mary Ann Smart's excellent
   *Mimomania: Music and Gesture in
   Nineteenth-Century Opera* (Berkeley,
   Calif., and Los Angeles, 2004) for a
   stimulating discussion of the subject.
9. Scott D. Paulin, 'Piercing Wagner:
   the *Ring* in *Golden Earrings*', in
   Wagner & Cinema (n. 4), p. 228.
10. See Neil Lerner, 'Reading
    Wagner in *Bugs Bunny Nips the
    Nips*', in *Wagner & Cinema* (n. 4),
    pp. 210–24, for an incisive critique of
    the political and racist representation

inherent in this and similar
cartoons.
11. Daniel Goldmark, *Tunes for 'Toons:
    Music and the Hollywood Cartoon*
    (Berkeley, Calif., 2005), esp.
    pp. 140–42.
12. The Reuters report, quoted
    by Matthew Wilson Smith in
    'American Valkyries: Richard
    Wagner, D. W. Griffith, and
    the Birth of Classical Cinema',
    Modernism/Modernity, XV/2
    (2008), p. 229, describes the
    exercise as 'a bizarre musical
    reprise' from *Apocalypse Now*.
13. See Marc A. Weiner, 'Hollywood's
    German Fantasy: Ridley Scott's
    Gladiator', in *Wagner & Cinema*
    (n. 4), pp. 186–209.
14. See Paul Fryer, '*The Life and Works
    of Richard Wagner* (1913): Becce,
    Froelich, and Messter', in *Wagner
    & Cinema* (n. 4), pp. 65–84, for full
    details about the film.
15. See Patrick Carnegy, *Wagner
    and the Art of the Theatre* (New
    Haven, Conn., and London, 2006),
    pp. 323–29, and Joy H. Calico,
    'Wagner in East Germany: Joachim
    Herz's *Der fliegende Holländer*'
    (1964), in *Wagner & Cinema* (n. 4),
    pp. 294–311.
16. See Carnegy (above, n. 15),
    pp. 375–94, for a lucid discussion
    of Syberberg.

**28. Swastikas Over Bayreuth:
Wagner and the Third Reich**

1. *Sunday Times*, 6 Aug. 1933.
2. Hans von Wolzogen, *Nach 1913*,
   quoted in Hartmut Zelinsky,
   *Richard Wagner: Ein deutsches
   Thema* (Berlin and Vienna, 1983),
   p. 128.
3. Letter of 7 Oct. 1923, repr.
   in Zelinsky, *Richard Wagner*
   (above, n. 2), p. 169.
4. Letter of 21 April 1927. See
   Dietrich Mack, *Der Bayreuther
   Inszenierungsstil* (Munich, 1976),
   p. 98.
5. See Patrick Carnegy, *Wagner and
   the Art of the Theatre* (New Haven,
   Conn., and London, 2006), p. 151,
   and Fabian Kern, 'Soeben gesehen.
   Bravo Bravissimo': Die Coburger
   Theatermalerfamilie Brückner und
   ihre Beziehungen zu den Bayreuther
   Festspielen* (Berlin, 2010).
6. Quoted in Frederic Spotts,
   *Bayreuth: A History of the Wagner
   Festival* (New Haven, Conn., and
   London, 1994), p. 161.
7. Brigitte Hamann's exemplary
   biography, *Winifred Wagner: A Life
   at the Heart of Hitler's Bayreuth*
   (London, 2005), charts Winifred's
   affairs in detail, drawing on many
   previously unpublished letters.

8. Quoted in Spotts (n. 6), p. 173.
9. Quoted in Hans Mayer, *Richard Wagner
   in Bayreuth: 1876–1976*, trans. Jack
   Zipes (London, 1976), p. 135.
10. The veracity of Hitler's claim to have
    initiated the invitation to Roller has
    been questioned, but the claim is
    independently verified by the testimony
    of Winifred: see Hamann (n. 7),
    pp. 214–16.

**29. Regime Change: The Grandsons
Usher in the Era of New Bayreuth**

1. For more details see Brigitte Hamann,
   *Winifred Wagner: A Life at the Heart
   of Hitler's Bayreuth* (London, 2005),
   pp. 377–82, and Jonathan Carr,
   The Wagner Clan (London, 2007),
   pp. 235–39.
2. Ingrid Kapsamer, *Wieland Wagner:
   Wegbereiter und Weltwirkung* (Vienna,
   2010).
3. The original essay, 'Überlieferung und
   Gestaltung', appeared in the Bayreuth
   Festival handbook for 1951. The English
   translation was published the following
   year in a brochure edited by Herbert
   Barth: *Life, Work, Festspielhaus*
   (Bayreuth, 1952).
4. Quoted in Wolfgang Wagner, *Acts:
   The Autobiography of Wolfgang
   Wagner*, trans. John Brownjohn
   (London, 1994), p. 106.
5. Testament SBT2 1390, SBT4 1391,
   SBT4 1392 and SBT4 1393.
6. Wolfgang Wagner, *Acts* (n. 4), p. 159.
7. Quoted in Patrick Carnegy, *Wagner
   and the Art of the Theatre* (New Haven,
   Conn., and London, 2006), p. 344.
8. Quoted in *Boulez in Bayreuth: The
   Centenary 'Ring'* (Baarn, 1981), p. 50.
9. *Ibid.*

**30. Renewing the Legacy: Bayreuth
Today and in the Future**

1. Nike Wagner, *Wagner Theater*
   (Frankfurt am Main and Leipzig, 1998);
   Eng. trans. Ewald Osers and Michael
   Downes (London, 2000), p. 304.

Select Bibliography

This select bibliography consists largely of titles consulted in the writing of the present book and/or cited in the endnotes.

Adorno, T. W., and Horkheimer, Max, *The Dialectic of Enlightenment* (London, 1972); trans. John Cumming

Adorno, T. W., *In Search of Wagner* (London, 1981); Trans. Rodney Livingstone

Barker, John W., *Wagner and Venice* (Rochester, N.Y., and Woodbridge, 2008)

Barth, Herbert: *Life, Work, Festspielhaus* (Bayreuth, 1952)

Bauer, Oswald, *Josef Hoffmann: Der Bühnenbildner der ersten Bayreuther Festspiele* (Munich and Berlin, 2008)

Bülow, Marie von, *Hans von Bülow in Leben und Wort* (Stuttgart, 1925)

Burk, John N. (ed.), *Letters of Richard Wagner: The Burrell Collection* (London, 1951)

Carnegy, Patrick, 'Designs on the Ring', *The Wagner Journal*, iv/2 (2010), pp. 41–55

Carr, Jonathan, *The Wagner Clan* (London, 2007)

Cole, G. D. H., *Jean-Jacques Rousseau: The Social Contract and Discourses* (London, 1913)

Cornelius, Peter, *Ausgewählte Briefe*, II (Leipzig, 1905)

Deathridge, John, 'Wagner's Sketches for the *Ring*', *Musical Times*, CXVIII (1977), pp. 383–89

Deathridge, John, 'Cataloguing Wagner', in *The Richard Wagner Centenary in Australia*, ed. Peter Dennison, *Miscellanea Musicologica: Adelaide Studies in Musicology*, XIV (Adelaide, 1985), pp. 185–99

Devrient, Eduard, *Aus seinen Tagebüchern: Berlin–Dresden 1836–1852*, ed. Rolf Kabel (Weimar, 1964)

Dreyfus, Laurence, *Wagner and the Erotic Impulse* (Cambridge, Mass., 2010)

Dreyfus, Laurence, 'Siegfried's Masculinity', *The Wagner Journal*, IV/3 (2010), pp. 4–26

Du Quenoy, Paul, *Wagner and the French Muse: Music, Society, and Nation in Modern France* (Palo Alto, Calif., 2011)

Du Quenoy, Paul, '"Honeymoon to Bayreuth": French Appreciations of Richard Wagner in the Interwar Era', *The Wagner Journal*, v/1 (2011), pp. 46–64

Eichner, Barbara and Houghton, Guy, 'Rose Oil and Pineapples: Julius Cyriax's Friendship with Wagner and the Early Years of the London Wagner Society', *The Wagner Journal*, I/2 (2007), pp. 19–49

Ellis, William Ashton, *Life of Richard Wagner* (London, 1900–08)

Emslie, Barry, *Richard Wagner and the Centrality of Love* (Woodbridge and Rochester, N.Y., 2010)

Emslie, Barry, 'Puppy Love' [review of Michael Tanner's *Faber Pocket Guide to Wagner*], *The Wagner Journal*, IV/3 (2010), pp. 83–86

Feuerbach, Ludwig, *The Essence of Christianity* (repr. Amherst, N.Y., 1989); trans. George Eliot

Foster, Daniel H., *Wagner's 'Ring' Cycle and the Greeks* (Cambridge, 2010)

Gauldin, Robert, 'Tracing Mathilde's A♭ Major', *Richard Wagner for the New Millennium: Essays in Music and Culture*, ed. M. Bribitzer-Stull, A. Lubet and G. Wagner (New York, 2007), pp. 27–42

Gautier, Judith, *Wagner at Home* (London, 1910); trans. Effie Dunreith Massie

Gleaves, Ian Beresford, 'Liszt and Wagner: an Exploration of a Key Relationship', *Wagner*, VI/3 (1985), pp. 77–99

Goldhill, Simon, 'Wagner's Greeks: The Politics of Hellenism', chap. 4 in *Victorian Culture and Classical Antiquity: Art, Opera, Fiction, and the Proclamation of Modernity* (Princeton, N.J., 2011), pp. 125–50

Gregor-Dellin, Martin, *Richard Wagner: His Life, His Work, His Century* (London, 1983); trans. J. Maxwell Brownjohn

Gregor-Dellin, Martin, 'Neue Wagner-Ermittlungen (Das Geheimnis der Mutter)', *Programmhefte der Bayreuther Festspiele* (1985): *Parsifal*, pp. 21–32 (Eng. trans.)

Grey, Thomas S., *Cambridge Companion to Wagner* (Cambridge, 2008)

Gutzkow, Karl, *Rückblicke auf mein Leben* (Berlin, 1875)

Hamann, Brigitte, *Winifred Wagner: A Life at the Heart of Hitler's Bayreuth* (London, 2005); trans. Alan Bance

Hartford, Robert, *Bayreuth: The Early Years* (London, 1980)

Haymes, Edward R., *Wagner's 'Ring' in 1848* (Rochester, N.Y., 2010)

Heller, Erich (ed.), *Thomas Mann: Pro and Contra Wagner* (London, 1985)

Hilmes, Oliver, *Cosima Wagner: The Lady of Bayreuth* (New Haven, Conn., and London, 2010); trans. Stewart Spencer

Hornstein, Robert von, *Memoiren* (Munich, 1908)

Horowitz, Joseph, *Wagner Nights: An American History* (Berkeley, Calif., and Los Angeles, 1994)

Joe, Jeongwon and Gilman, Sander L. (eds), *Wagner & Cinema* (Bloomington, Ind., 2010)

Kapsamer, Ingrid, *Wieland Wagner: Wegbereiter und Weltwirkung* (Vienna, 2010)

Kellermann, Berthold, *Erinnerungen* (Erlenbach and Leipzig, 1932)

Köhler, Joachim, *Richard Wagner: The Last of the Titans* (New Haven, Conn., and London, 2004); trans. Stewart Spencer

Kempis, Thomas à, *Of the Imitation of Christ: Four Books* (Oxford, 1849)

Kern, Fabian, 'Soeben gesehen. Bravo Bravissimo': Die Coburger Theatermalerfamilie Brückner und ihre Beziehungen zu den Bayreuther Festspielen* (Berlin, 2010)

Kinderman, William and Syer, Katherine R. (eds), *A Companion to Wagner's 'Parsifal'* (Rochester, N.Y., and Woodbridge, 2005)

Kregor, Jonathan, 'Liszt's Wagner', *The Wagner Journal*, v (2011), pp. 17–43

Kusche, Ludwig, *Richard Wagner und die Putzmacherin oder Die Macht der Verleumdung* (Wilhelmshaven, 1967)

Lippert, Woldemar, *Wagner in Exile: 1849–62* (London, 1930); trans. Paul England

Litzmann, Berthold, *Clara Schumann: ein Künstlerleben nach Tagebüchern und Briefen*, 3 vols (Leipzig, 1902–8)

Lockspeiser, E. (ed.), *Lettres inédites à André Caplet* (Monaco, 1957)

Mack, Dietrich, *Der Bayreuther Inszenierungsstil* (Munich, 1976)

Magee, Bryan, *The Philosophy of Schopenhauer* (Oxford, 1983)

Mann, Golo, *The History of Germany Since 1789* (London, 1968); trans. Marian Jackson

Mann, Thomas, 'Versuch über das Theater', repr. in *Im Schatten Wagners: Thomas Mann über Richard Wagner: Texts und Zeugnisse 1895–1955*, ed. Hans Rudolf Vaget (Frankfurt am Main, 2005)

Margret, Arthur W., 'Liszt and *Parsifal*', *Music Review*, XIV (1953), pp. 107–24

Mayer, Hans, *Richard Wagner in Bayreuth: 1876–1976* (London, 1976); trans. Jack Zipes

Meysenbug, Malwida von, *Memoiren einer Idealistin* (Stuttgart, 2nd edn 1877)

Millington, Barry, 'Nuremberg Trial: Is there anti-semitism in *Die Meistersinger?*', *Cambridge Opera Journal*, III (1991), pp. 247–60

Millington, Barry, *The Wagner Compendium* (London, 1992)

Millington, Barry, 'After the Revolution: *The Ring* in the Light of Wagner's Dresden and Zurich Projects', *University of Toronto Quarterly*, LXXIV/2 (2005), pp. 677–92

Millington, Barry, 'Happy Families: A Wagner Singspiel Rediscovered', *The Wagner Journal*, I/3 (2007), pp. 3–18

Millington, Barry, and Spencer, Stewart (eds), *Wagner in Performance* (New Haven, Conn., and London, 1992)

Parly, Nila, *Vocal Victories: Wagner's Female Characters from Senta to Kundry* (Copenhagen, 2011)

Pecht, Friedrich, *Aus meiner Zeit* (Munich, 1894)

Richardson, Joanna, *Judith Gautier: A Biography* (London, 1986)

Rieger, Eva, *Richard Wagner's Women* (Woodbridge, 2011); trans. Chris Walton

Röckl, Sebastien, *Ludwig II und Richard Wagner*, I (Munich, 1913)

Sagarra, Eda, *An Introduction to Nineteenth-Century Germany* (Harlow, 1980)

Schopenhauer, Arthur, *The World as Will and Representation* (Indian Hills, Colo., 1958, repr. 1966); trans. E. F. J. Payne

Schuré, Edouard, *Richard Wagner: Son oeuvre et son idée* (Paris, 1933)

Shapiro, Alexander H., 'McEwan and Forster, the Perfect Wagnerites', *The Wagner Journal*, V/2 (2011), pp. 20–45

Shaw, George Bernard, *The Perfect Wagnerite* (London, 1898, 4/1923/ repr.)

Skelton, Geoffrey, *Wagner at Bayreuth* (London, 1965)

Skelton, Geoffrey, *Wagner in Thought and Practice* (London, 1991)

Smart, Mary Ann, *Mimomania: Music and Gesture in Nineteenth-Century Opera* (Berkeley, Calif., and Los Angeles, 2004)

Spencer, Stewart, *Wagner Remembered* (London, 2000)

Spencer, Stewart, '"Er starb, – ein Mensch wie alle": Wagner and Carrie Pringle', *Wagner*, XXV/2 (2004), pp. 55–77

Spencer, Stewart, 'Wagner and Gaetano Ghezzi', *The Wagner Journal*, I/1 (2007), pp. 18–32

Spotts, Frederic, *Bayreuth: A History of the Wagner Festival* (New Haven, Conn., and London, 1994)

Tchaikovsky, Modeste, *The Life and Letters of Peter Ilich Tchaikovsky* (London, 1906); trans. Rosa Newmarch

Vazsonyi, Nicholas, *Richard Wagner: Self-Promotion and the Making of a Brand* (Cambridge, 2010)

Voss, Egon, 'Die "schwarze und die weiße Flagge": zur Entstehung von Wagners "Tristan"', *Archiv für Musikwissenschaft*, LIV/3 (1997), pp. 210–27

Wagner, Nike, *The Wagners: The Dramas of a Musical Dynasty* (London, 2000); trans. Ewald Osers and Michael Downes

Wagner, Wolfgang, *Acts: The Autobiography of Wolfgang Wagner* (London, 1994); trans. John Brownjohn

Walker, Alan, *Hans von Bülow* (New York, 2010)

Walton, Chris, 'Voicing Mathilde: Wagner's Controlling Muse', *The Wagner Journal*, I/2 (2007), pp. 3–18

Walton, Chris, *Richard Wagner's Zurich: The Muse of Place* (Rochester, N.Y., 2007)

Warrack, John, 'Behind "The Flying Dutchman"', ENO Opera Guide to *Der fliegende Holländer*, ed. Nicholas John (London, 1982), pp. 7–12

Weiner, Marc A., *Richard Wagner and the Anti-Semitic Imagination* (Lincoln, Nebr., and London, 1995)

Weiner, Marc A., 'Wagner and the Perils of Reading', *Wagner*, XVIII (1997), pp. 59–82

Weissheimer, Wendelin, *Erlebnisse mit Richard Wagner, Franz Liszt und vielen anderen Zeitgenossen nebst deren Briefen* (Stuttgart and Leipzig, 1898)

Wille, Eliza, *Richard Wagner an Eliza Wille: Fünfzehn Briefe des Meisters nebst Erinnerungen und Erläuterungen von Eliza Wille* (Berlin and Leipzig, 1908)

Zelinsky, Hartmut, *Richard Wagner: Ein deutsches Thema* (Berlin and Vienna, 1983)

Select Discography

Die Feen (CD)
*Edward Downes/BBC Northern
Singers and Symphony Orchestra.
Cast includes April Cantelo, John
Mitchinson, Lorna Haywood, Della
Jones and Elizabeth Gale (Ponto, 2004).*

Impressive 1976 concert performance
by BBC forces under the fine Wagnerian
Edward Downes. A curious but
welcome bonus features extracts
from a Viennese performance of 1983
starring Gundula Janowitz as Ada.

Der fliegende Holländer (CD)
*Joseph Keilberth/Bayreuth Festival
Chorus and Orchestra. Cast includes
Hermann Uhde, Astrid Varnay,
Ludwig Weber and Rudolf Lustig
(Decca, 1955).*

Hermann Uhde is a superbly
tormented Dutchman, as is
Dietrich Fischer-Dieskau in Franz
Konwitschny's 1962 recording for
Berlin Clasics.

*Marek Janowski/Berlin Radio Choir
and Symphony Orchestra. Cast includes
Albert Dohmen, Ricarda Merbeth,
Matti Salminen and Robert Dean
Smith (PentaTone, 2011).*

The first of a new edition of the ten
major Wagner operas, this highly
impressive recording challenges other
catalogue contenders of recent decades,
including Barenboim, Sinopoli,
Dohnányi and Levine.

Der fliegende Holländer (DVD)
*Woldemar Nelsson/Bayreuth Festival
Chorus and Orchestra. Cast includes
Simon Estes, Lisbeth Balslev, Matti
Salminen and Robert Schunk (DG/
Unitel, 1985).*

The strength of Harry Kupfer's
landmark Bayreuth production, a
thrilling piece of music theatre, easily
outweighs any reservations about
musical values.

*Hartmut Haenchen/Netherlands
Opera Chorus, Netherlands
Philharmonic Orchestra. Cast includes
Juha Uusitalo, Catherine Nagelstadt,
Robert Lloyd and Marco Jentzsch
(Opus Arte, 2011).*

Provocative and insightful
production by Martin Kušej.

Das Liebesverbot (CD)
*Wolfgang Sawallisch/Bavarian Radio
Chorus and Symphony Orchestra. Cast
includes Hermann Prey, Wolfgang
Fassler, Robert Schunk, Sabine Haas
and Alfred Kuhn (Orfeo, 1995).*

Heavily cut but otherwise
recommendable performance from
the 1983 Munich Opera Festival.

Lohengrin (CD)
*Rudolf Kempe/Vienna State Opera
Chorus, Vienna Philharmonic
Orchestra. Cast includes Jess Thomas,
Elisabeth Grümmer, Dietrich Fischer-
Dieskau, Christa Ludwig and Gottlob
Frick (EMI, 1962–63).*

Fischer-Dieskau and Ludwig
are outstanding in Kempe's classic
recording.

*Semyon Bychkov/WDR Chorus and
Sinfonieorchester Köln. Cast includes
Johan Botha, Adrianne Pieczonka, Falk
Struckmann and Petra Lang.*

Arguably the finest of modern
recordings, not least for Bychkov's
superb realization of the layered
orchestration. Also strongly
recommendable are the versions by
Abbado (DG, 1994) and Barenboim
(Teldec, 1998).

Lohengrin (DVD)
*Sebastian Weigle/Cor and Orquestra
Simfònica del Gran Teatre del Liceu.
Cast includes John Treleaven, Emily
Magee, Hans-Joachim Ketelsen and
Luana DeVol (EuroArts, 2006).*

Peter Konwitschny's celebrated
'schoolroom' production is a terrifying
examination of the irrational fervour
of a crowd and the charismatic power
of a leader.

Die Meistersinger von Nürnberg (CD)
*Rafael Kubelik/Bavarian Radio
Symphony Chorus and Orchestra.
Cast includes Thomas Stewart, Sándor
Kónya, Gundula Janowitz, Thomas
Hemsley and Brigitte Fassbaender
(Myto, 1992).*

Kubelik's warmly eloquent, humane
1967 performance, though not released
until 1992 by Myto (and subsequently
also by Calig and Arts), is one of
the finest recordings of the work.
A superlative cast features Thomas
Stewart as the wise cobbler-poet.

Later notable recordings include
those under Sawallisch (EMI, 1994)
and Barenboim (Teldec, 1999).

Die Meistersinger von Nürnberg (DVD)
*Sebastian Weigle/Bayreuth Festival
Chorus and Orchestra. Cast includes
Franz Hawlata, Klaus Florian Vogt,
Michaela Kaune and Michael Volle
(Opus Arte, 2008).*

Katharina Wagner's iconoclastic
production grapples with the
problematic ideological issues and
performance history of the work,
reaching a shocking but powerfully
dramatic climax.

Parsifal (CD)
*Hans Knappertsbusch/Bayreuth
Festival Chorus and Orchestra. Cast
includes Jess Thomas, Hans Hotter,
Irene Dalis, George London and
Gustav Neidlinger (Philips, 1962).*

The later of two classic versions by
Knappertsbusch, the earlier dating
from 1951. Both sets have their
adherents and both exemplify mid-
20th-century Wagner conducting at
its most intensely spiritual. The earlier
version is more monumental, the later
one more fluid, while still expansive –
and better recorded.

*Christian Thielemann/Vienna State
Opera Chorus and Orchestra. Cast
includes Plácido Domingo, Falk
Struckmann, Franz-Josef Selig and
Waltraud Meier (DG, 2006).*

Thielemann's authoritative reading
is responsive both to the musico-
dramatic argument and the overriding
architecture of the work. Also
recommendable are the versions by
Daniel Barenboim (Teldec, 1991)
and Valery Gergiev (Mariinsky, 2010).

Parsifal (DVD)
*Kent Nagano/Baden-Baden Festival
Choir, Deutsches Symphonie-Orchester
Berlin. Cast includes Christopher
Ventris, Matti Salminen, Waltraud
Meier, Thomas Hampson and Tom Fox
(Opus Arte, 2005).*

Intelligent, thought-provoking
staging by Nikolaus Lehnhoff, seen
in London (ENO), San Francisco
and Chicago before being filmed at
the Baden-Baden Festival.

Rienzi (CD)
*Heinrich Hollreiser/Dresden
State Opera Chorus and Dresden
Staatskapelle. Cast includes
René Kollo, Siv Wennberg, Nikolaus
Hillebrand and Janis Martin
(EMI, 1976).*

Decently conducted East German
performance featuring Kollo in good
voice but marred by an Irene not up
to the taxing tessitura.

Rienzi (DVD)
Sebastian Lang-Lessing/Deutsche Oper Berlin Chorus and Orchestra. Cast includes Torsten Kerl, Camilla Nylund, Ante Jerkunica and Kate Aldrich (Unitel, 2010).

The production by film director Philipp Stölzl powerfully underlines the proto-fascist ideology of Wagner's early attempt at grand opera through images of Nazi propaganda, including Leni Riefenstahl's *Triumph des Willens*.

Der Ring des Nibelungen (CD)
Joseph Keilberth/Bayreuth Festival Chorus and Orchestra. Cast includes Hans Hotter, Astrid Varnay, Wolfgang Windgassen, Ramón Vinay, Gré Brouwenstijn and Josef Greindl (Testament, 2006).

Recorded at Bayreuth in 1955, but not released for over half a century, this enthralling recording by Keilberth, with stellar performances by Varnay, Hotter and others, immediately secured a place as one of the finest of the tetralogy of all time.

Daniel Barenboim/Bayreuth Festival Chorus and Orchestra. Cast includes John Tomlinson, Anne Evans, Poul Elming, Nadine Secunde and Günter von Kannen (Teldec, 1993–94).

Barenboim's prowess as a Wagnerian of the highest order is always evident in this recording, made in conjunction with Harry Kupfer's Bayreuth production of 1988–92. Also recommendable are the versions of Christian Thielemann (Opus Arte, 2009) and the landmark first stereo recording of Georg Solti (Decca, 1958–65).

Der Ring des Nibelungen (DVD)
Pierre Boulez/Bayreuth Festival Chorus and Orchestra. Cast includes Donald McIntyre, Gwyneth Jones, Manfred Jung, Peter Hofmann and Jeannine Altmeyer (DG, 2005).

The 1976 centenary staging at Bayreuth was a trailblazing production by Patrice Chéreau that brought an unprecedented level of realism and theatricality to the operatic stage. High-calibre performances, too, from McIntyre, Jones and many others.

More recent productions of note include the Stuttgart *Ring* of 2002 (EuroArts), notable for the combining of its four directorial visions, and the Copenhagen *Ring* of 2008 (Decca), a wonderfully imaginative, witty and moving realization by Kasper Holten, placing Brünnhilde at the centre of things.

Tannhäuser (CD)
Georg Solti/Vienna State Opera Chorus, Vienna Philharmonic Orchestra. Cast includes René Kollo, Helga Dernesch, Christa Ludwig, Victor Braun and Hans Sotin (Decca, 1971).

First recording of the 'Paris version', strongly cast, as was Bernard Haitink's later recording for EMI (1985) and Daniel Barenboim's for Teldec (2001).

Tannhäuser (DVD)
Friedemann Layer/Royal Danish Opera Chorus and Orchestra. Cast includes Stig Andersen, Tina Kiberg, Susanne Resmark, Tommi Hakala and Stephen Milling (Decca, 2011).

Kasper Holten's production is an engrossing take on the familiar theme of the minstrel as contemporary artist. David Alden's Munich production (Arthaus Music, 1995) is also worth investigating.

Tristan und Isolde (CD)
Wilhelm Furtwängler/Chorus of the Royal Opera House, Covent Garden; Philharmonia Orchestra. Cast includes Ludwig Suthaus, Kirsten Flagstad, Dietrich Fischer-Dieskau, Blanche Thebom and Josef Greindl (EMI, 1953).

The first complete performance of the work on record, this one has always held legendary status, in part for the authority and spontaneity of Furtwängler's conductng, in part for the magnificent Isolde of Flagstad.

Carlos Kleiber/Leipzig Radio Chorus, Dresden Staatskapelle. Cast includes René Kollo, Margaret Price, Dietrich Fischer-Dieskau, Brigitte Fassbaender and Kurt Moll (DG, 1982).

Several earlier live performances under Kleiber, including those at Bayreuth, 1974–76, have also been issued, but this studio version from Dresden – with Margaret Price as a sublime Isolde – is as sensual, penetrating and electrifying as any.

Tristan und Isolde (DVD)
Jiří Bělohlávek/Glyndebourne Chorus, London Philharmonic Orchestra. Cast includes Robert Gambill, Nina Stemme, Katarina Karnéus, René Pape and Bo Skovhus.

Nikolaus Lehnhoff's ravishingly minimalistic Glyndebourne production, stripped of all illusionistic references, focuses on death rather than erotic love but is utterly mesmerizing nevertheless.

Picture Credits

Key: a=above b=below l=left r=right

akg-images 8, 13, 18b, 25a, 37, 51, 53, 71a, 71b, 125, 148, 164, 165, 235, 242, 259
akg-images/De Agostini Picture Library 29a
akg-images/IAM 31
akg-images/Stefan Diller 222
akg-images/ullstein bild 22, 71b
The Art Archive/Alamy 9, 77
Mary Evans Picture Library/Alamy 52a
© imagebroker/Alamy 74
Lebrecht Music and Arts Photo Library/Alamy 189
© Oso Media/Alamy 301
Associated Press 297
Photo Tato Baeza 270
© Dorothée Baganz, Burghaun 76
© Clive Barda/ArenaPal.com 41, 48, 50, 115
Schloss Neuschwanstein, Bavaria 59
Bayerische Staatsbibliothek, Munich, Germany/De Agostini Picture Library/Bridgeman Art Library 167
Bayerische Verwaltung der staatlichen Schlösser, Gärten und Seen 156
Historisches Museum, Bayreuth 271, 290a & b, 298, 299
Nationalarchiv der Richard-Wagner-Stiftung, Bayreuth 11al, 11ar, 11br, 12, 14, 16, 17a, 19, 20, 23, 25, 26, 28, 39, 47, 67, 80, 89, 112, 118, 128, 129, 136, 151, 161, 177, 178r, 195a, 199, 202, 203, 205a, 206, 207, 208, 210, 211a, 215b, 223, 224, 232, 234, 240, 246, 247, 257a, 260, 272, 275a, 280, 283, 284, 285, 286a/Thomas Kohler 107
Bildarchiv Bayreuther Festspiele, Bayreuth 289b, 291, 292, 294, 295/photos Siegfried Lauterwasser, Wilhelm Rauh 34a, 66, 114, 278a, 288/photo Ramme 289a
Bayreuther Blätter, January 1878 256
© Bayreuther Festspiele/Enrico Nawrath 52b, 69, 91, 172, 241a, 261, 300a & b, 30b
© Bayreuther Festspiele/Jörg Schulze 320a
© Bayerische Staatsoper/Wilfried Hösl 45
Photo Antoni Bofill 236
Rheinische Landesmuseum, Bonn 124
Stadtmuseum Bonn 145b
bpk 275b, 282
Briefe an Mathilde Maier, Leipzig 1930 150b
Charivari, Paris 1861 86
Bildersammlung des Staatsarchivs Coburg 228
Theatermuseum des Instituts für Theaterwissenschaft, Universität Köln, Cologne 173
Theaterwissenschaftliche Sammlung Schloss Wahn, Cologne 44b, 46, 158
Theaterwissenschaftliche Sammlung,

Universität zu Koln, Cologne 281
© Marcus Fuehrer/Corbis 233
© Robbie Jack/Corbis 237
© Susana Vera/Reuters/Corbis 166
Stapleton Collection/Corbis 92b
Hessische Hausstiftung, Kronberg, Schlossmuseum Darmstadt 42, 56, 103, 174, 176
DEFA Foundation/Heinz Wenzel 268
Reuter-Wagner-Museum, Eisenach 108, 178l, 250
Photo Elliot and Fry 139
Erich W. Engel, *Richard Wagners Leben und Werke im Bilde*, Leipzig 1922 75a
Escenarios del Teatro de Bayreuth, ed. C. Martínez Pérez, Barcelona 181
FORBES Magazine Collection, New York/Bridgeman Art Library 85
Photo Karl Forster 61
Gaumont/TMS Film GMBH 269
© Gavin Graham Gallery, London 110b
Photo Alastair Muir, Glyndebourne Productions Ltd 180
König Ludwig II Museum, Neues Schloss Herrenchiemsee, Herreninsel 219
Photo © Ken Howard/Metropolitan Opera 87
Illustrated London News Supplement 92a
Kikeriki, Vienna 1882 184
ZM/Zoetrope/Kobal Collection 264
Foto-studio Koch, Lucerne 152
König Ludwig II und die Kunst. Exhibition catalogue, Prestel-Verlag 1968 57
Ernst Kreowski and Eduard Fuchs, *Richard Wagner in der Karikatur*, Berlin, 1907 135, 138, 163, 196, 212
Museum für Geschichte der Stadt Leipzig 38, 143
British Film Institute, London 263
Royal Academy of Music, London 197
The Yellow Book, vol. III, Oct. 1894. Victoria & Albert Museum, London 252
Barry Millington 226, 296
Münchner Stadtmuseum/Bibliothek 274a
Münchner Stadtmuseum/Fotomuseum 274b
Bavarian State Art Collection, Munich 160
Bayerische Stadtsoper, Munich 62a
Deutsches Theatermuseum, Munich 24
Stadtmuseum/Graphiksammlung, Munich 101
Wittelsbacher Ausgleichsfonds, Munich 95
Rights Friedrich-Wilhelm-Murnau-Stiftung; Distributor Transit Film GmbH 266
Musée de la Ville de Paris, Musée Carnavalet, Paris/Giraudon/Bridgeman Art Library 154
National Geographic, May 1944 44a
The Burrell Collection, Curtis Institute of Music, New York 21, 29b
Metropolitan Museum of Art, New York 134

New York Clipper, 13 November, 1904 265b
Den Norske Opera & Ballett/photo Erik Berg 58
By kind permission of Tony Palmer 267b
Bibliothèque-Musée de l'Opéra, Pari 170
Collection Tom Phillips 7, 10, 32, 54, 63b, 84, 121, 157, 190, 239, 262
Paul Pretzsch 257b
Preussen-Museum Nordrhein-Westfalen 75l, 185
Private collection 79, 179, 216, 278b, 279, 286b
Private collection, Munich 110a, 230
Private collection/Bridgeman Art Library 109
Private collection/Noortman Master Paintings, Amsterdam/Bridgeman Art Library 205b
Private collection/Photo Agnew's, London/Bridgeman Art Library 82
Museum of Art, Rhode Island School of Design, Providence, R.I. 253
Republic Pictures 267a
Dan Rest/Lyric Opera of Chicago 169
Richard Wagner's Bühnenwerke in Bildern dargestellt von Hugo L. Braune, C. F. W. Siegel's Musikalienhandlung R. Linnemann, Leipzig 49
Photo Martin Mydtskov Rønne 65
Photo Max von Rüdiger, Gotha 187
Matthew Rye 198, 200, 201
Dr Hans Scholz, *Richard Wagner an Mathilde Maier (1862–1878)*, Theodor Weicher, Leipzig 1930 132
Photo Jörg Schöner 36
Photo © Michael Scott-Mitchell 102
Verlag B. Schott's Söhne 211b
Nationalmuseum, Stockholm 100
Skizzen aus Bayreuth, 1876 231
© Bettina Stoess, Berlin 40
Richard Wagner Museum, Triebschen 34b, 123, 153
Photo Lauterwasser, Überlingen 277
ullstein Bild 15
Museo-Palazzo Mariano Fortuny, Venice 99
Historisches Museum der Stadt Wien, Vienna 149, 150b
Österreichische Nationalbibliothek, Vienna 142
Universitätsbibliothek, Vienna 227
Egon Voss, *Die "schwarze und die weisse Flagge" Zur Entstehung von Wagner's "Tristan"*, Archiv für Musikwissenshaft, 54. Jahrg., H.3 (1997), Franz Steiner Verlag 195b
Library of Congress, Washington, D.C. 265a
Liszthaus Weimar 117, 122
Schlossmuseum, Weimar 116
Archiv Wille, Mariafeld 137, 147, 168
Baugeschichtliches Archiv der Stadt Zurich 126

Index

Page numbers in *italics*
indicate illustrations

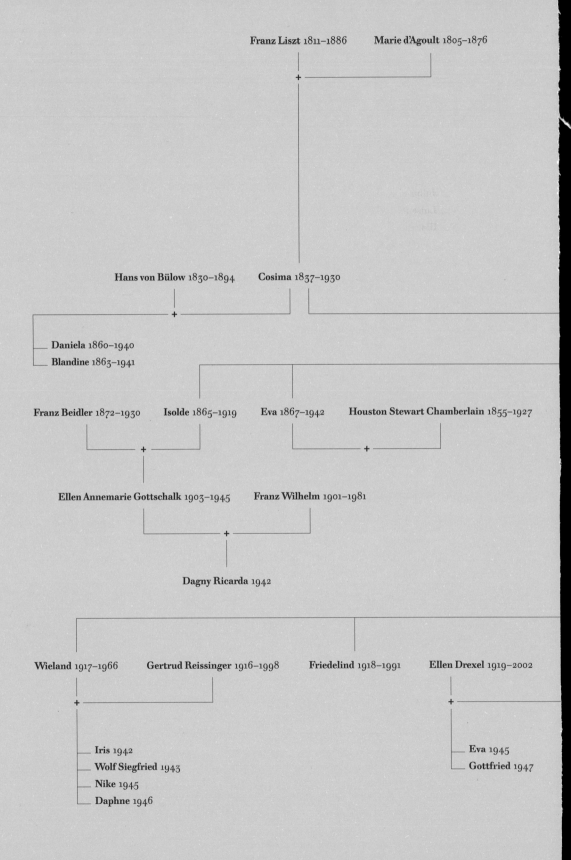

Franz Liszt 1811–1886   Marie d'Agoult 1805–1876

Hans von Bülow 1830–1894   Cosima 1837–1930

Daniela 1860–1940
Blandine 1863–1941

Franz Beidler 1872–1930   Isolde 1865–1919   Eva 1867–1942   Houston Stewart Chamberlain 1855–1927

Ellen Annemarie Gottschalk 1903–1945   Franz Wilhelm 1901–1981

Dagny Ricarda 1942

Wieland 1917–1966   Gertrud Reissinger 1916–1998   Friedelind 1918–1991   Ellen Drexel 1919–2002

Iris 1942
Wolf Siegfried 1943
Nike 1945
Daphne 1946

Eva 1945
Gottfried 1947